40th Bombardment Group (VH)
History

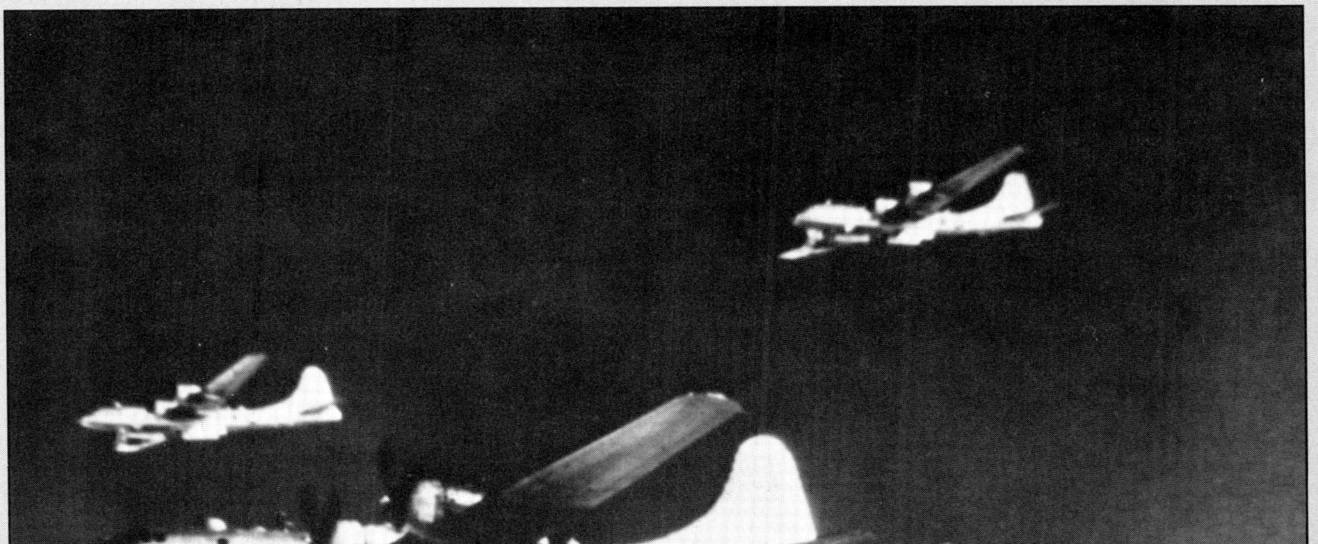

Bombers of the 40th bomb group hit targets of opportunity. (Courtesy of J. Ivan Potts, Jr.)

Turner Publishing Company
Publishers of Military History Books
P.O. Box 3101
Paducah, KY 42002-3101

Book Staff:
G. M. Etherington
Harry M. Changnon
William A. Rooney
Ivan Potts
Father Bartholomew Adler

Created and designed :
Mark A. Thompson, Independent
Consultant for Turner Publishing Company
Book Design: Elizabeth Dennis
Book Author: Keith Todd

Library of Congress Catalog
Card No. 88-051133

ISBN: 0-938021-28-1

Printed in U. S. A.
Limited Edition of 1000 Copies

Additional books may be purchased directly from Turner Publishing

Above: Daniel T. Rogers Crew #351, Chakulia, India. (Courtesy of Walter Messersmith) Right: Staying in tight formation, the 40th Bomb Group fly over Japan. (Courtesy of J. Ivan Potts, Jr.)

Table of Contents

At left: The crippled B-29, "Rankless Wreck," No. 420, 25th BS, limps toward Iwo Jima, 5 June 1945. After landing the crew was unharmed, but the B-29 never flew again. (Courtesy of J. Ivan Potts, Jr.) Above: Major Weschler and his bomber crew. (Courtesy of Everett E. Swansoon)

ACKNOWLEDGEMENTS

Many people have contributed to make this book a reality.

Special mention should go to the 40th Bomb Group Association Newsletter Editor, Bill Rooney, who not only hepled promote the idea of the book through repeated inserts in our Newsletter, but also handled much of the liaison with Turner Publishing Company.

We owe a debt of gratitude to that close gorup of old 40th Bomb Group friends, Flo Mallory, Ira Matthews, Pete Lowman, Louise Jones, Walter Lucas, Larry Eustis and John Kelly, who organized the first 40th Bomb Group Reunion in 1980. From this grew our 40th Bomb Group Association. Without it this undertaking would not have occurred.

Our Past President, Bill Hunter, is acknowledged for having established our initial contact with the Turner Publishing Company. We also thank our current President, Bob Copley, for following this project to completion. Our Historian, Harry Changnon, is recognized for his help and participation.

Last and most of all we thank and recognize all of you who have submitted your pictures, biographies, and other input to make this book possible.

May God bless you all.

G.M. (Bud) Etherington
Past President
40th Bomb Group Association

DEDICATION

The 40th Bomb Group, 58th Wing, 20th Air Force served with valor and distinction in Puerto Rico, Panama, Pratt, Kansas, Chakulia, India, Cheng-tu, China and the Island of Tinian in the Marianas.

This book is a reminder of the effort put forth by the 40th Bomb Group during World War II and is dedicated to those members of the Group who gave their lives in defense of their Country.

"From this day to the ending of the world,
we in it shall be remembered....
we band of brothers;
For he today that sheds his blood with me
Shall be my brother"
King Henry V

Fr. Bartholomew Adler, Chaplain

Introduction

At our fifth reunion in Williamsburg in 1985. Victor Agather spoke to the members attending. He said that in his assignment during WW II, it was necessary for him to visit every B-29 Group in the XXth Air Force. In none of them did he find the espirit-de-corps that existed in the 40th. Those thoughts confirm something all of us have known. We experienced, in a compressed period of four short years, an intensity of experience which called for everyone to give of themselves in the interest of the Group and of their comrades. Since then, there has been a period in which we engaged in establishing a livelihood and building a life for ourselves. Now we have emerged into our senior years to find that those brief years of WW II which we survived were a period of comradeship that will endure for all time.

Once a speaker at a seminar for prospective retirees told the gorup he was addressing that if they could count three good, true friends in their life, they should regard themselves as very lucky. The esprit of the 40th shows us how many times over we are blessed with good frineds. That gives meaning to this volume. It helps us remember those war years and the people who contributed so much to what we have become. It gives us an opportunity to remember also our deceased comrades whom we cared for just as certainly as we care for those whom we read about in this book.

William A. Rooney

A B-29 is readied for departure overseas. (Courtesy of H.W. Eppler)

The ground crew of the 40th Bomb Group prepares a B-29 for a mission. (Courtesy of John A. Bailey)

40TH BOMBARDMENT GROUP (VH) HISTORY

In a 1956 summary of 40th Bombardment Group activities during World War II, Air Force historians said, "The history of the 40th Bombardment Group is, in a sense, the history of the development of the B-29 Superfortress which was thought out and planned as a high altitude long range bomber to attack Japan, her cities and industrial key points."

In August 1943, when the 40th Bomb Group became the first bombardment unit of the Air Force to be assigned the B-29 aircraft, the capabilities of that plane as a long-range strategic bomber were not known. As one of four pioneer bombardment groups of the XX Bomber Command, the 40th had the task of proving the capabilities of the B-29 and of launching effective strikes against the Japanese Homeland.

Operating first from India and China and then from Tinian in the Mariana Islands, the Group carried the war to the Japanese people. Its long-range attacks, which helped to cripple the enemy's war effort, illustrated the value of strategic warfare.

During the course of operations in World War II the unit received credit for participating in five campaigns and was awarded Distinguished Unit Citations for outstanding performance of duty on three occasions.

Just as the history of the 40th Bomb Group is the history of the development of the B-29, it becomes apparent that the story of the B-29 is so intertwined with the story of the 40th Bomb Group as to be one and the same.

The 40th Bombardment Group

When the 40th Bombardment Group formed on 1 April 1941, the unit had little way of knowing that it would play a part in taking World War II to the Japanese mainland.

Organized mainly from members of the 25th Bombardment Group, the 40th was initially stationed at Borinquen Field, Puerto Rico under the command of Colonel William Souza.

The unit's home at Borinquen lacked some of the amenities of other bases, so much so that the flyers dubbed it "tent city." After five months in temporary quarters, the day in August the Group moved into its new barracks was a memorable one. The barracks provided new comforts and life took on a brighter hue.

The December attack on Pearl Harbor found the 40th still at Borinquen Field, but on continuous alert. Daily activity that had taken on a certain monotony now gained new significance, including frequent blackouts and air raid warnings. The men were hardened by long hours without sleep, and calls to duty at various odd hours during the day and night.

The Group got its first taste of combat in the Battle of Borinquen. "It happened after dark and machine gun fire was aimed in our direction with tracer bullets lighting the sky adding to our sudden tension," recalled Floyd Park. "Small caliber gun fire was returned toward the source of the invisible invasion but there was no further action until a pistol shot was heard in the officers housing area. The shot caused the only casualty of the battle and came from an officer hearing an intruder attempting to enter his habitat."

Park continued, "The shot wounded his maid who came to seek shelter from the fray. The next day it was revealed that the firing was an accidental discharge from our own friendly forces." The Battle of Borinquen was a reminder of just how jumpy everyone had become in the uncertain days after December 7th.

In May of 1942 the 29th, 44th, 45th and 395th Bombardment Squadrons of the 40th Group were redesignated to heavy bombardment status because they were flying B-17s and B-24s on patrol duty. The real purpose of the new designation and the use of the heavy bombers on patrol would not become apparent until months later when the Group would encounter the B-29 Superfortress and be elevated to very heavy (VH) bombardment status.

May brought a move by ship to the Panama Canal area through the sub-infested waters of the Caribbean. Enemy submarines became a minor worry early in the voyage. The sea was rough and the majority of the complexions aboard ship were a perfect match to the blue-green water around them. Later the water began to calm down and the chow lines extended in direct proportion. On the last night out from Panama, the guns of the convoy let loose with a heavy barrage. Whether or not there were submarines lurking nearby was yet to be learned.

Firmly based in the Canal Zone, the 40th patrolled waters of the Caribbean and Pacific in B-17s, B-18s and B-24s. The 40th also used a base in Guatemala and at the rock, better known as one of the Galapagos Islands. "The Rock" (actually Baltra Island) was held up to later recruits as an outstanding example of rugged living even worse than the unit had faced earlier at Borinquen Field.

Living conditions aside, the 40th Bomb Group was fulfilling an important function on the rock. The security of the Panama Canal was a major concern. During a defensive assessment of the canal in early 1942 British radar expert Watson Watt said that the canal, ". . . being unique in the world, possessing only four vital points, each of small area, but each so fragile that a single projectile on any of the four could cut this vital line of communications and two projectiles on any one of three could prevent its re-establishment for up to two years."

The canal was considered vulnerable to attack by submarine-borne German commandos from the Atlantic, and to air attacks launched by Japanese carriers on the Pacific. The Group was assigned to maintain daily patrols to alert the canal defenses to approaching enemy ships. These long monotonous flights served to prepare the 40th for more eventful long-range flights that would come later. However, not all of the patrol flights were uneventful.

After following a convoy of four shallow draft tankers from Venezuela to Oranjestad harbor for six hours the crew of a B-18 landed at the Aruba Airport to refuel and catch a meal.

"As we ate, the bombardier, Sgt. James E. (Buck) Dozier glanced over my shoulder toward the harbor," said Ira Matthews. "His eyes widened as he yelled, 'SUBMARINE IN THE HARBOR' I whirled to look. A mottled gray submarine with a German insignia on the conning tower was fully surfaced, very near the west end of the runway. Crew members were coming down the conning tower ladder, moving toward their 88 MM deck gun. We were unaware the crew had already fired a torpedo at the berthed tankers. Luckily it missed, skidding onto the shore without exploding, coming to rest very near the Harbor Masters office, which housed the Allied anti-submarine operations. It appeared obvious, the crew intended to shell the tankers, Oranjestad and perhaps the airport at point blank range. Ours was the only plane on the field at the moment."

Dismal but necessary living quarters at Borinquen Field, 1940. (Courtesy of Floyd Park)

"I vaulted the window sill, calling 'Let's go!' to the others. They were close on my heels as I sprinted some 200 feet across the runway to the B-18. Bennie Slonia, still pumping gas, looked up in surprise." Matthews continued, "I pointed to the sub and yelled, 'Move that fuel truck and clear the props.' I clambered through the rear hatch, followed by our Navigator, Lt. David Snow. Sgt. Dozier ducked into the bomb bay, pulled the four depth charge pins and entered the nose compartment through the forward hatch (along with Sgt. Bennie Slonina)."

Matthews admits he was probably the greenest pilot in the Group. Only five months out of flying school, with only a couple of hundred hours in a B-18 he had made only five landings in the plane. With pilot Colonel Ivan Palmer nowhere in site, Matthews decided to take off down wind, a move that would take the plane straight over the sub.

"I released the parking brakes and started to advance power for take off. Suddenly I glimpsed a khaki clad figure in the dust directly in front of the plane. It was Col. Palmer. I cut the throttles to Idle and locked the brakes. He ducked under the left wing, opened the hatch and climbed aboard," said Matthews.

As Matthews moved to the co-pilot's position he explained that he planned to take off down wind. Palmer replied, "Lieutenant, that tail wind is too strong (Easterly trade winds gusted to 20 mph). We could never get off the ground. We 'll taxi to the other end. There's plenty of time." Palmer released the brakes and taxied toward the submarine.

Matthews said, "We reached the halfway point and that sub looked awfully large to me, particularly that big deck gun, surrounded by its crew. Anxious beyond measure, I blurted, 'Co-pilot to bombardier, start strafing the sub with the nose gun, force them away from that deck gun'. Colonel Palmer cut in, 'Disregard that bombardier, this is the Pilot, we will be turning in a moment and you might hit a prop as we turn.' The bombardiers subdued, 'Roger Sir!' matched my sinking feeling completely. By this time, we were less than 500 feet from the sub. Some of the crew was climbing the ladder and four men were still at the gun controls. Some glanced nervously at us. An officer in a white, visored cap, stood in the conning tower, visible from the waist up. He ignored us, signaling to the gun crew with both hands. Binoculars hung from a cord around his neck."

Palmer turned the plane and proceeded to check the engines. Matthews remembers thinking how odd it was being that close to the submarine and Palmer taking time for an engine check. "I could barely conceal my emotions. We were almost within pistol shot of a German sub, yet the Colonel was delaying take off for routine engine checks," Matthews said.

The co-pilot was relieved when the plane started rolling and the cloud of dust from the engines offered some concealment from the Sub's 88 MM shells. The B-18, buffeted by the strong wind, climbed slowly.

Matthews added, "I looked back. The submarine was slanting toward the harbor channel, bow submerged. It was crash diving for the safety of deeper water outside the short channel. I called across the aisle, 'Colonel, he is diving into the channel, we have to hurry if we can get there in time.' Palmer did not reply and continued the shallow turn. The bombardier called, 'Pilot I can see the periscope wake, center the PDI and level off here. Hold 130 miles per hour and give me a level.'

"I could see a faint sub wake, merging with the seething waves at the channel mouth, we were still a good half mile from the wake. The bombardier calmly called his pre-release angles from the fixed bomb sight and the bomb bay doors opened. He called, 'Pilot from bombardier, the doors are open, hold this heading and speed, keep it level.' His voice lost its customary confidence as he continued, 'I have lost the wake, I'll try to estimate the release point, stand by for bombs away.'"

As the four depth charges fell away, the plane lurched upward, released from the 1,200 pound load. Palmer went into a steep left turn as the concussion of the explosions thudded in their ears.

The water's surface was covered with tossing whitecaps and foam. The subs wake was not visible. Well below the surface, they could see four circles from the explosions, in a neat line, well beyond the channel entrance. The 40th had bombed in deep water. As the plane continued to circle the channel mouth, the men strained to see an oil slick, air bubbles, or possibly wreckage, as evidence the submarine had been damaged. They saw nothing but waves, whitecaps and foam streaks.

After being debriefed by the Allied Naval staff, the crew refueled their plane, loaded more depth charges and headed out on their afternoon patrol. Later, the Navy would grudgingly give a plane from the 40th Bomb Group (piloted by Chick Koenig with bombardier Bill Lessin) credit for sinking a submarine near the Panama Canal.

In January 1943 Colonel Palmer was transferred to 2nd Air Force Headquarters and Colonel V.C. Smith took command. The 25th Bombardment Squadron (H) was assigned to the 40th Bomb Group while the 29th Squadron was reassigned to the 6th Bomb Group. Colonel Henry K. Mooney became commander with the later transfer of Colonel Smith to the 744th Observation Group.

The change in command brought rumors of an impending move back to the states which "were met with much enthusiasm." The move began on 15 June with an uneventful voyage to San Francisco, taking the 40th Bombardment Group one step closer to its meeting with the B-29. From San Fransisco the 40th headed directly to Pratt, Kansas where members learned they were to be among the first flyers to train for B-29 service. The first meeting with the B-29 instilled new pride in the men of the 40th.

Pratt, Kansas. (Courtesy of Robert E. Watson)

AAF Pratt, Kansas, September 1944. (Courtesy of John M. Backes)

Plans for the aircraft that would become the B-29 had first materialized in mid-1938 after Boeing's first test flights of the B-15 and B-17. The idea was to develop a long-range strategic bomber that could maintain a speed of 400 miles per hour with a range of more than 5,000 miles and up to one ton of bomb capacity.

While the B-29s would play a large role in winning the war with Japan, they were originally designed to provide even more power and bombing capacity than B-17s and B-24s against Germany and the Axis Powers. With the war in Europe turning more in favor of the Allies, there was a much greater need for the B-29 in the Pacific where it could help overcome the obstacle of fighting a war over great distances.

In early 1941, 250 of the huge planes were ordered. With the Japanese attack on Pearl Harbor the order was doubled. More than 1,500 were on order before the first Superfortress rolled off the assembly line. Production delays kept the men of the 40th from meeting up with their first fully functional B-29 until July 1943. The crash of one of the first B-29s during a test flight contributed to the delays and was the first indication that the plane had a weak spot.

Boeing's chief test pilot, Eddie Allen took the second XB-29 prototype for an afternoon test flight in February 1943 along with ten key members of the company's engineering team. Allen reported an engine fire but told the tower it was not serious. A short time later he asked for emergency equipment to be called out for the landing. The plane caught a power line short of the Seattle runway and crashed into a nearby meat packing plant.

An investigation blamed part of the problem on magnesium engine parts that could catch fire, burning with such intensity that they could practically cut the wing off a plane. The crash resulted in the government taking a greater role in the development of the plane, but engine problems would continue to plague the huge bombers.

Serious doubts existed about whether enough of the planes would be in service in time to get the 40th and other groups in the 58th Wing into combat by mid-1944, much less have a significant impact on the war effort.

The arrival of the 40th at Pratt, Kansas meant the beginning of a long and intensive program of classroom instruction, practical maintenance, and flying; a program made more difficult because of the fact that so few B-29s were available. The plane was at best out of the experimental stage and not yet in mass production.

Members of the unit spent months scattered across the country in various training schools to learn intricacies of a plane that was barely off the drawing board. Navigators were forced to train in medium bombers and bombardiers trained in heavy bombers with an occasional run in a YB-29 (Y being the designation for aircraft under "Service Test"). Pilots and new recruits had to get by flying in B-17s for flight crew training. To become more familiar with the nose landing gear, as opposed to tail draggers that were common to most WWII aircraft, crews used a few B-26s that were available on the flight line.

By the early months of 1944 ground school was almost complete. The Group started to emerge as an organized outfit ready for combat, with most personnel able to function in a dual capacity. Bombardiers were often interchangeable with navigators, a flight engineer could double as maintenance officer, on the ground a gunner could become an engine mechanic.

The first tactical B-29s arrived at Pratt from the Boeing plant at Wichita in February. With some of the ground crews already heading for ports of embarkation the flight crews and a few ground personnel were left to fight what would later be called the Battle of Pratt (or sometimes "the Battle of Kansas") on their own.

Aided by civilian personnel, flight crews were faced with making seven major modifications, plus 40 to 50 minor adjustments to the aircraft in the cold and snow of March 1944. The change-out list included one minor modification that wasn't so minor, the replacement of all engines with the "war engine." In addition to the personnel shortage the fight against time, fatigue, confusion, and the ever present cold weather presented serious problems.

The huge planes finally started rolling off the assembly line, but most weren't complete. To get production plants running with some kind of regularity engineers decided to produce the basic airplane shell, then finish final modifications as needed on each plane. That way, if an internal component was not available on the assembly line it could be added later.

The process was frustrating to the men. But, through it all the 40th was instrumental in preparing the plane for war. The members of the 40th were responsible both for suggestions and carrying out many of the minor modifications of the new long-range bomber. Changes in the design of the airplane continued even through combat operations, helping to make the B-29 an effective long-range bomber.

Some of the procedures were developed almost by accident. Gunner Neil Coleman joined a crew ferrying a B-29 to the Birmingham, Alabama modification center in December with the hope some of the men might spend Christmas with the family of one of the crewmen. Coleman said, "On our arrival (at Wichita) the Boeing ground crew stated that the B-29 had been refueled and was ready to go. We had been briefed that the weather was forecast to be clear all the way to Birmingham but just after crossing the Mississippi we suddenly encountered solid overcast." He continued, "Interphone conversation was at a minimum, Frank Rutledge (the other gunner/spotter) reporting only a slight oil leak on number four engine. After flying for three and a half hours the plane suddenly broke out of the overcast. Looking out of the left blister, I saw we were very close to the ground, barely above the tree tops. Just then Captain (Marvin W.) Goodwyn called for a gear check and moments later we reported the gear down and locked. It then occurred to me that the flaps had not been lowered nor had the flight engineer requested Frank to start the put-put (auxiliary power unit), so I told Frank to go back and start it."

"I tried to call the flight engineer but received no reply, so I switched to the Interphone command position and called Captain Goodwyn to report the condition of the flaps, but again received no response." Coleman said, "Then Frank yelled that number three engine was out. I quickly glanced out the left blister only to see the end of the runway pass quickly underneath, only 10 or 15 feet below the plane. Seconds later I looked up and saw number one prop windmilling."

He added, "Suddenly the left gear slammed onto the runway, the left wing dropping to within two feet of the concrete. Then the plane bounced, rocked onto the right gear and the left wing went high in the air. Again, the plane rocked onto the left gear, the wing tip nearly scraping the concrete. On the third bounce, Frank yelled that number four engine had just quit. As the B-29 screamed down the concrete strip, it flashed by several crash and emergency vehicles beside the runway which began following us. As the plane began to slow down, I saw number two prop stop turning just seconds before the B-29 braked to a stop."

"Being very new crew members, on only our third flight in a B-29, I figured that Frank and I had done something wrong, so we were reluctant to get out of the plane. Finally, we decided to get out and take our chewing out."

"We joined a large crowd of men who had gathered around the nose wheel, still wondering what had happened. As soon as Captain Goodwyn came down the forward hatch ladder, a Lt. Colonel rushed forward, shook his hand vigorously and congratulated him on the great job he had done in bringing the plane in safely," Coleman concluded.

Coleman and Rutledge asked the radio operators what had happened. Sgt. Donald Gilbreath explained, "The navigator got lost in the Memphis area because of the bad weather and when the flight engineer reported that our fuel was getting very low, I radioed Birmingham who gave us a heading to the airport. "As we started to descend, all the cockpit windows iced over (defrosters were to be part of the modifications in Birmingham) so Captain Goodwyn told me to grab a crash axe and chop out two of the thick plexiglass panes so he could see to land the plane. By then we were low on fuel, so the pilot radioed the control tower, declared an emergency and requested a straight-in approach. The flaps were not lowered so the plane would be able to maintain sufficient airspeed in cased of an engine failure."

A check of the gas tanks proved they were dry. "Captain Goodwyn became furious, knowing that the 'feather merchants' at Wichita had obviously short-changed the gas load."

Later the engineer told Coleman that if he and Rutledge hadn't started the put-put, ". . . the airplane would probably have ran off the end of the runway and perhaps crashed due to the loss of hydraulic pressure when the inboard engines stopped" thereby losing the brakes.

According to Coleman, "This fiasco quickly brought forth several changes in preflight procedures and requirements."

Through the winter the mechanics and crew chiefs continued their super-human battle against the elements, parts shortages and fatigue. Realizing many of the planes were still not ready for combat, Major Victor Agather was assigned to get things on track.

Agather went down the line writing down serial numbers and compiling a list of missing components. Armed with a "shopping list" he shanghaied civilians from aircraft plants to help with the work. Small plants that produced the missing components were ordered to put a priority on delivering the missing parts.

1st Lt. Robert "Con" Conley, co-pilot "Ding How," Chakulia, India. (Courtesy of John P. Brusco)

Back on the modification line at Pratt, Agather was known for working along side the mechanics. On one occasion a mechanic crawled into a plane to inform Agather an officer in a well pressed uniform was outside wanting to talk to him. Agather responded, "If he wants to talk to me tell him to climb up here." When the mechanic delivered the message it was not well taken by the General waiting outside. The General cited the Major for insubordination but the urgency of getting the planes ready for war took priority. Agather's willingness to join the exhausted and often grease covered ground crews in their overwhelming task gained their respect.

During January 1944 Colonel Louis R. Parker, who had become commander of the Group on 15 July 1943, departed for England where he studied tactical problems and techniques of air operations in the European Theater. It was thought that he should fly at least five European missions in order to command a B-29 Group.

Parker was expected to join the 40th in India. Instead, he was reported missing during a mission over Germany. Lt. Colonel Louis Coira was acting CO, but after Parker was shot down Colonel Leonard Harman took over.

Easter 1944 became D-Day for the 40th. General Arnold showed up a few days before the departure to prepare a proper send-off for the big planes. He suggested a seven day furlough for the flyers, but this never materialized and he was not around when the planes departed. More than a few of the flyers were disappointed, all were left wondering what happened to the seven day furlough.

There were only nine planes for 15 flight crews, so six crews in each of the four squadrons had to travel by boat or air to Africa. They flew the rest of the way in C-54 transports. Some of the crews that traveled by boat were amused that they arrived in India before most of the B-29s.

The 40th Bomb Group in 38 Superforts left Pratt on the first leg of a trip that would take them to an appointment over Japan and eventually around the world. The first stop-over was Gander Lake, Newfoundland.

At about the time the planes were leaving Pratt, half of the ground echelons were approaching India after being bombed by Germans while in the Harbor at Naples, Italy. Near misses caused slight damage but no casualties. Other ground crews went by way of the Pacific and Australia. The B-29s were of such strategic importance to the war effort that commanders chose the separate routes in case ships carrying the crews went down. The loss of a single ship would not keep the huge bombers from being deployed.

Flying the B-29s to their new home became an almost constant struggle with engine problems. Engineers were already aware that the new R-3350 engines needed many modifications.

"Oil would not reach the rocker arms and valves of the top-most cylinders to lubricate and cool them," acting CO Louis Coira recalled. "As a result, we were plagued with broken valves dropping into the upper cylinders and beating the pistons and causing engine failures and fires."

Each plane that left for India carried an extra engine in the bomb bay. Many of these engines had to be used to replace defective engines on the way to the Group's new home at Chakulia, India.

In 1943 General H. H. "Hap" Arnold ordered intelligence to identify strategic sites that, if destroyed, could speed up the defeat of the Japanese. Ten groups of B-29s were expected to be functional by October of1944 and10 more in May of 1945. Under the time table set for 1943 and 1944 there weren't likely to be any U.S. occupied islands in the Pacific

Crew of the first B-29 raid on Japan, 15 June 1944. Front row l to r: Fesler, Middleton, Skousan, Glen, and O'Keefe. Back row l to r: Martin, Aaron, Wilson, Halas, Gershone, and Miller. (Courtesy of Paul Gershone)

within B-29 range of Japan. Basing the planes in China became the natural alternative.

While moving the B-29s through India into China was a logistical nightmare, the plan was supported by political considerations, including the need to improve morale of the Chinese people and encourage the troops of Generalissimo Chiang Kai-shek to keep up the fight. If the Chinese army could be encouraged to continue pressing the fight on their front, the Japanese would be tied down in China and Manchuria and that meant fewer Jap troops would be available to defend important islands in the Pacific.

Under a plan code named "twilight" the first B-29 strikes against Japan were set to begin in June 1944. The schedule was much slower than President Roosevelt and his strategists back in Washington had promised Stalin, Churchill and Chiang Kai-shek, but it was deemed the earliest practical date by commanders in the China-Burma-India (CBI) Theater.

By November 1943 a list of strategic targets in Japan had been outlined. Six basic priorities existed: Merchant shipping, industrial cities, electronic manufacturers, ball bearing plants, aircraft plants and steel mills.

Delays were expected because of security considerations at bases in China and the ever present problems of ferrying gas and other supplies to the forward bases. The advance bases in the Chengtu Valley of western China were within striking distance of Japanese fighters and too close to enemy held territory. However, the plan was considered better than an earlier proposal to improve and use 14th Air Force bases which were overrun by the Japanese in the summer of 1944.

Eventually the strategists decided to base the planes in India. The planes could then be refueled in China for the final leg of the trip to Japan. This would bring the B-29s into striking distance of the Japanese mainland, however they would still not be able to reach the Emperor's Palace and some of the more strategic targets on their hit list.

The need for longer airstrips also threatened to further delay the use of the B-29s. A shortage of construction equipment created a great deal of manual work. Even in the relatively safe rear base areas of India, construction was difficult. The British had constructed airstrips to handle their aircraft and B-24 Liberators for bombing missions over Burma and flying supplies into China. After a review of sites, engineers chose airfields at Kharagpur, Piardoba, Dudhkundi, Charra, Kalaikunda and Chakulia. The Chakulia airstrip, a former B-24 base, was to become home to the 40th Bomb Group.

While Japanese intelligence was aware of the airstrip construction in India and China, the 40th flew a round-about route to their new home. After a hop from Kansas to Newfoundland, the B-29s set out across the Atlantic as part of a cover plan to confuse the enemy.

Intelligence leaks were designed to indicate the B-29 had not worked out on shakedown flights and would be used as a transport hauling supplies over the Himalayas, the Hump, instead of as a heavy bomber.

To complete the cover, one B-29 was put on display in England and within an hour the Germans had pictures of it. Meanwhile, the rest of the planes quietly headed for India by way of stops in Marrakech, Cairo, and Karachi.

April and May 1944 found members of the 40th Bomb Group facing plenty of adjustments. Just as Merrill's Marauders had already discovered in the jungle, the CBI Theater was not very hospitable.

Due to the closeness of the Japanese lines, crews were on 24 hour alert. Many of the men had gone through army infantry training before being transferred to the Army Air Corps, so while there was concern about a potential ground attack they had some idea about how to defend themselves and the planes.

The heat was terrific at Chakulia. With the average daily temperature above 100 degrees Fahrenheit, it was almost impossible for the men to work outside during the day, especially between 1000 and 1500 hours.

The extreme heat hindered the aircraft too. Engines (already plagued with problems) were prone to overheating because of improper cooling. The 40th Bomb Group ground crews were again called upon to make modifications that would correct the problem. They came up with an engine cowling change to force more air over the piston heads.

Ground crews attempting to get the Superforts in top condition for their first missions were also plagued by differences in the planes. Design improvements developed during production were added as they became available. The dozens of modifications, added by different crews, at different places, and at different times also created discrepancies in each plane.

Electrical systems on the planes could be very different, depending on the wiring harness used. It often meant diagrams did not match what electricians found inside the planes, forcing them to spend hours tracing down each wire and drawing their own diagrams as they went.

Add a list of dozens of other problems that were amplified by the heat and you had almost impossible living and working conditions.

The base wasn't ready to house the Group. The flight line was almost five miles from the original living quarters, making travel an additional factor in efforts to maintain any kind of schedule.

Despite the difficulties, flying commenced in mid-April, even though the operational runway was only partially paved. Native laborers continued around the clock trying to finish the main (north-south) runway, the hardstands and taxiway. During this time the aircraft remained lined up in two parallel rows, wing tip to wing tip. They looked and indeed were, extremely vulnerable to enemy attack. "It worried us sick we would be attacked," recalls William Rooney.

Security considerations deemed that the B-29s remain stationed primarily in India with the establishment of bases in China for the final hop to Japan.

Most of the crewmen still could not communicate with local natives at the forward bases. During a year of intensive training few of the men had been given training in the Chinese language. At the time Crew Chief Floyd Park admitted to knowing only a few words, "'Ding how' meant good guy or thumbs up, 'Poo how' meant bad buy or thumbs down."

In early May a contingent of ground personnel moved to Hsinching, China to establish the 40th Group Forward Base Detachment (code named "A-1"). This created a situation similar to the problems that occurred in Pratt when too few ground personnel were left behind. Ground crews trained to do the work always seemed to be somewhere else when they were needed.

With the regular ATC transports busy hauling vital cargo to China and resupplying ground troops in Burma, the 40th and other 58th Wing Groups had to transport most of the supplies for B-29 operations in China.

While the B-29s hauled some supplies over the hump into China for ground operations, ground commanders were not inclined to return the favor. In addition to a sometimes critical shortage of transports and supplies, ground commanders were aware the B-29 was considered a strategic weapon for attacking the Japanese mainland and would rarely be available for tactical operations in direct support of ground troops in the CBI Theater.

A B-29 departs for another bombing mission. (Courtesy of John P. Constandy)

Ground forces were responsible for protecting B-29 bases and providing logistical support, but did not get the benefit of using the big planes for combat support.

It became apparent that hauling gas, oil and supplies over the Hump into the advance operations base and stocking up for future combat missions would become the top priority of the 40th.

"There was no such thing as a typical Hump trip," explains George E. Lowry who made 34 Hump flights. "After 17 round trips and a one way ticket to Tinian, I still could not say what was typical over the Hump."

Even the routes changed through the war. The monsoon season from June into September changed the character of the trip. Just before departing Chakulia the planes were able to use the more southern of the routes where terrain allowed flights at lower altitude.

"The scenery was most spectacular along the northern route - if it could be seen," Lowry remembers. "A wonder of the world, not well know to western civilization, was a hazard on the northern route near Likiang. Still not clearly identified on maps 40 years later, the hazard is a spectacular shard of rock split down its length in nearly equal proportions. It is my impression that it is anchored near a distinctive turn in the Yangtze River. It overlooks a sort of large valley, extends a couple of miles above the level where it is anchored, and reaches to an elevation estimated at 18 to 20 thousand feet. It is not a cliff, since it is not supported by anything except the mountain ridge in which it is anchored. I do not know its name, so I must refer to it as "The Rock." Because its extreme height caused severe turbulence for a long distance I, for one, did not venture close to it. Those who flew only the more southerly route over the Hump did not see it."

On one trip up to the forward base and back Lowry spent almost half of the 12 hour flight on instruments, often unable to see his wing tips. When the crew checked the fuel, they were able to deposit only 1,000 gallons at the A-1 base after navigating some of the most treacherous mountains in the world.

The extraordinary effort needed to take the war to the Japanese mainland did not go unnoticed. The 40th Bomb Group got three Presidential Unit Citations in the fall of 1944 in recognition of the Hump flights.

"We flew 20 missions from our A-1 China base, and since it took at least six Hump trips to haul fuel, bombs, and other supplies from B-4 to A-1 for each mission, we saw lots of the 'rock pile'," explains Harry Changnon who flew the Hump 33 times. "We lost nine B-29s and several friends on the 'aluminum trail' between Chakulia and Hsinching."

The 40th and other groups went to work converting combat B-29s into tankers. Engineers and mechanics spent most of the month of May overcoming base technical problems and outfitting the tanker conversions.

At a time when B-29s were rare, spare parts were even more rare and a shortage, coupled with chronic engine problems kept many aircraft on the ground during May. As the Group became more organized and ready for combat, morale improved in spite of the continuing difficulties.

On 5 June 5 1944 the Group struck its first blow against the Japanese enemy, two and a half.years after the attack on Pearl Harbor. The mission's objective was to the Makason Railway Workshops at Bangkok, Thailand.

The bombing results on that first shakedown mission were very disappointing and by some accounts terrible. Confusion over the target resulted in droping the bombs by radar, only a few of which entered the target area. Still, it was a beginning, what everyone had been preparing for. Perhaps for the first time, everyone felt some sense of achievement. Each man felt the importance of his job in the team effort and the necessity of doing it well.

The Group paid heavily for the first mission. The 395th Squadron was particularly hard hit. It lost three B-29s, one on take off and two in the Bay of Bengal, losing a total of 20 crewmen.

The months of training, working under extreme cold at Pratt, then the extreme heat of India had created an unusual relationship between ground crews and flight crews. Since the men had been trained to fill multiple roles they often worked side by side. It helped to amplify the impact of the Group's first combat losses.

Father Bartholomew Adler had been with the 40th Bomb Group since it was formed in Puerto Rico. He wrote his impressions of the first mission and the first combat losses for **Sign** Magazine, a story that was later reprinted in **Catholic Digest**. Because of security considerations the article had to omit names and specific references to the mission to get past censors.

The night before the mission he took note of a subtle, yet noticeable change in the way the men played cards. "The boys are not thinking much about the cards," Father Adler observed. "You can tell by the way they play. Joe, who never before drew to an inside straight, does it now. Maybe Joe feels that his luck is good, that it will have to be good tomorrow. Bill, who always jokes when he is playing, hasn't much to say. After the game he comes to me and hands me his wallet. 'Keep this for me Padre,' he says. He's never done that before."

The next morning Father Adler joined the ground crews to watch the huge planes wait their turn to thunder down the dusty runway and disappear in the distance.

"You can tell what the men flying the planes are thinking as one after another raises the thumb of his right hand into the air. That signal means, 'This is it.' It is hard to control your emotions. Now the planes are lined up, one behind the other, their huge propellers turning. There is going to be a minute interval, two minutes at the most, between take-offs. You drive over to the side of the east-west runway, and you stand and wait and 'sweat.' Your mouth feels dry when you try to speak, and when you notice it you can feel your heart beating faster. Here comes the first plane; it is taking its position. Slowly, majestically, it wheels into place. A few seconds are spent in the final warming up; then the plane begins to move. You are thinking of the short runway with the ditch at the end. You yell, 'Give her the gun, Wimpy boy, get her rolling.' Faster and faster she moves. By the time she passes you she is going 90. Carrying tons of metal, bombs, traveling on six wheels with 11 human beings aboard," said Father Adler.

"The mechanics, who have labored long hours to get these planes ready; long, hard hours with the sun blistering their backs, causing the dust and grease to run in tiny trickles down their spines. Some of them have worked 36 straight hours preparing their planes for this morning."

Father Adler continued, "Now they stand on the sidelines, tired, dirty, hungry, but happy. Not only the mechanics, but all of us are there. The weather men, the medics, the bomb handlers, the cooks, the fuelers, the clerks - we all stand watching the last word in heavy bombers take to the air. We are in the nose with the bombardiers, or back with the tale gunners, or sitting in the waist, watching the engines."

"And then it happens. Maybe John figures because of the cloud of dust at the end of the runway that the plane ahead of him hasn't cleared the runway so he is trying to lift his plane as early as possible. The plane doesn't respond. Instead, her tail skid drags the concrete, causing bluish flames to leap up from it. John puts her nose down again, but by dragging the skid the plane has lost precious speed. The end of the runway is coming up fast; he will have to raise her now. Again John tries to lift her off the concrete, she rises slowly and is airborne."

"Johnny is away. He got out of that one nicely. But no, he isn't out of trouble yet. He rises to about 150 feet, and the plane is slipping toward the left. Johnny's left wing is down. 'Bring her up, Johnny, bring up your left wing or you will crash. Dear Mother of God help him,' you murmur. And then, as the plane slips down behind the trees that lie west of the runway, you raise your hand in absolution, 'Ego vos absolvo...in nomine patris, et filii, et Spiritus Sancti. . . ' The words are hardly out of your mouth when a huge column of flame shoots into the sky, and then over the sound of your racing car you hear the dull thud of the explosion as the plane blows up."

Frantically Father Adler drove down the road toward the wreck. He could hear the popping of ammunition set off by the terrific heat of the fire. He drove as close as he could, then ran across the field to the twisted wreckage.

Father Adler said, "Suddenly you are thrown on your face by the impact of a bomb which 'cooks off.' Bullets whistle overhead. For a minute or so you hug the ground. Finally you circle and come to the wreck in another direction. It is a gruesome scene. Sadly you make out various forms among the scattered, burning debris. John is there, and Willie. Your scarcely recognize them."

"As you have difficulty recognizing them, so you bend down to look at their identification tags. They are Burt and Al, co-pilot and flight engineer. Burt is still strapped to his seat. He was thrown clear by the explosion, with his safety belt still fastened. His legs are broken, and he has a deep gash over his eyes, but he is still breathing. You look a little more closely at Al. You can tell he doesn't have much of a chance. But, he is still living. In no time at all the doctor and his assistants are giving both men morphine and injecting plasma. Frantically they work over them, even while the stretcher-bearers carry them tenderly to the ambulance, a slim chance. All the rest have gone. Having paid the price of freedom, they have gone to the reward promised to men who lay down their lives for their friends," Father Adler continued.

The final planes to take-off on the mission pass directly over the wrecked plane, ". . . a once majestic bird with glistening silver wings, now broken and shattered in a smoldering heap."

"Back at the field, you run into Johnny's crew chief, Father Adler said. He is the man who was in charge of maintaining Johnny's airplane. He has a dazed, hurt look in his eyes. It is the first plane he ever had charge of that crashed. You can't think of anything to say to him, so you just pat him on the shoulder."

The ground personnel then waited nervously for the return of the planes and crews. Some slept, others prayed, but they all gathered anxiously to listen for the first signs that the planes were returning.

". . . you hear a sound. There is no mistaking it. A plane is approaching the field. The sound grows louder. It is one of our own. You can hear it pass overhead; it is above the rain. The pilot cannot see the field. 'Has he contacted the tower?' someone asks, as the sound of the plane fades. 'No' comes the reply, 'the radio operator reports his set is dead, knocked out by the storm.' 'Someone start the emergency power unit,' yells the Operations Officer, and two men dash out into the rain. Again you hear the sound of engines. The plane is coming back. 'Dear God, please let this stuff lift!'"

Father Adler continued, "The rain does slacken slightly; there is a slight rift in the clouds, and the pilot takes advantage of it to come in to the field. The water on the runway rises in great splashes, as the giant wheels roll into it. The first plane is home. You want to cheer, but you don't. As the plane passes, you look anxiously to see if it is damaged. It isn't."

"Then you hear the sound of another plane. By this time the weather has cleared sufficiently for it to come right in. After landing, the plane rolls about 1,000 feet, and the propellers, all four of them, slow down and stop. Old Luke, the pilot, had just enough gas to get his plane home. A tractor rumbles out, and as they tow the plane past, there springs up within you an immense liking for that airplane." Father Adler said, "You can't help thinking of her as a huge bird, giving its all to bring the men home, and then being too tired to move."

The first mission brought the first ditching of a B-29. A crash landing brought danger, but going down in the sea multiplied the hazards. Co-Pilot Lt. Ashley Briggs, Navigator Lt. Jim W. Evans, Bombardier Lt. Barney Wotipka, Engineer Lt. Joseph Phalon, Radarman Lt. Jesse C. Beal, Right Gunner Sgt. Gilbert Bleyl, Rear Gunner Sgt. William F. O'Connell and Left Gunner Wayne Wiseman were on board the plane piloted by Major Alex N. Zamry when it went down killing Zamry and radio operator Joseph W. Harvey.

The fuel transfer system malfunctioned. Tail gunner William F. O'Connel who was also a mechanic came forward to figure out the problem. With the fuel pump down, the plane could only fly for an hour or two. Unable to fix the problem, they were forced down.

". . . the pilot brought the plane down and made a beautiful landing considering the high waves," Wayne Wiseman related a few days after the ordeal. "The co-pilot later told me Major Zamry was smiling up to the last. (Truly a great pilot in my estimation and the reason the others of us are here now) the radio operator was continually sending out an SOS and when we started to hit the water he braced himself, for it was his job to pull the life rafts. On contact with the water, some object hit the radio operator and that was the end of him and I presume the pilot hit his head against something, for he had no time to put a pillow or anything in front to protect himself."

The impact threw all but two of the men out of the plane. Lt. Ashley Briggs and Lt. Joseph Phalon escaped through a window and managed to pull the life rafts out of the top of the ship.

44th Bomb Sqd. personnel, India, 1944. Left to right: George Hyde, Jack W. Lewis, Robert L. Tam. (Courtesy of Howard Eppler)

"They began to pick up everyone which was a bad job, trying to paddle those little light rubber rafts in such waves," Wiseman continued. "It seemed I was being carried further away by the waves. I saw Lt. Beal float by one time perfectly still and I thought he was gone. I kept hollering. The waves were so high I couldn't see anything and I know the boys on the raft couldn't see me. I heard Lt. Beal hollering in a few minutes and recognized his voice, but I still didn't hear the boys in the life rafts. They later told us they all paddled until they were given out. Some were throwing up blood from the salt water and some had broken bones. They were forced to give up getting to Lt. Beal and me and left us there to die."

The plane went down about 4:30 in the afternoon. Wiseman kept yelling then listening to see if he could hear his buddies on the rafts. Eventually, he heard a voice. Making his way toward the sound he recognized it as Beal's voice.

". . .we both kept hollering and I kept trying to get to him. Finally, it seemed the waves changed and brought us right together. He grabbed hold of me. He was nearly gone and he had an oxygen bottle under one arm. I took that and put it under his head. This brought him out of the water enough to get air."

Beal had a broken arm and leg. Using the oxygen bottle as a makeshift pillow-float, Wiseman was able to keep their heads above water. "We floated around with the waves rolling over us and kept drinking the salt water and throwing up blood. We would go as long as we could and Lt. Beal would say he had to have some air so I would tell him to hold on, and with my legs I would turn us around so our

A heavy bomber of the 40th flys through the smoke of Yokahoma, Japan, 1945. (Courtesy of J. Ivan Potts Jr.)

heads would be into the waves. The bottle would break part of the wave and I would push Lt. Beal up as high as I could and jump myself until we got some air."

A storm came up after dark. The waves got higher and Wiseman declared it was the blackest and darkest night he ever spent, with lightning flashing through the pouring rain. When they tried to catch rainwater in their mouths the waves would roll over their heads, forcing them to swallow more saltwater. It became calm, then another squall hit.

The next day the pair tried paddling toward where they thought land might be. About noon they sighted an island and thought they could swim to it, but the wind changed and they had to give up.

"It was some feeling being so close but yet so far from land. We kept on trying and about two o'clock we saw a small boat of some kind so we started toward that. We couldn't tell what kind of boat for the saltwater and sun, also the blows we had in our eyes had them nearly closed so we couldn't see well. After seeing the boat we were both encouraged."

At first the downed flyers thought it was a Japanese boat. They were so desperate they started swimming toward it anyway. They were relieved to find it was the rest of their crew and they placed Beal in one raft, Wiseman in the other.

"They had just a little water. They weren't able to find our big water can out of the wreckage. All they had was a few little half pint cans that were in the life raft, four to be exact and most of those were empty," said Wiseman. "We were in sight of land and we thought we could get water when we hit land so they gave Lt. Beal and me all the water and boy it was good. My tongue was swollen so much from the salt water I could hardly close my mouth."

The other crew members sprinkled Wiseman's cuts with sulfanilimic powder and covered him with the sail to protect him from the sun. As the hours passed, the flyers tried to paddle to an island they spotted. The wind and the tide worked against them and they had to give up. Eventually, they put up the sail attempting to hit another island. Again their efforts were thwarted by the tide.

After missing the second island, they started for another they saw in the distance. The two rafts were untied with the hope that each raft could better navigate independently.

Wiseman continued, "We hit that island but when we got close to it we could see high rocks with the waves beating against them and we knew the waves would end us if they caught and smashed us against the rock, but it was a chance we had to take. Just as we got close to the island, it seemed a big wave just caught our little raft and put it down gently on the rocks."

The exhausted survivors tried to make their way to a clearing. Belcher's bad leg forced him to crawl around on all fours. Wiseman was so weak he fell when he tried to walk. They tried to build a fire but all their matches were wet. Efforts to find water were useless. They finally settled in for the night, but the wet, cold and pestering mosquitos kept them from getting much sleep.

The next day they tried floating up a nearby river to find fresh water and food. The tide carried them up stream but the water was still too salty to drink. Dejected, they stumbled back to their original campsite. That night they prepared the sail to catch rain water in case a shower came through.

"The rest of the time on the island was much the same, no water and we were all too weak to attempt to get in the life raft to try to paddle to another island or anywhere. We just had to hope for rain but none came. That is really a miserable feeling to want water so badly and not be able to get any. All this time we didn't know where the other fellows in the other raft landed."

The next day they spotted some natives off shore. Lt. Wotipka signaled them with a mirror and waved. The natives waved back,raised their sail and moved away dashing

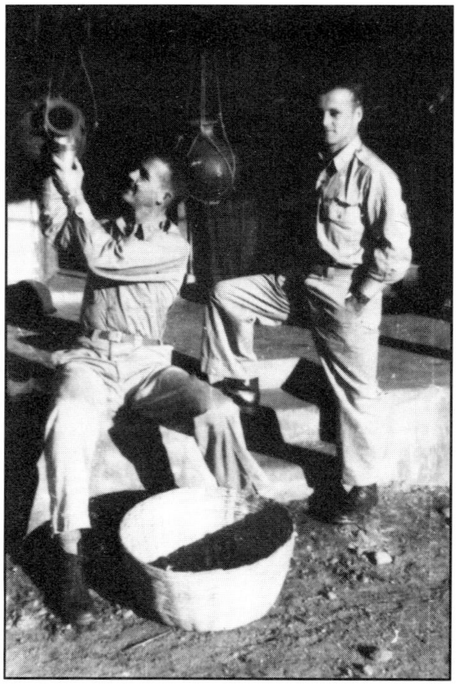

John E. Child and Long at Chakulia, India, December 1944. (Courtesy of John E. Child)

hopes again. The flyers could only hope the natives had gone for help.

"Next morning after a bad night with no rain, we heard a whistle and someone hollering for Lt. Wotipka. We were all about done for with no water and no luck fishing. Lt. Wotipka answered and started down to the water and found Lt. Briggs and Lt. Phalon who had contacted some natives. The native chief had found an interpreter and gotten a boat and had come after us for the little native boys had told them about seeing us that afternoon before on the island. The native men and the chief had with them on the boat water and coconuts which they would open and give us the juice. They wouldn't let me drink but a little at a time, but when I first got water I couldn't help but cry like a baby with joy."

The survivors in the other raft had also been discovered by the natives. Beal had been taken to a small dispensary. The others were taken to a village where according to Wiseman they were treated royally.

"They asked Lt. Briggs if he wanted some fish and he said yes, so they went out in the channel and in a few minutes they brought back two great big fish and put them on the floor in front of Lt. Briggs. The fish were still flapping. He said they were very nice so the natives took them and prepared us some stuff to go with it. All ate much, but I drank tea and water for I was afraid to start putting much hard food in my stomach yet. I ate only a small piece of the fish but it was certainly delicious. The natives put some of the prettiest green banana leaves I have ever seen over the table for a table cloth and the food was really clean. They were certainly wonderful to us and you should have seen them gather around me and talk to one

John E. Child takes a moment to relax on a makeshift cot in Chakulia, India, 1944. (Courtesy of John E. Child)

another and point to my cuts. I will never forget those people. They did everything they could for us."

Later that day an amphibious plane flew over and Wotipka signaled it. As the flyers were carried out to the plane hundreds of natives followed along.

"The natives all seemed to be enjoying the show and had a good time watching us take off. Guess we owe our lives to them for it seemed they came just in time, and did all they could."

As it turned out, severe weather on that first mission was almost as dangerous as the enemy for it was the start of monsoon season. G.M. Etherington recalled, "The weather on the first mission was terrible. It not only created problems for the planes out on the mission, but did considerable damage at the base in Chakulia as well." What some ground crew members described as a tornado like wind swept across the home base.

With only rare attacks by Japanese fighters, the B-29s had not proven their defensive capabilities. Still, crews had gained confidence in the planes and were eager for the next sortie.

Some of the flyers expected the first battle use of the B-29 to attract the attention of newspapers back home. However, the mission didn't receive as much publicity as expected in June 1944. The significance of the flight was overshadowed. Newspapers back home were filled with headlines focusing on D-Day - the Allied invasion of Europe and the continuing struggle along the Normandy coast.

The wait for the next mission was a short one. On the 13th, 14th and 15th of June 20 combat readied B-29s took off for the advance base (A-1) at Hsinching, China. The target on 15 June was the Imperial Iron and Steel Works at Yawata, Japan.

This trip provided the first real test of the aircraft and the men. Eleven general officers and numerous war correspondents present at the "A-1" base lent emphasis to the fact that this mission was one of the big events of World War II. This was the first strike against the Japanese homeland by land based American bombers. It was the first American attack on the Japanese mainland since Jimmy Doolittle's carrier based B-25s struck at Tokyo in April 1942.

One General called it, "The beginning of the organized destruction of the Japanese industrial empire." However, Sgt. Lou Stoumen, a **Yank Weekly** magazine correspondent who went along on the trip noted that , "...to the crews of the B-29s who bombed Yawata, it was just one long series of sweat outs."

The flight was to mark several firsts for the war. "It was the first official combat use of the B-29 Superfortress, the biggest bomber in the world. It was the longest bombing raid of the war, and it was the only solid Sunday Punch America has yet to land at the industrial heart of Japan."

Correspondent Stoumen was issued the same equipment regular crew members would take on the trip. He said, "My parachute was replaced with another, for mine had no jungle kit attached. I also drew a helmet with earphones and oxygen mask, a Mae West life jacket, a survival kit containing such items as fish-hooks and water purifying tablets, a shrapnel-proof flak suit, a 'pointee talkie' book for emergency conversations with the Chinese and a number of other handy gadgets."

"I grabbed my parachute and rushed out onto the field. The silver-skinned Superfortress to which I was assigned looked enormous and deadly in the afternoon sun, like a B-17 with a case of gland trouble which had grown to twice normal size."

Captain Ronald A. Harte of Lafayette, Indiana, the plane commander and pilot, lined up the crew for a last minute inspection. "We stood under the big black letters K-26 on the ship's long nose as Captain Harte made sure each of us had his dogtags and an extra pair of socks in case we should come down some place in Jap-occupied China and have to walk out."

Just as they were about to climb aboard the huge Superfortress, Stoumen thought to ask where they were headed. "A place called Yawata, about 300 miles south-southwest of Tokyo," came the reply from 2nd Lt. Emanuel M. Greenberg of Brooklyn, New York. "They told us it is to Japan what Essen is -or was - to Germany, a center of the nation's war industry. Our target is the Imperial Iron and Steel Works there."

The bomb run to Japan created mixed feelings for Brigadier General Kenneth B. Wolfe, the congenial commander of the 20th Bomber Command. As the planes began their trip down the taxiway, Wolfe "....was sitting in a jeep with a gloomy look on his face. Everyone knew why and couldn't blame him. After supervising the B-29s from the first rough sketches on the drafting board all through their construction, testing and mass production, then directing the organization of the Double X Command and all the work that brought it to this final take-off point, he had just received orders from Washington not to fly the mission."

Wolfe was replaced as commanding officer on the raid by Brigadier General La Verne "Blondie" Saunders, a wing commander who had won six decorations as fighting head of the 11th Bomb Group in the Solomons during earlier Pacific battles.

Each plane's four 2200 horse-power Wright Cyclone engines roared to life, one by one, the huge bombers bumped along the taxiway and turned to face the runway.

"Three other ships had already take off, barely lifting themselves off the ground after hugging almost the entire length of the gravel strip. We craned our necks to watch them and then we began sweating out our own take-off more than we had sweated out any other take-off in our lives."

Even without a bomb load the B-29 needed a longer runway than any other plane made at that time. "Ahead of us stretched almost two miles of runway - we would need every foot of it. Captain Harte gunned the engines, our B-29 started rolling. With quickened pulses and clammy palms, we all held on."

"The world's heaviest airplane pounded and blasted its way down the runway, the strip unfolding itself beneath us like a never ending drive-belt on a factory motor. It seemed we'd been roaring down that endless runway at least

B-29 40th Bomb Group Bomber

10 minutes without leaving it. The end of the runway - where was it? And then, just as the dusty orange blur beneath us changed to green, we were airborne, skimming a few feet over the trees and rice paddies of China."

Lou Stoumen made his observations from the waist compartment where he was joined by 2nd Lt. Frederick Tasch (the bombardier) from New York City; S/Sgt. Algernan Matulis (chief gunner) from Manhattan; Sgt. Dale L. Johnson (right gunner) of Rio, Illinois; and Sgt. Ronald G. Hurlburt (left gunner) of Gaines, Pennsylvania.

When Lt. Tasch went forward to take his seat in the bombardiers "greenhouse," Stoumen decided to tag along. He said, "We crawled forward on hands and knees through a long padded tunnel over the bomb-bay that connects the front cabin of the ship with the waist. He took his position in the glassed in nose and I kneeled on a hatch cover behind the pilots, next to 2nd Lt. George P. Appignani (the engineer) of New York City.

"The 'front office' of a B-29 seemed to have more instruments than a B-17 and B-24 combined. As I looked around I remembered the crack made by Sgt. Phil Berchad of Brooklyn, a public relations man back at the field. When he had examined the dozens of instruments that clutter up a B-29 cabin he had shaken his head and remarked, 'The B-29 is a wonderful gadget all right. But, it'll never replace the airplane'."

There was still light in the sky as the B-29s crossed into Japanese occupied China. The planes flew higher now, beginning their next "sweat out" scanning the sky for Japanese fighters.

The crews only occasionally glimpsed the other planes in the distance on the long flight. The B-29s didn't fly in formation until they reached their target and were preparing for their bomb run. Flying to and from the target the planes flew singly, allowing engineers to get optimum efficiency out of the engines, conserving fuel. Plus, the huge planes could use the extra room (with 141 foot wings) to maneuver. The B-29s were mostly on their own heading to the target, depending on well placed guns and speed to evade enemy fighters.

The B-29 was to become a model for airliners of the future. One of its well kept secrets (revealed for the first time by Stoumen's **Yank Weekly** article) was that it had a pressurized cabin to allow the crew to breathe and work normally at high altitude.

Stoumen observed, "I wouldn't need my oxygen mask except in some sort of emergency. The ride was Pullman comfortable at any altitude."

A smoking engine caused some concern among the crew that they would have to turn back, missing their first appointment over Japan. Several planes did have to turn back, returning to the field only a few hours after take off. Some crew members got out with tears in their eyes. According to one account, "Some were really crying, all were cursing," the malfunctioning engines or equipment that forced them to abort on the important raid.

As darkness set in so did the monotony of the hours. As they moved over enemy territory, crews speculated that the speed of the B-29 was discouraging Japanese fighters from pursuing them.

"They might have climbed to meet us but couldn't catch us. Nevertheless, we still sweated them out, straining our eyes through the pitch-black moonless night."

"We're four and a half hours from Japan," reported 2nd Lt. Elmer K. Johnson (the navigator) of Portland, Oregon. Sgt. E.A. Gisburne of Norway, Maryland (the radioman) broke out a carton of rations over the Yellow Sea, passing out candy bars. Some crew members took Benzedrine tablets to help them stay alert.

As the hours droned on some crew members may have thought about their families back home with some apprehension considering what lay ahead on the mission. It's likely there were some thoughts about what happened to some of the first Americans to bomb the Japanese mainland. Two years earlier eight of Doolittle's Tokyo Raiders were captured and executed by Japanese in occupied China. The same fate would likely await the crew of any plane that went down after a strike on mainland Japan.

Stoumen recalled a comment he heard a pilot make back at the field, "If the Japs hit our plane so badly we couldn't get back I'd dive the ship right into the target rather than let them take me prisoner and give me the works." Others in the group at the time nodded with silent approval.

A disembodied voice came over the intercom, "We're approaching the target." The signal put the crew to work struggling into their flak suits that looked something like catcher's chest protectors and were so heavy with flak proof metal that we could hardly stand up with them on. The pilot and co-pilot were too busy to put theirs on.

The planes were at last over Japan. Through breaks in the clouds crewmen could see Japanese real estate for the first time. The blackout of the city below was total. "The B-29s that had preceded us must have given the little Sons of Heaven plenty of worrying."

Japanese searchlights started piercing the night sky near the target. The planes were headed straight toward the lights. S/Sgt. F.C. Hodgen (the tail gunner) from Houghten, Maryland noticed the searchlights caught the B-29s tail section several times but lost the plane as it passed through patchy clouds.

Suddenly, looming ahead was another hazard. Ack-Ack guns were flashing thousands of feet below. The shells rifled up to burst around the plane.

"Our waist and rear gunners reported that the dark sky on both sides of and behind us was

Lt. Robert Pollard peers through the bombardier nose of his B-29 Chakulia, India. (Courtesy of J. Brusco)

The navigator of a B-29 basks in the sunlight after a successful mission. (Courtesy of J. Brusco)

The port hole of Renfro's crew. India. (Courtesy of J. Brusco)

Tail gunner S/Sgt. Al Ebert sits in the tail of a B-29 Indian. (Courtesy of J. Brusco)

21

The 25th BS over Japan. (Courtesy of John P. Constandy)

lighting up with pink and orange flashes of flak."

Later the returning crews would learn that one of the last planes of the group had been caught in the powerful searchlights, held in a bracket of light, and shot down with all four motors streaming fire.

The **Yank Weekly** correspondent continued his account of the mission, "Our bomb bay doors were swinging open now, noiselessly and without sending any vibration through the ship. The bombs tumbled out and angled down and through the wispy clouds. One. By one. By one. By one..."

"Bombs away," came the call on the interphone.

Loosed from the heavy load the B-29 accelerated, ". . . almost like an elevator shooting up to the 50th floor of a sky scraper, our plane hurled forward and down, whipped into a sharp left turn that made some of us think we had been hit, and raced back across Japan toward the Yellow Sea at fighter plane speed."

"The big moment was over as quickly as that. A few seconds after we left the target area Hodgen, the tail gunner reported over the interphone, 'I can't see much through the clouds, but I can make out a big glow over the target. And it isn't any searchlight.'"

"Planes that followed us a little later, when the clouds weren't so thick over the target, reported seeing columns of smoke and fire from as far as 50 miles away, rising 5,000 feet in the air."

As the planes streaked back toward China the crews figured Japanese fighters would be laying for them on the trip home. The fighters, alerted by reports of the air raid would have plenty of time to gas up and climb to a position where they could pounce on us.

The crews could barely make out the dark outline of the China coast, a landmark that would become a welcomed site on later trips.

Stoumen noted, "Our gunners actually seemed to want Jap fighters to come around now to relieve the tense strain of the waiting and watching."

Members of the 40th speculated that a B-24 bombing run on Japanese fighter bases in China the day before had been effective. But, there were still questions about the absence of fighters over Japan.

"We decided they had either been caught with their pants down or they had been warned away from B-29 fire-power by Jap fighters that ran across a Superfort over the Hump several weeks before and turned tail after getting in a few hurried shots."

While shooting pictures Lou Stoumen observed how the crew had seemingly changed during the flight that had lasted almost half a day.

"I suddenly realized how different everyone looked the morning after the longest bombing mission in history. Especially Captain Harte and Lt. Haddow. Their bloodshot eyes seemed to be mounted over pouches that looked like squashed prunes. Their skin was pale in the morning light. They looked as though someone had been beating them about the head with a rubber hose. Everyone looked

Fuel being pumped out of bombay tanks into 55 gallon drums. Chengtu, China, December, 1944. (Courtesy of Ivan Potts, Jr.)

droopy and old and gray from the nervous strain and lack of sleep."

The description would later apply to other crews returning from equally tiring missions.

The crews piled out of hatches to the greeting of ground crews, other flight crews, reporters, and other visitors.

Later, the crewmen were treated to a feast of egg sandwiches during debriefing. "When intelligence reports were finally tallied, we learned that four B-29s had been lost- one shot down over the target, one unreported and two lost in accidents. The entire crew of one ship which force-landed just inside occupied China after the mission, came back two days later, the pilot with shrapnel eye wounds from a Jap bombing of his grounded plane."

Within hours of the raid newspapers back in the states would hail the raid with all kinds of superlatives, for strategically it was, as General Wolfe had declared, "the beginning of the organized destruction of the Japanese industrial empire."

Photographs would later show disappointing results. But, as crews headed to a well earned rest they could reflect on the millions back home who were getting a much needed morale boost from reading of the first raid on the Japanese homeland since the famous Doolittle raid early in the war.

There were no more missions in June. There was still much to be done to get the bases in order for the long haul.

There were still parts shortages. But, support transportation was catching up and by the end of June the 40th Bombardment Group had 78% of its authorized equipment. Also, by the end of June Group and Squadron Operations moved into the new "E" building on the line. The move provided the first real Group Headquarters. It was considered, "...a great improvement in spite of leaks in the roof and other minor irritations."

While the group continued to settle in during July only two more raids were scheduled: One on July 7th against Sasebo and Kyushu, the other a full scale daylight attack on the Showa Steel works at Anshan, Manchuria on the 29th.

The Chakulia base continued to improve. The north-south runway was at last complete. A new housing area within a mile of the flight line was also complete so personnel were able to move out of the old area.

The new thatch-roofed living quarters came none too soon. The renowned India monsoons had commenced and were shortly in full swing. A total of 17.7 inches of rain fell during the month. While the rain caused problems of its own, it brought relief from the searing heat which had hampered the group for the previous three months.

The big social event of the month came on the 4th of July. No less than 10 white girls were courageous enough to attend a dance marking the opening of the officers club. Most

Men of the 40th Bomb Group enjoy a few laughs between missions, Officers Club, Chakulia, India. (Courtesy of J. Brusco)

of the 400 officers who attended who didn't care for dancing or couldn't find a dance partner, found a pleasant alternative in the liquid refreshments that were offered.

The first week of August brought another change of command. Colonel William H. Blanchard became CO, succeeding Colonel Harman. Lt. Col. Henry R. Sullivan became Deputy Group Commander replacing Col. Louis E. Coira. Coira, one of the older members of the Group, was transferred to the XX Bomber Command.

The first mission of August was flown out of Ceylon on the 10th. The raid on Palembang, Sumatra was considered, ". . . the longest range bombing operation in the history of aerial warfare."

A companion mission headed for Nagasaki on the same day. It was hoped that a successful strike against the targets, more than 4,000 miles apart, would demonstrate the increasing ability of American bombers to strike at the industrial heart of Japan and cause concern among the Japanese people.

On August 20th the 40th undertook another mission to Yawata. The group lost four out of the 22 aircraft dispatched during the maximum-daylight strike but luckily not all personnel were lost.

This second trip to Yawata was perhaps the roughest mission of the Group's overseas tour to date. The flyers faced high altitude barrage balloons, air to air phosphorus bombs, ramming attacks by fighters and the usual AA which was more intense than previous missions.

September 1944 marked another turning point. Major General Curtis E. LeMay took over the XX Bomber Command. He immediately began to initiate some of the practices that had proven successful in Europe.

Plans were laid for a 12 plane formation to improve firepower and improve the bomb pattern. The old four plane diamond formation was dropped. Training was also stepped up with lead crews specially picked for their ability to pilot, navigate and bomb.

The new training effort still allowed time for two strikes at the Showa Steel Works at Anshan, Manchuria.

The Japanese continued to be frustrated in their efforts to down B-29s in the air. The enemy adopted new tactics, including strikes at the advance B-29 bases in China in an effort to destroy the huge planes on the ground.

Evidence of "5th Column" activities around the airfields just before and during the Japanese raids was alarming. Flares, were set off and rice paddies were set ablaze to help enemy planes accurately locate the runways and parking areas. The absence of anti-aircraft defenses and fighter protection at the forward staging area created some uncomfortable moments for the men in the forward detachment.

The Chakulia base also attracted occasional visits from Japanese bombers and fighters based at Rangoon. Flyer Ed Buagh, a former Julliard Music School student and opra singer, was closing out the entertainment on Christmas Eve 1944 when air raid warning sirens sounded. The men piled into slit trenches as a Japanese Betty dropped several bombs around the field. Harry Changnon said, "Our Indian Anti-Aircraft crews fired their guns for what seemed like all night, the Betty was probably back in Rangoon by the time they quit."

The 25th Armament Squadron, September 1944, Chakulia, India. (Courtesy of Robert E. Watson)

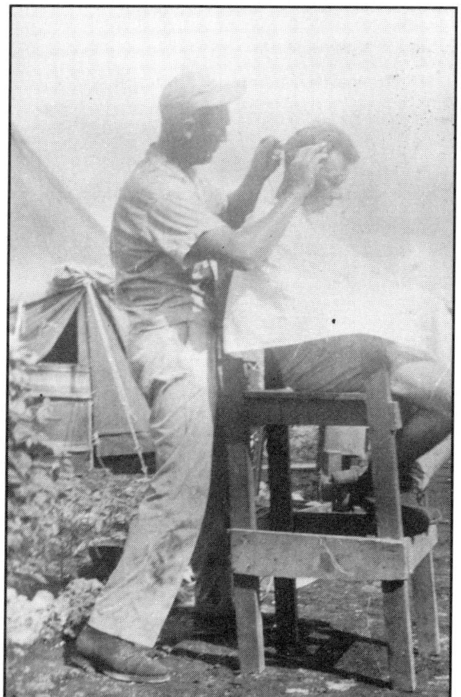

Virgil Tullos, the 40th Bomb Group barber cutting Kermit Conner's hair at Chakulia, India. (Courtesy of Floyd Park)

The Japanese attacks prompted an uneasy Floyd Park to observe, "Night guard watch of the aircraft was maintained by 'Ding How' Guy, who was our ally, until a Japanese night air raid bombing attack near our base in which many ground lights suddenly surrounded our runway giving the Japs the correct bombing point. We later learned the Japanese paid them better than we did."

The Japanese raid may have fostered some suspicion of the natives. However, as Cpl. Charles Wayne Sullivan wrote home in a letter that was uncensored, the relationship between Americans and Indian locals often developed into friendship.

"I guess you wonder what sort of a place this is," he wrote. "Things aren't so bad, they could be a lot worse. It's pretty warm at this time and I guess it will get warmer as time goes by."

"We have a few natives around. Six boys and myself have three little boys called 'bearers' do our work. They come sweep, make up our beds and take out our laundry for us. We pay them for it of course [3 rupees or $1.00 a week]. It isn't much but a little."

"They know a few words of our speech. That's more than I can say about myself and their lingo. What gets me is the way they all work, that is the women and kids included. You should see my hair cut, it's about one fourth inch long. Love Wayne."

While the early raids on Japan hurt enemy pride more than damaging the war machine, perhaps the group's most significant contribution to the war effort up to this time was the support for General MacArthur's invasion of the Philippines in mid-October 1944.

The B-29s made two strikes against enemy installations on the Island of Formosa on the 14th and 17th. The Okayama Airfield and Arsenal were considered, " . . . the most important target south of Japan," along with the Einansho Airfield and Repair Depot, and harbor at Takao. The strike at the plant and associated supply depots was credited with cutting supply lines and aiding the Philippine invasion effort.

A third mission on October 25th hit the aircraft plant at Omura, Japan. The day after the mission a B-29 was sent back to Omura on a reconnaissance mission. In addition to confirming damage to the target, the trip confirmed the effectiveness of the Central Fire Control (CFC) System developed by General Electric.

CFC allowed control of gun turrets to be switched from one gunner to another to concentrate firepower where it was most needed. Some crew members and old line officers were suspicious of the remote controls and there had

Flying crew and ground crew of Smiling Jack, 25th Sqdn. Tinian, 1945. (Courtesy of J. Ivan Potts)

been talk of converting the planes back to a manual system to save weight so bomb loads could be increased.

The running gunbattle that developed between the crew of #582 and more than two dozen Jap fighters became known as the mission that saved the CFC.

Major John C. Eigenmann and his crew liked to refer to themselves as "Smiling Jack and his ten Jokers." They were supposed to take part in the Omura bombing mission on the 25th but had to abort because of mechanical problems. With the problem repaired they were first in line the next day for a reconn mission to check damage at the target.

The flight to the target was uneventful. As the plane crossed the China Sea the crew spotted a large number of enemy fighters lined up along air strips on some of the islands. Major Eigenmann recalls counting 40 or 50.

As they approached the target the cloud cover became solid. They tried taking pictures through some breaks in the undercast. Eventually, the observer Col. Edward J. Potter noticed another break in clouds to the north. The flying was good so there was no complaint when Potter asked to take a look at the break for additional pictures. That's when the flight started to change.

"Just as we turned north, (Cliff) Bell reported nine fighters coming up through the clouds behind us, and while they were climbing up to get in front of us, he reported seven more coming up," remembers CFC Gunner John K. Jensen. "As we approached the new target, the first nine were in position to attack. Donahue and I coordinated the use of the upper forward turret so we could use it to the maximum. The first group came at us singly and in pairs so we each used it at different times.

"The first pass was a single and he came in at 12 o'clock level. Donahue took both forward turrets, and the fighter made the mistake of climbing so Donahue could get both turrets on him. He was smoking as he passed just over our right wing - so close, in fact, Eigenmann said he could almost read his dog tags. This was very likely the one damaged plane which Donahue got credit for."

"On the next pass two came in, one high and one low. Donahue took the lower turret and I the upper turret. The one that came in high rolled over and started into us just as I fired both upper turrets. He never made it all the way around before his nose dipped down and he went into a dive, straight down. In the meantime, Donahue had gotten his fighter, as confirmed by Douglas. As this was happening one of the second group attempted a tail attack, and Cliff Bell shot him down. Lagoy was taking pictures with the spare K-14 (I think this was the number of the camera) of the fighters as they went by."

Lagoy was considered something of a free spirit by the other crew members. Bill Baker recalled thinking at the time, "What the hell is Lagoy taking pictures for at a time like this." With other gunners controlling the lower aft turret Lagoy was free to play photographer.

Jensen continued, "Another one came in on us from 12 o'clock high, and as he rolled over and started his attack, I fired at him with both upper turrets and his plane just seemed to stop, and after a second his nose dropped and he went down. I thought to myself, 'Another one of the Emperor's little slant-eyed yellow devils sent into oblivion.'"

"At this time, or just shortly afterward, three came in from one o'clock level, and here is where Eigenmann's ability came to the fore. He either turned right or left, went up or down, and adjusted the speed either faster or slower to either throw off the timing of the attack or to bring into play the upper turrets' fire power. Donahue fired at all three and hit every one hard as we saw smoke streaming from all of them. We are certain that he got all three; either Lagoy or Douglas reported seeing them disappear through the clouds still trailing smoke. However, the powers that be credited him with two shot down and one damaged," said Jensen.

Jensen managed to hit another fighter then came at them, but not before the attacker came so close that he hit their radio antenna and snapped it off.

By this time the B-29 gunners had worked their way through the first swarm of 16 fighters that had come up to challenge them. Luckily, additional fighters that had come up to join the attack were far less aggressive.

Jensen continued, "With some time to think now, I became concerned about our ammo supply, primarily in the upper and lower forward turrets, so we decided that Donahue and I would just fire at the fighters that posed a threat to us. We all felt that if we had more ammo we could have gotten some more of their fighters. Later, when I did check the ammo supply, the upper turrets were almost out, and the lower forward had no more than 100 or 200 rounds left."

As they journeyed over the China Sea the fighters they had seen on the islands on the way out started coming up.

"Up to this time Lagoy and Douglas really had not had many chances to shoot at anything, but the change in tactics now gave them several good chances. Lagoy reported that one was coming up from six o'clock low and he had him in his sights," Jensen said. "I remember thinking after a while, 'My God, why doesn't he shoot?' However, when he felt he had him in range, he fired at him and down he went smoking badly. Douglas got his about this time, and I remember the fighter just nosed over and went down. One of the last ones to come up Lagoy shot at and hit real hard as we saw him going down smoking very badly."

He continued, "After we crossed the China coast and the fighters had stopped coming, we sort of collapsed in a daze, the intercom was silent, and no one spoke."

During the running gunbattle the B-29 had been attacked by 30 or 40 fighters and the crew had spotted dozens more. They were officially credited with downing nine Japanese fighters and damaging two more during the almost 14 hour flight. But, the crew members believed they shot down 11 and damaged four or five.

Jensen believes the count was based on the old flexible gunnery formula. Plus, pandemonium that erupted during the debriefing when everybody tried to give their version of the trip may have caused confusion when intelligence officers tried to figure out what happened.

"The reason for this discrepancy, I feel, was because up to this time the gunner system had not really been put to such a severe test and no one really knew of its tremendous potential. We CFC gunners knew, because we knew the system so well and how it worked," Jensen declared.

As missions picked up during the next three months so did the training schedule. Crews were becoming familiar with the B-29s unique flying characteristics under combat conditions and gaining confidence in the plane's superb defensive capabilities.

The Japanese were also gaining a healthy respect for the B-29. The Japanese had been unable to catch up with American ingenuity and technology to create a fighter that could match the B-29s speed and altitude.

As B-29 raids became more common heading into December, Japanese flyers took more desperate measures. Japanese fighters could occasionally climb to B-29 altitudes but lacked power for attack maneuvers. After several near collisions it quickly became obvious that the Japanese pilots were deliberately trying to ram American bombers in fighters stripped of armor and loaded with explosives.

Morale during the last months of 1944 was probably higher than since the Group arrived a Chakulia. One factor was the need to transfer some tankers and battle-scarred B-29s back to the states. Crews with the most combat time were in line to make the trip home. The continued improvement of base facilities and what some considered a country club atmosphere, compared to earlier living and working conditions, didn't hurt either.

The morale of the enlisted men got a particular boost from completion of the Base Service Center that included a baseball diamond, tennis and volley ball courts, an outdoor theater with a stage and lighting facilities, a social room bar, orientation room and reading room.

By the end of 1944 the 40th Bomb Group had participated in 22 missions over 12 primary targets.

A November 5th mission against the Graving Dock at Singapore brought another long flight covering 3,790 statute miles. The bombing accuracy on the Graving Dock raid was also deemed the best performance of all the missions conducted, with the target being breached from an altitude of 25,000 feet.

The mission was so successful that General LeMay visited the 40th to personally commend lead bombardier Frank McKinney and the crew of the "Bombing Buggy II" (#541) flown by Captain Bill Hunter.

The most disastrous mission came on 14

Picture painted on the outside of the enlisted men's club, Chakulia, India. (Courtesy of Rodolfo Hemander)

40th Bomb Group members take time out to play a game of volleyball. (Courtesy of J. Brusco)

Back row l to r: Haas, Larson, Grof, Knight, Penn, and Barton. Front row: l to r: Lacko, Bailey, Lowry, Burrows, and Wotipka. (Courtesy of John A. Bailey)

December 1944. Despite the protest of almost everyone else on the staff, Col. Butch Blanchard, the CO, insisted on a mixed bomb load. Each plane was loaded with 12 1,000-pound and six 500-pound demolition bombs. Some officers, including Captain Frank Redler (the armament officer) and Lt. Col. J.I. Cornett (commander of the 44th squadron and of the mission), complained that the mixed load was dangerous and unnecessary.

Faced with conflicting advice and information from his staff (opposing the mixed bomb load) and the XX Bomber Command staff (supporting it, but granting Blanchard the option to change the load), Col. Blanchard ordered the mission to proceed with the mixed load - a controversial command decision that has left some crew members bitter to this day.

The planes made two passes over the Rama VI Bridge in Bankok, but cloud cover prevented sighting of the primary target. The formation headed for the secondary target, the central Rail Yards in Rangoon, Burma.

Seconds after bombs away there was a tremendous explosion just below the formation. Many flyers speculated that heavy and accurate flak hit some of the bombs causing premature detonation. More than 50 burst of flak were observed about the time the bombs were dropped. The Rangoon area was always considered a dangerous target by the flyers because of the many gun installations and both heavy and accurate fire.

The official investigation would conclude bombs collided just beneath the formation causing a huge explosion. Flight Engineer G. M. "Bud" Etherington aboard # 293 agreed with the mixed bomb theory. "The weather was clear as we approached Rangoon. Apparently we had taken the Japanese by surprise as

Plane and crew of "Shoot your faded." (Courtesy of J. Brusco)

Standling l to r: Robert Conley, John Brusco, Major Moss and David Miles Lustig. (Courtesy of J. Brusco)

Engine repair on B-29

there was no defensive action. Seconds after bombs away there was a tremendous explosion. We were hit and hit bad."

He continued, "The exact events of the next several minutes are not clear in my mind. I guess all four engines had been hit. Two engines were on fire. The gunners reported there was a big hole in the right wing and the control surfaces were badly damaged. Bob (Pilot Robert Shanks) and Fletch (Co-pilot Harold Fletcher) had a lot of trouble flying the plane but managed to control it. There were several holes in the plane but miraculously nobody was seriously hurt. I had a scratch on my left arm and Julian Cochran had a small piece of metal in the sole of his shoe and a small wound on his leg. His parachute was shredded, and he went through the tunnel to get a spare chute which just happened to be in the back."

"We managed to fly 15 or 20 minutes after being hit and were somewhere over the delta of the Irrawaddy River at about 6,000 feet with a higher mountain range ahead of us when #2 engine started to burn," said Etherington.

With the plane losing altitude the crew bailed out and were captured by the Japanese. Eleven planes were in the doomed formation. Four B-29s were lost and seven others damaged. Only Major Doyles's plane was able to return directly to Chakulia, the others had to land at other air fields. The human loss was even more devastating. Seventeen men were killed and 29 wound up as prisoners of war.

Ironically, as was the case at Rangoon, most of the early aircraft losses came not from enemy fire but from take-off and landing mishaps, equipment malfunctions or other similar accidents.

A total of 33 B-29s were lost during the first seven months of operations with only four (possibly as many as six) due to enemy action, the rest were operational with the exception of one shot down by mistake by a British Beaufighter [#335 piloted by Maj. Bob Moss, the first B-29 to arrive in the CBI]. Another B-29 burned on the ground when spilled fuel was ignited by an electrical drop cord.

Claims against the enemy amounted to 35 aircraft destroyed, 14 probably destroyed and 29 damaged.

January 1945 was to become the most active month of the group's combat tour of the CBI Theater. Six missions were completed during the first 17 days of the month. A seventh mission later during the month capped the record.

On 14 January 1945 another tragedy resulted when crews were unloading fragmentation bombs from one of the 44th Squadron aircraft.

Difficulties were common with the M-47 Cluster Anti-Personnel Bombs. Each bomb contained 10 fragmentation bombs that were held together by metal bands in two five bomb clusters. The bands would often become loose

A bomb loading accident on the ground in India. 1944 (Courtesy of Paul Gershone)

A bomb exploded on the ground at Chakulia, India, January 1944, (Courtesy of Walter Maurer)

and the bombs would shift during handling. Since they were armed and could explode on impact a mistake during loading could be fatal.

Two back up planes were generally prepared for each mission in case one of the primary aircraft failed to make take off. Group Armament Officer Frank Redler did not want crews to off-load the bombs because of the loosened condition of the bands.

Redder said, "I vehemently protested, citing the danger of the additional handling of these clusters, and I recommended flying the aircraft and dropping on the bombing practice range. My recommendation was denied."

One of the clusters broke and one or more bombs fell to the ground exploding on contact. The explosion caused a fire in the aircraft [#583] which in turn ignited and caused other frag bombs to explode completely destroying the aircraft being unloaded.

Crew Chief Nathan Kritzer was working on #394 on the same hardstand. He said, "Still to this day I do not know exactly what happened. I do know that all hell broke out. (#582

Crew Chief Carmine) Merolla started to run toward his plane, but I grabbed him as there was nothing he could do over there. I also saw that there was nothing I could do with my plane either."

The plane (#394) was on jacks and could not be taxied away. The tragedy left nine dead and 21 wounded, most badly. The loss was great but also brought some of the most heroic acts members of the 40th witnessed during the war.

Father Bartholomew Adler, who was visiting the operations office when the explosion rocked the building, received special praise. Later Father Adler would recall the horror of that Sunday morning.

"Rushing outside I saw a column of smoke in the vicinity of where the planes of the 44th Squadron were parked. I drove to the scene and on arrival saw a horrifying sight. The bomb bay of an airplane was on fire. As near as I can recall, four or five men were lying on the ground. They were badly burned, with wisps of smoke floating from their clothing. Several men were trying to drag them to safety; other men were trying to rescue those still trapped beneath the bomb bay. I joined in the effort. I distinctly remember helping Cpl. (Aloysius) Schumacher to get away from the plane, assisting him to crawl under a command car that was parked some distance away. Although badly wounded he kept asking me to help his buddy, Sgt. Edward Donnelly, who was still back at the plane. As it turned out, Sgt. Donnelly was killed almost instantly. When a second explosion occurred, someone jumped into the command car under which Cpl. Schumacher lay and drove away leaving him quite exposed."

Those who were at the field agreed that as fire trucks and ambulances arrived there was plenty of confusion.

"Cpl. Schumacher was quite a man," said Father Adler. "Later that dreadful Sunday afternoon I found him at the Base Hospital, clutching his stomach where he had been struck by shrapnel, telling medics to take care of another buddy of his, Pvt. Edwin Elefant, whom he considered more seriously wounded than he." Schumacher and Elefant were among the nine who died.

On 6 February 1945 an accident report on the explosion documented the bravery that gained the Soldier's Medal for several of the men.

Private Cleo I. Askins, a cook in the Base Dispensary, immediately left his post to assist two medics. He said, "They parked their ambulance approximately 75 yards from the exploding aircraft. Pvt. Askins immediately proceeded to the tail of the aircraft where five seriously injured men were lying. He assisted administering morphine to the men, despite the fact that explosions threw sharpnel all around him and 50-caliber ammunition was going off nearby."

S/Sgt. Morris Backer who was working on a nearby aircraft went to the men with no thought for his personal safety, and immediately attempted to rescue those who had been seriously injured. He was successful in removing a seriously injured man who was lying alongside the rear bomb bay, where the explosion took place. He removed the injured man during this time a series of explosions of gas tanks, bombs and ammunition occurred and S/Sgt. Backer was wounded in the the left thigh.

Sergeant Stephen A. D'Addio, a medical NCO ". . . proceeded to the tail of the aircraft where five seriously injured enlisted men were lying. Despite the fact that bombs were still exploding, throwing shrapnel all around him, ammunition was going off wildly."

Master Sergeant Emil Dobrowolski, ". . . was successful in removing seriously injured men to an ambulance. Despite a series of explosions of gas tanks, bombs and ammunition, he attempted to return to rescue other personnel and was wounded in the head, back and leg by shrapnel, forcing him to retreat."

Private First Class Elias T. Flessor was working on a nearby plane and fled the explosion with two other seriously wounded men when one of the wounded men fell and could go no further Flessor ran to the ambulance, obtained a stretcher and with the services of another enlisted man, ran back to the injured man, placed him on a stretcher and carried him to the ambulance. Attempting to rescue others, a series of explosions of gas tanks, bombs and ammunitions felled and wounded him, and he was forced to retreat.

Left to right are the pall bearers for the funeral of a friend: Erie Baker, Walter Maurer, Edwin, Cody, Frank Sunderland, Chas. Selugiki, and Calvin Pedder.

Bomb loading accident casualities, India 1944

First Lt. Michael Knezevich was credited with rescuing four of the wounded accomplished at great personal risk in the face of a series of explosions of gas tanks, bombs and ammunition. His courage and utter disregard for his own safety were meritorious.

Sergeant Charles McCarthy a medical NCO proceeded to the tail of the exploding aircraft, where five enlisted men were lying seriously injured. Despite the fact that ammunition was going off wildly and explosions were occurring repeatedly all around him, Sgt. McCarthy administered morphine to the men, relieving their pain, and then bandaged them before sending them to the ambulance.

Corporal Irvin A. Miller, who was working on #582 when the explosion occurred, immediately attempted to rescue those who had been seriously injured. He was successful in removing two seriously injured men from the aircraft. Wounded himself, Cpl. Miller remained with an injured man and placed him on a stretcher during a series of explosions.

S/Sgt. Mayo W. Young without regard for his own safety assisted in removing two seriously injured men from the vicinity of the burning aircraft, despite a series of explosions.

It was just days later that a message arrived from the ordnance department back in the states declaring that the cluster bombs were unsafe and use of the M-47 should be discontinued.

The accident had an impact on the flyers. Captain Fountain Brown said, "I suppose scenes of wounded personnel were common in a ground pounder's combat experience, but bomber crews and support personnel expected to be spared such trauma while in the sanctuary of their home base. He continued, "Witnessing this dark moment in the history of the 44th Bomb Squadron was a sobering experience, and it seemed to serve notice that anyone, anywhere at any time could become a casualty of this war."

The explosion turned what otherwise would have been a welcomed break from the war into a dark day. Pianist and conductor Andre Kostelanitz and opera singer Lily Pons made a USO stop at the Chakulia base that Sunday evening. The performance, while entertaining, couldn't block out what the men of the 40th Bomb Group experienced that morning. The sound of the explosions and the smell of the smoke was still too vivid.

In addition to the human loss, the accident claimed another B-29, "The Last Resort," parked nearby. It had to be salvaged. Four other B-29s were damaged by the explosions. The XX Bomber Command's new boss, Brigadier General Roger M. Ramey, personally came to Chakulia the next day to pin the Soldier's Medal on 11 survivors.

The last of January brought with it orders to evacuate the 147 enlisted men and 10 officers stationed at Hsinching. Japanese forces were moving toward western China threatening the B-29 forward bases. Besides, the Group was about to begin preparations for a move to another theater of operations. By the end of the month most of the forward echelon was back at the Chakulia base in India.

Back row l to r: Abbott, Hilton, Leonard, Netzong, Peyton. Front row l to r: Wiget, Brant, Simpson, Reed, Kekseon, Mansko. (Courtesy of Zane L. Abbott)

Reflecting on the month's work over enemy territory left crews with mixed feelings. The raids were during poor flying weather over almost all of the targets. Radar bombing had been the rule, hampering effectiveness of the bomb runs. Bomb sights were seldom used during this period.

The unique long-rang capabilities of the B-29 continued to create additional demands on the Group. Some B-29s and their crews were pressed into special service for photo reconnaissance missions to Singapore. These missions were requested by Lord Louis Mountbatten who had become aware of the B-29s capabilities during his visit to the bases.

Two award ceremonies during January brought 253 medals to members of the 40th.

February brought the start of a major transition. The Group was moving to a new base of operations. The move reduced the Group's offensive effort and cut combat flying down to four missions with two additional photo reconnaissance assignments that required general sorties back to the Singapore. area.

The flyers of the 40th had been gaining more confidence in the battle worthiness of the B-29. That confidence was bolstered by the experience of a crew on one of the Singapore bombing missions.

Singapore was regarded as an especially tough target. It required a flight covering 2,000 miles from base, most of it over enemy held territory. Singapore was well defended by experienced fighter pilots and was surrounded by accurate anti-aircraft batteries.

The 40th Bomb Group over Osaka. (Courtesy of John P. Constandy)

Robert L. Hall who was a gunner on the "Winged Victory II" (aircraft #538), with pilot Fountain L. Brown and co-pilot O.W. Burchett, recalls that there weren't any of the expected fighters around when the planes released their bombs about 20,000 feet above the target. Things changed very quickly.

Hall said, ". . . anti-aircraft fire started bursting around us at the time of bombs away," "I was sitting in my swivel chair in the upper blister, scanning the sky for fighters. After bombs away, as we turned away from the bomb run, there was the 'plunk' noise of flak striking us and a strange sensation as the cabin suddenly depressurized. At the time of the sudden noise I was facing to the left of the plane. I spun around trying to see where we were hit, and I saw a gaping hole, perhaps five or six feet in diameter, like a bite out of the trailing edge of the right wing behind number three engine nacelle. We had taken a direct hit of an exploding anti-aircraft shrapnel shell. Strips of sheet metal from the wing were waving like small flags in the wind, but all propellers were still turning and we were flying straight and level."

Hall tried to contact the pilot through the intercom. It was dead. Being out of contact with the pilot was the most frightening problem to the young gunner.

Hall continued, "Every so often I would look at the damaged area to see if there was any sign of fuel or oil leak, but I saw none. I also looked through the tunnel, without success, for any sign of activity up front. I saw no one. I had the panicky thought that they could be bailing out up front. If the intercom and emergency intercom were both out, then the alarm bell could be out, too. How would we know if they put the plane on autopilot and bailed out?" Hall strained to watch for parachutes below.

Air rushing across and through dozens of small holes punched in the fuselage by the exploding shell raised the noise level in the plane. Right gunner Everett Nygard tried to yell something to Hall. All Hall heard was ". . . hit . . . Moncrief, wounded. . . ." Hall misunderstood, thinking that Nygard meant radar operator Lloyd Moncrief was wounded, ordered Nygard to, go help him. Later Hall would learn it was Nygard, not Moncrief who was wounded and needing help.

Another B-29 pulled along side to escort the crippled plane. It meant someone would be able to report their position to rescuers if they went down. It also reduced Hall's concern about fighter attacks with no gunner for protection on the right side. Without an intercom, Hall was unable to contact rear gunner Harrell Moore and had no way of knowing his condition.

Away from the target area and with another plane in sight, Hall felt comfortable enough to try to contact crew members at the other end of the forward tunnel.

Hall said, "I climbed down from my seat and saw the Navigator, Leonard Jellis, at the other end of the tunnel. I tried by hand signals to get him to come aft. After some delay, perhaps to contact Brown, he did crawl back through the tunnel. He said Brown wanted me to come forward."

In the cockpit, Hall described the grave condition of the wing, but noted that there was no sign of a fuel or oil leak.

Some time later, with both engines and plane in stable condition, someone (Hall believes probably flight engineer Leonard Morris) suggested they should repair holes in the fuselage to increase cabin pressure. The pilot wanted to maintain altitude to save fuel so the crew was having to stay on portable oxygen. Stuffing the holes with chewing gum and pieces of insulation would increase cabin pressure and minimize their need for extra oxygen. Crew members chewed dozens of sticks of gum from the supply kit to plug smaller holes in the fuselage.

Bomber crew of the Eddie Allen II, March 1944 after coming from Japan on two engines. (Courtesy of Mrs. C. Sullivan)

It was about half way home that Brown turned the plane over to the co-pilot and made what Hall recalls as a calm and leisurely trip to the rear of the plane to survey the damage. Psychologically it helped reassure less experienced crewmen in the rear of the plane.

Brown made detailed plans after consulting with the crew. Fearing damage to the flaps would cause them to break loose if lowered, he

Bobby Shank's Crew, Chakulia, India, 1944. Back row l to r: Sommers, Majors, Ogelsby, Lentz, Basche, and Poplaski. Front row l to r: Shanks, Fletcher, Cochran, Benedict, and Etherington. (Courtesy of G.M. Etherington)

chose to land at high speed with flaps up. A parachute was rigged to throw out the rear of the plane to help slow the huge ship.

If all the holes weren't enough, as they prepared to land a cockpit indicator light failed to show the right gear locked down. After visual checks they decided to land anyway.

Hall described the landing as, ". . . the smoothest that I have ever experienced." Until the touchdown the plane's safety was in doubt. The crew kept the plane in the air for nine hours after the flak hit.

"I remember watching with amusement the faces of ground crews as we taxied past them and they saw the extent of the battle damage, and at this point I could take some pleasure in their sagging jaws and awed whistles," Hall continued.

Recalling the strain of those nine hours Hall said, "I think that I have never felt so tired as I did the next day, probably partly as an hangover from the hypoxia and partly from tension. For many hours I had had too little oxygen while working feverishly a good part of the time. My jaws ached for a couple of days from chewing so much gum while short of oxygen."

After they were safely on the ground the crew realized the full extent of the damage. Several pieces of shrapnel had gone completely through the gunnery compartment, one lodging in Hall's parachute just inches from his back.

The official damage report included severe damage to the right wing flap and adjacent wing structure, the right landing gear strut failing, a fuel transfer line, instrument lines including fuel quantity, a few control cables, numerous electrical wires including main power busses in the bomb bay, oxygen lines and bottles, pressurization ducts, bomb racks, right and top blisters, the IFF unit, the right stabilizer, and hundreds of holes through the fuselage and tunnel.

The damage to "Winged Victory II" was so severe that Fountain Brown requested, and

A little rest and relaxation in Calcutta. L to R: Leslie F. Savage, James I. Potts, Jr., William E. McQueen, Rudolf C. Zubach. February 1945. (Courtesy of J. Ivan Potts, Jr.)

L to R: Lt. John P. Brusco, Lt. David Miles Lustig, Hsinching, China. (Courtesy of John Brusco)

Renfro's crew, Chengtu Area

Calamity Jane, Chakulia, India, Jan. 1945. 25th BS. Standing L to R: James I. Potts, Jr., Reginald A. Manning, Leslie F. Savage, Rudolph C. Zubach, Wm. E. McQueen, Zane E. Bloom, Myrel D. Massey. Kneeling, Irving M. Craig, George E. Kelly, Donald C. Jones, and Robert Mrugala. (Courtesy of J. Ivan Potts, Jr.)

got, another plane. The successful landing with a five foot hole in the wing was another example that the B-29 could take a tremendous beating and still stay in the air.

On February 24th and 25th two ground and crew detachments of about 1,300 men, including 74 flying crew members, boarded a train with their equipment and headed for Calcutta enroute to an unknown destination. This loss of maintenance personnel at Chakulia forced cuts in flight time, even for training.

The outstanding social event in February was a visit by Admiral Lord Louis Mounbatten. Lord Louis was quite proud to be the first theatre commander to have some control of the B-29s for reconnaissance use and the missions at Saigon, Bangkok, and Singapore.

February 23rd bought the departure of nine combat crews for the states in eight B-29s. The loss of experienced combat veterans was a blow to the group but no one begrudged their going. Some replacement crews fresh from training in the states were arriving at a steady pace. The total strength of the Group thus remained about the same with about 60 flight crews.

February brought fewer sorties, but increasing effectiveness. Lord Mountbatten praised the group for two important strikes.

The floating dry dock at Singapore had been the target of cameras on earlier reconnaissance runs. This time the B-29s made a return appearance loaded with bombs.

The main target was the dry dock, the largest in the world, capable of handling repairs on the largest of Japanese Naval vessels. As an added attraction the 70 B-29s from the 58th Wing that made the trip bagged a transport that was sitting in the dock for repairs. The dock was of major importance because it was Japan's main source of repair to their largest naval vessels outside Japan and by its sinking the Japs were materially hampered in their movements in the Pacific.

The Rama VI Bridge at Bangkok was the second key target to feel the wrath of the 40th Bombardment Group, as well as ammunition dumps at Rangoon. The Rama VI Bridge was of strategic importance for the impending allied invasion of Burma.

Two additional photo missions were scheduled for the Singapore area. The reconnaissance sorties were no small undertaking. The B-29s long-range capabilities provided military strategists with one of the few sources of aerial intelligence deep in enemy territory. That also meant the Superforts were often on their own far from home base and without protective fighter cover.

Several of the huge planes were shot up by Japanese fighters during these missions, with one being shot down. Still, the flights were critical for obtaining photo coverage of that area for the impending invasion operations by the British. During the month the Group lost two B-29s and 14 of their personnel.

Even with the recon missions, time moved slowly for crew members left behind at Chakulia. The pending move meant little activity beyond the minimum needed to keep up already low-key operations. About the only other activity was the continual packing of equipment and supplies for shipment to the new base. With most of the equipment in crates, even ground training practically came to a halt.

On March 20th four lead crews were headed to the new base somewhere in the Marianas. Members of the 40th were again pioneering the way for others. What the lead crews learned operating under new conditions would help

Pyote Army Air Field, TX. April. Standing L to R: Richard C. Fischer, F/O Gerald C. Frybarger, Capt. Thomas E. Turner, Lt. John P. Constandy, Lt. Nathan Hicks. Back row L to R: S/Sgt. George R. Brown, Cpl. William E. Hixenbaugh, Cpl. Thomas J. McMillan, Cpl. Carroll T. Rabb, Cpl. Melvin S. Shirley, and Cpl. Harold Morgan. (Courtesy of N. Hicks)

train fresh B-29 crews who would arrive later.

Like people the world over, the flyers were shocked and saddened by the death of President Franklin Roosevelt on 13 April 1945. They were sure the President had been a casualty of war just as surely as if he had been killed by a Kamikaze attack.

April 1st brought April Fools Day, Easter and 40th Group Organization Day all rolled into one. Only a few old timers were able to recall the formation of the 40th in Puerto Rico four years earlier.

The 40th Bomb Group's new home was to be West Field on Tinian Island, among the Marianas.

On 16 April 1945 General Ramey addressed the men, briefing them on conditions they would face on Tinian. The General served notice that the group and wing as a whole would be operating on a shoestring, hat they would be using makeshift buildings and green maintenance personnel for awhile. A great deal would be expected from the four original B-29 groups as befitted their reputation.

During the last week of April the 40th Bomb Group completed its movement of B-29s as part of the reactivated 58th Bomb Wing.

The change of stations meant an unprecedented flight of 3,960 statute miles including several hundred miles over enemy territory and enemy controlled waters. Only one plane failed to make non-stop trip. The "Eddie Allen" made a forced landing in the Philippines to quickly repair some mechanical problems.

The April move brought combat missions to a halt. By the end of the month only a small contingent was left in India awaiting orders. The 40th Bombardment Group was settling into its new headquarters on Tinian.

Like the Group's previous moves, the new station provided a change of scenery but not much else. "From Borinquen Field to the Galapagos Islands to Pratt to Chakulia to Hsinching to Tinian, there was nothing but primitive living conditions and misery that was just a cut above the worst," recalls Willaim Rooney. "If it ever got livable, we moved. If anyone laughed at the misery it was because there was nothing else to do."

The base on Tinian reminded the few old timers still around of "tent city" where the 40th

T/Sgt. William Houts with Calamity Jane of the 25th BS, Chakulia, India, 1944. (Courtesy of William S. Houts)

started out, or maybe the Rock that had provided them with plenty of stories about primitive living to tell the newcomers at Pratt. Everyone lived in tents but Quonset Huts were promised.

Enlisted men and officers alike shared a cramped mess hall and although it was crowded the food that the mess officers served was a definite improvement over that to which the group had become accustomed in India. Such items as fresh butter, corn-on-the-cob, pork chops, celery and ice cream more than made up for the crowded conditions in the mess hall.

Although it was hot at mid-day the weather was pleasant. Almost constant trade winds made it seem cooler, especially at night. The men of the 40th were also able to give up the mosquito netting that had become a nightly chore at bases in the CBI area.

The entertainment was also greatly improved. In India and China USO shows were few and the troupes that did make it were not exactly first rate. On Tinian there was swimming as well as additional entertainment by several orchestras formed by members of the various bomb groups.

Morale was generally good. However, some of the crews had been overseas for 18 months and some had more than 500 hours of operational time. That, plus the knowledge that they now needed 35 missions to be rotated, and even then might not get a break, created some quiet concern.

After a one-month break from combat the men of the 40th were as anxious to get back to work as any other GI. May brought eight combat trips to the Japanese mainland - a record for the 40th, but one which from all indications would not stand for very long. The cost was high: 43 men missing, four wounded, and three injured after bailing out at Iwo Jima.

Operating procedures for the 40th Bombardment Group changed. Now under the XXI Bomber command everything accelerated.

On April 29th it became known that the group might participate in its first mission from Tinian on the 30th. Subsequent to the first information received there were two delays in take off date and a complete target change. With subsequent missions it became apparent that the good old days in India, where the group had a week to ten days to prepare for a mission, were gone forever. Changes in dates and targets could be expected up to within a few hours of take-off.

May brought four night missions and five daylight raids. Two night raids on Tokyo were the most challenging. They also brought the most punishment to man and machine.

Two of the largest fire-bombing missions of the war came against Tokyo on May 24th and 26th. The 40th bomb Group contributed 30 B-29s to the more than 500 that dropped almost 4,000 tons of bombs on Tokyo during each of the two missions.

Anti-aircraft and automatic weapons fire was the most intense and accurate the group had ever experienced and enemy searchlight activity was excellent. According to one crewman, "The flak was so thick you could get out and walk on it."

"Batteries of searchlights picked us up shortly after we started our run," recalls J.E. "Dusty" Child, pilot of the "Tabooma II" (Aircraft # 233). "Each battery of lights would walk us into the next battery as we proceeded on course."

"By the time we reached the immediate target area fires were building up rapidly. There were patches of fire on the eastern outskirts of Tokyo and larger areas of fire in the center of the city. There was enough light to see certain key portions of the city. On the whole, it was one horrendous area of fire."

The huge firestorm on the ground created some of the roughest flying the B-29s encountered during the war. Some flyers described what they saw as a surrealistic fireworks display, with fire so high in the air it was impossible to tell where the ground ended and the sky began. Heat and smoke billowing up from the conflagration below created extreme turbulence and thermals.

"We were like a cork on the ocean, bouncing in every direction," Child continued. "We entered the cloud at the prescribed bombing altitude, which was 10,000 or 11,000 feet, as I recall. We came out of the smoke a few minutes later at 16,000 or 17,000 feet. At our speed that meant the smoke cloud was some 10 to 15 miles in diameter. The odor of smoke was very evident inside the aircraft."

Pilot Carter McGregor with the 45th Squadron observed what he termed a black area on the flight path. "As we plunged into the

Officers quarters, Tinian, May 1945. New Mess Hall in background. (Courtesy of J. Ivan Potts, Jr.)

Tinian, May 1945. 40th BG area looking west. 25th BS tent city behind quonsets. (Courtesy of J. Ivan Potts, Jr.)

Crew of Tabooma III. (Courtesy of Lewis Fussell

West field looking back on 40th BG area. (Courtesy of John P. Constandy)

West field of the 40th BS, 25th BS. B-29s parked and ready for missions. (Courtesy of John P. Constandy)

stygian darkness, it was as though a giant hand had grabbed our plane and was attempting to tear it to shreds. We had entered the smoke cloud from the burning city, and I had never experienced such turbulence, not even in the most viscous thunderstorm. I yelled for the co-pilot to get on the controls with me, and we had no thought of trying to maintain altitude or direction. We were just struggling to keep the plane from turning on its back."

The May 24th raid brought evidence of a new threat to the B-29s. Intelligence officers initially thought the Tokyo firestorm had sparked overwrought imaginations of the crew members. Further interviews and investigation brought a different evaluation.

Several crews reported seeing tremendous explosions in the air. A number of B-29 losses on the mission were unexplained. The planes disappeared without issuing a distress call.

"Our intelligence officers sorted through the interrogation reports, details of a crude, small aircraft captured on Okinawa, radio messages broadcast by raving Japanese military leaders, and came up with "the Baka Bomb," a suicide plane which could be launched from the belly of a bomber such as the Betty, a standard Japanese medium bomber," recalls 25th Squadron bombardier James O'Keefe.

In its desperation to stop the B-29s, the Japanese Command armed the fighters with more than 2,000 pounds of explosives. They added rockets to provide the suicide planes with a last moment burst of speed to ram the faster B-29s.

O'Keefe recalls the description of the Baka Bomb tactics offered during a briefing for the second fire bomb mission.

"The Baka can be aimed and released at you when you're caught in and illuminated by ground searchlights. But, before you come in range of those searchlights beware of the mother plane which we think also carries a powerful searchlight capable of picking you up at a distance. And, of course, if the mother plane is one of the fast Bettys, it can keep up with you, hold you in its light while its Baka is released and overtakes you. And. . . uh," the intelligence officer's voice trailed away, "You're welcome to look at these diagrams and pictures of this. . . uh, new weapon."

O'Keefe and the other flyers at the briefing were keenly aware of the beating the Navy had taken at the hands of Kamikazes. The intelligence officer was unable to offer a means of defense to the suicide attacks.

Gunners became trigger-happy worrying about the flying bombs. After the next flight O'Keefe admitted to bringing four 50 caliber machine guns to bear on a bright light he thought was a mother ship. He later realized it was the planet Venus shinning in the pre-dawn sky.

There were also reports of a B-29 firing on another Superfortress with an engine on fire. The gunners apparently mistook the engine blaze for the trail of an oncoming rocket propelled fighter.

One co-pilot later described seeing one of the Japanese suicide machines taking its toll. "As I looked at a B-29 about a quarter mile to the right I saw the tail gunner firing furiously at a target above and behind him. There was a ball of fire, which seemed to be following down the tracks of the incendiary bullets. It kept coming and rammed the B-29 just in front of its tail section, exploding with such terrific force that we rocked from it. Parts of both planes rained down."

As rough as the flights over Japan could be, the flight to and from the target was often unnervingly peaceful.

"As we moved along our flight path which would take us over Tokyo again, my mind went back to the previous months," Ivan Potts recalled on his last flight over Japan. "The long lonely nights on the way to the target, the blackness of the ocean, and the tropical weather front which seemed to always rest between Iwo Jima and Japan. I remembered the beautiful rings of neon-like light around our props and the seemingly millions of specks of light on our windshield from the static electricity as we passed through the front. Also the reports from our gunners when the electrical charge built high enough to escape through our wing tips bursting in great globs of fire."

Potts continued, "I would never forget the

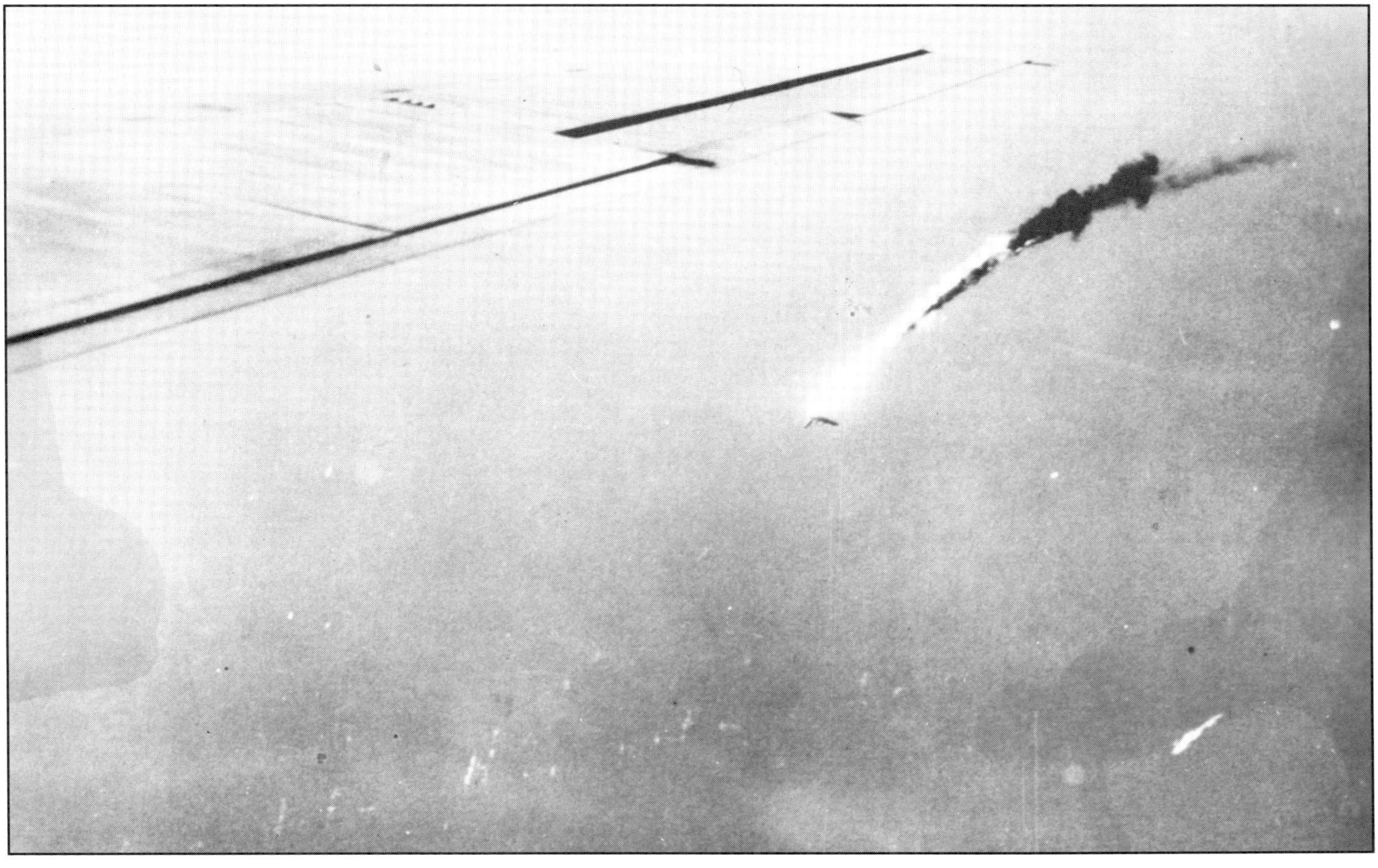

An enemy plane falls to the ocean after a hit by the gunners in a B-29. (Courtesy of Everett E. Swanson)

Lt. Otto Kerstner the 25th BS sitting on a 4,000 pound bomb, Tinian. (Courtesy of Otto Kerstner)

sun rising through the scattered cloud banks which explained the Japanese flag. I remembered also that with the dawn how utterly beautiful Chicijima, the largest of the Bonin Islands would appear, not knowing at the time that it was the site of unspeakable cruelty to our airmen who happened to go down there."

"Japanese Lt. General Yosi Tachivana, commander of the garrison there, ordered the death of dozens of American Airmen by beating, bayonetting, and beheadings and the cannibalizing of their bodies."

May 8th and VE Day brought the end of the war in Europe. VE Day also brought a new point system for rotating flight crews and ground personnel home. However, an announcement that the system would not apply to B-29 crews, caused morale to drop considerably.

Despite major successes against Japan on land, sea, and in the air, the end of the war in the Pacific was nowhere in sight.

June brought a blitz against the Japanese mainland. There was a sense that some of the resources that had been directed against Hitler would soon be headed toward the Pacific Theatre. The Group flew ten missions (a new record) including seven more fire bomb strikes against urban areas.

The fire bombing raids brought a new dimension to the war. While there were some weight restrictions due to fuel requirements for each raid, a B-29 loaded with up to 12,000 pounds of incendiaries could wipe out more than 15 acres. The rain of fire effectively destroyed Japan's ability to resist.

Under the plan promoted by General LeMay, the first wave of planes carried jelled-gasoline bombs (napalm) that started a series of small fires around the target. Another wave then dropped oil cannisters that sprayed additional fuel on the blaze. Still another wave dropped magnesium thermite bombs to increase the intensity of the fires even more. Through trial and error the fire bomb attacks were perfected.

In Japan's closely packed cities the fire storms were far more effective than bombing with traditional explosives. By massing planes by the hundreds for the raids the devastation was incredible. The planes also went in at lower altitude to improve accurracy. The raids left Tokyo 86% destroyed. One raid by 175 Superforts destroyed almost 99% of Toyama.

June 11 provided a welcome change. Censorship of out going mail was relaxed, allowing many of the men to tell their families with some accuracy where they were and what they were doing for the first time since leaving the states.

Censorship had attracted the ire of the flyers since their arrival in India. The men circulated a "Love Letter" inspired by the censorship:

B-29 Out of Service (Courtesy of Robert M. Harchett)

Can't write a thing - the censor to blame,
Just say I'm well and sign my name.
Can't tell where we flew from
Can't mention the date
And, can't even number the meals that I ate.
Can't say where we are going,
Don't know where we'll land,
Couldn't inform you if met by a band.
Can't mention the weather,
Can't say if there's rain,
All Military secrets must remain.
Can't have a flashlight to guide me at night,
Can't light a match except out of sight,
Can't keep a diary for such is a sin,
Can't say for sure just what I can write,
So I'll call this a letter and close with "Good Night."

The Group historian reported that the easing of censorship, along with word that crews that had completed 35 missions, would not be required to make additional combat sorties, brought improved morale.

To celebrate the anniversary of the 40th Bomb Group's first visit to the skies over Japan on June 15, General "Hap" Arnold dropped in to award the four groups of the 58th Wing the Distinguished Unit Citation.

Thus, for the second consecutive month, the 20th consecutive mission and the 649th consecutive sortie ended without a casualty or the loss of any air-borne plane - a record that is believed unparalleled in any B-29 group.

The third month of the "blitz" against Japan brought more changes in Air Corps operating structure, changes that were taking the U.S. another step closer to an Air Force separate and independent of military ground forces. Many of the changes were brought about by the unique combat operations of the B-29s.

The XXI Bomber Command became a part of the 8th Air Force. Both were under the command of the new United States Army Strategic Air Forces.

At the end of the month Allied forces started using a psychological tactic. Future targets were announced to the Japanese people in advance. The move came after the unconditional surrender ultimatum was issued at Potsdam. It succeeded in causing some panic among the Japanese people. Many left their homes in the crowded cities, deserting factory jobs that were crucial to Japan's war industry.

By the time the ultimatum was issued the Japanese fleet was reduced to a few scattered light units by Admiral Halsey's American and British carrier aircraft. However, at the end of the month Japanese radio reported that the war lords would ignore the surrender ultimatum.

At the end of the month almost a hundred combat personnel who had traveled overseas in early 1944 were still with the 40th. Combat crews with more than 35 missions were being rotated back to the states, some for additional training, some for 30 day leave, others for discharge or reassignment.

The departure of a large contingent of mechanics, technicians, and ground crewmen for home raised the morale of the remaining men. The improvement in living conditions didn't hurt either. Tents were quickly being replaced by Quonset Huts for living quarters.

The month of July included a series of night incendiary raids against Kure, Takamatsu, Chiba, Sendai, Utsunomiya, Numazu, Fukui, and Tsu.

The only daylight raid of the month on the 24th to Osaka was also one of the group's most effective of the war.

"The largest number of aircraft the Group had ever put into the air, 43, were airborne, and of this number, 40 reached the primary target in four large formations. A total of 240 tons were released on the target with excellent results.

L to R: Pvt. Montefusco, T/Sgt. James A. Knox, Capt. William E. Drislane, Lt. Donald Q. Sammis, Cpl. Charles K. Ridge, Sgt. Carroll F. Coleman, and T/Sgt. Rodolfo Hernandez.

The first formation had 85% of its bombs within 1000 feet of the aiming point, the second had 81.5% , the third had 88% and the last had 94%. The Group average was 85.4% of its bombs within 1000 feet of the aiming point and all four formations bombed within a time interval of approximately two minutes. Damage assessment photos showed 95.5% of the target destroyed.

Things moved quickly going into August 1945 as climax followed climax and the war moved quickly to a close.

On 2 August more than 800 B-29s dropped an unprecedented 6,000 tons of bombs on the Japanese Empire; on 6 August the first Atomic bomb was dropped, on 8 August Russia entered the war against Japan; on 9 August the second A-bomb was dropped on Nagasaki; on 10 August Japan offered to surrender under certain conditions; and finally on 15 August, after a tense, nerve-wracking period of suspense, President Truman announced the war was over.

The months spent on Tinian had been hectic. Members of the 40th Bomb Group were too busy keeping their heads down trying to win the war to pay attention to what the guys were doing over on North Field. The guys over on North Field, members of the 509th Composite Group, were preparing to drop the first atomic bomb. Just as the flyers of the 40th were unaware of the atomic bomb, they were also unaware that their work pioneering the development of the B-29 had been helping engineers perfect the only plane capable of delivering the "superbomb" to the Japanese mainland.

During what was to become the last month of the war there were four strikes. Bombing accuracy improved even more as Japan's resistance continued to falter. The two were interrelated. The effective strikes were cutting huge chunks out of the Emperor's war machine. As the wheels of Japan's war industry stopped turning, there were fewer fighters to confront the B-29s. Anti-aircraft crews were being pressed into service elsewhere preparing for what the Japanese Command believed would be an almost certain mainland invasion.

The four August missions also meant a continuation of the Group's safe return record in which the 40th suffered neither a fatality nor the loss of an airborne plane.

Ironically, the last mission on August 14 came as the Japanese were preparing to announce their surrender. All formations joined in one of the best coordinated performances for the Group with 68% of all bombs landing within 1000 feet of the aiming point. 42 planes in four formations bombed in less than one minute at Hikari under the direction of lead bombardiers James L. Payton, W.E. McQulen, W.W. Beck and Harold Dickerson.

As the B-29s turned to head home, ground crews on Tinian were getting word the war was ending. The code word "UTAH" was flashed to the planes, a signal that they were to jettison their bombs over the sea and return to base, but they had already hit their target and closed their bomb bay doors for the last time.

Planes of the 40th BG load supplies to drop on POW camps in Japan. Saipan, 1945. (Courtesy of J. Ivan Potts, Jr.)

POW camp in Taipan. (Courtesy of John P. Constandy)

Many hours before the planes returned radio Tokyo announced Japan's acceptance of the Potsdam Ultimatum and when the planes finally arrived home they were met by a large number of the ground personnel. The results of their mission and their reception was a fitting ending to the Group's combat efforts.

While the war was over, the Group was to record one more loss the last week of August. The B-29s were called to take part in a mission of mercy, delivering food and medical supplies to POW camps in Japan.

After months of dumping tons of destruction on Japanese cities, the flyers felt good about dropping relief to some of their own held captive behind enemy lines. The huge B-29s, no longer threatened by fighters or flak, were able to drop from the high altitudes where they had rained down so much destruction on the enemy. The POW relief effort, requiring low altitude drops, was a very different type of flying than the Group had experienced during the war.

"The Japanese envoys who met with U.S. representatives to arrange terms of the peace agreement were asked for, and provided, longitude and latitude of the POW camps," O.W. Burchett noted later. "Some aircrews in the

40th and other groups were immediately assigned and started loading aircraft with oil drums rigged with parachutes and loaded with medical supplies, food, and clothing. This was to be our first contact with our surviving comrades in the prison situations. Both bomb bays were loaded, and we were briefed with very little information as to the identity of our drop zone and very little information on the anticipated drop trajectory. It seems to me there were four other aircraft in addition to mine. We were assigned to drop on a camp at Taihokli, Formosa. We were briefed to fly direct to Formosa, locate the target, drop one bomb bay from very low altitude or less than 500 feet. After observing the results, we then could make some calculated corrections to drop the second bomb bay of supplies."

While circling looking for the camps, Burchett and his crew observed Japanese civilians on roads below, walking and riding bicycles in a very normal manner seeming to ignore the huge airplane overhead.

"We arrived over Formosa in good weather, but finding and properly identifying the POW camp proved to be difficult and time consuming. We did locate the camp at the base of some hills on the edge of a small stream. We observed a sign on a roof reading, TWO KILLED AVOID CAMP, and next to the camp was an open field with a sign reading, PW SUPPLIES DROP HERE. We took K-20 pictures of these signs. Then we dropped the first bomb bay satisfactorily, but the prisoners rushed the field in such panic that we had to delay the second drop until they cleared the field. This was an extremely tear jerking sight. We really would have enjoyed stopping to pick up a load of POW's."

But, even these mercy flights after the war were not without tragedy. The flyers were saddened to learn later some POW's had been killed during one of the earlier mercy missions. Parachutes on the supply crates failed to open. The falling boxes and 55 gallon drums hit desperately hungry prisoners who scrambled into the drop zone to retrieve food before all of the supplies fell to the ground. The deaths prompted the signs Burchett's crew spotted from the air.

Still another tragedy darkened the POW mercy missions. Bombardier Delmar Johnson volunteered for two of the flights between August 27 and September 20, 1945. He was aboard one of two planes that headed to Yatawa.

Johnson said, "Knowing some of each crew I had my choice of aircraft and crew. Since I had flown once before with Ken Dothage, I chose his crew, which was to be our good fortune. The flight was long and uneventful until we were approaching the Islands, which were completely 'socked in.' We stayed on top in almost clear weather, searching for openings to get down to our drop altitude of 800 feet. After a couple of hours of circling the target with no such opening appearing, we decided to go out over the water to get down under the heavy clouds, head into the harbor, make our drop, and immediately climb out."

He continued, "If my memory serves me correctly, our maps showed hills to be not over 600 to 650 feet nearby in the heading we were on. There was absolutely no visibility above our approximately 600 to 800 feet. Our drop was made and as we began climbing slowly, my recollection is that the radar observer screamed to 'pull up and turn right,' which Ken immediately did - with all throttles at the limit. Evidently the radar operator saw a dark left patch on his screen and lighter on the right. Not too many seconds later. . . we were about 1300-1350 feet altitude - and a brief second of clouds disappeared. Off our right wing, not more than 20 or 30 feet, were the trees, just as we cleared the top. Ken Dothage, John Laxton and I saw what in all probability John Cornwell and the others in the B-29 a few minutes behind us did not see - and they were killed in the crash of their plane."

It was only now at the end of the war that the 40th Bombardment Group was granted an unofficial nickname. There had been several requests for a designation to be used in news dispatches sent back to the states. But, the designation of the "Kagu-Tsuchi Bomb Group" came too late to be of much use.

The new nickname, however late in coming, was appropriate. Kagu-Tsuchi was ". . . the Japanese fire god who in mythological times had vowed to return some day and destroy Japan by fire. The B-29s of the 40th were the modern embodiment of Kagu-Tsuchi. They had done more than their share of destroying Japan by fire."

The Japanese surrender found the 40th Bombardment Group half a world away from where it came into existence.

According to the Group Historian Capt. Forrest G. Wood, "The Group had participated in 70 combat missions and had dropped a total of 9,218 tons of bombs on enemy targets. Its claims numbered 46.5 enemy planes destroyed, 92 probably destroyed and 64 damaged. The cost had been 32 B-29s lost in combat, 53 men killed, 26 wounded and 134 missing."

Within days of the surrender dozens of men were heading home. So many were leaving the group promotions were needed to keep some semblance of organization. The Group was able to promote 165 enlisted men and five officers during August.

As things continued to wind down, September became a month of rumors and speculation about when the Group would pull out for home.

In the meantime, the 40th joined in the "Show of Strength" flight over Tokyo during the signing of the surrender.

The Group contributed 36 aircraft to the day's formalities. Assembling over Japan, the aircraft, together with B-29s from all over the Marianas put on a magnificent power display during signing of the official surrender terms on the USS Missouri. It was a long and tiresome flight, but all agreed that it was well worth the trouble.

Figuring out how to get back to the states was suddenly the Group's biggest problem. There weren't enough B-29s to haul all of the equipment and men. Someone was going to have to take the slow road by ship.

Each aircraft was to have a crew of eight and was to carry 12 passengers. Those finally selected had to have over the critical point score, and if a crew member, at least 10 missions to his credit.

The 40th Bombardment Group that had seen so many firsts during the war contributed a plane and crew to another first after the end of the war. On September 13th three B-29s were to attempt a non-stop Japan to Washington, D.C. flight.

It was the kind of test flight Boeing engineers wanted to try before the B-29 went into battle.

Ivan Potts had become squadron "Gravel Officer." He was in command of three trucks and drivers charged with hauling crushed coral to spread on roads and walkways around the Tinian Air Base. Much of his time was spent searching for his trucks. They were often stolen by Marines who went joy riding around the island until the trucks ran out of gas and were abandoned.

After dispatching his trucks one morning Lt. Colonel William Kingsbury approached Potts to ask, "How would you like to go home?" It was the kind of question any homesick G.I. could answer without thinking, especially since the war had been over for a month.

A few days later Kingsbury told Potts they would head for Guam to represent the wing. However, he didn't mention that the trip home would be non-stop. Crews worked around the clock for 10 days to prepare the planes for the long flight.

The only field large enough to accommodate the B-29s was at Mizzutani on Hokkaido, the northern-most island of Japan. A tentative flight plan called for a trip of 6,762 miles.

Leaving Guam heading for the departure point in Japan by way of Iwo Jima the crew got one last glimpse of Tinian and Saipan. They were lying like two emeralds surrounded by the sparkling white shorelines and the beautiful blue Pacific.

During an overnight stop at Iwo Jima the crews were reminded of the thousands of Marines of the 5th Amphibious Corps who died taking the "pork chop" island. The island was still pock marked with craters, blasted in rapid succession by the naval assault on the island February 19, 1945.

The overnight stop at Iwo Jima had a practical purpose. The planes had to be loaded with as much fuel as possible when they arrived at Hokkaido because of the severe gasoline shortage in Japan.

The landing at Hakkaido generated some apprehensive feelings. Colonel Blanchard had determined the field would handle B-29s but there was some concern that the planes were so heavy with their load of fuel they would break through the concrete.

A brief encounter with Japanese troops at the Sapporo Airbase created a curious moment. "As we landed at Sapporo we were greeted by about 30 soldiers and the Japanese commander. They were all lined up and were very polite. When General LeMay stepped off the plane he was greeted by the airbase commander. The Japanese officer smartly saluted General LeMay, who made it very clear that he had no intention of returning the salute and the poor

B-29s over Tokyo, VJ Day, 2 Sept. 1945. 25th BS, 40th BG. (Courtesy of John E. Child)

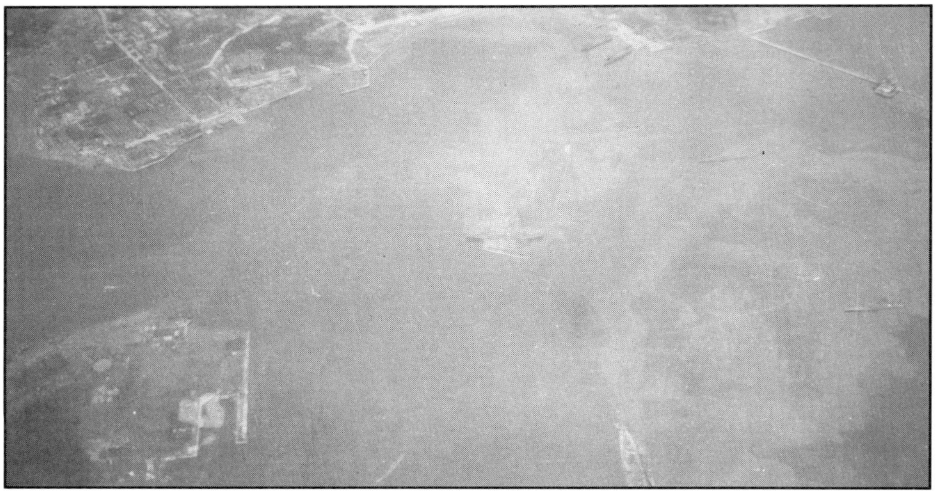

VJ Day fly over 20th AF at moment of treaty signing. USS Missouri. Tokyo Bay, 2 Sept. 1945. (Courtesy of John P. Constandy)

fellow stood there saluting for quite some time before he finally dropped his right hand."

Just as the B-29s had helped take the war to Japan the crews they now carried were the first Americans to be encountered by the Japanese at Sapporo.

Being in enemy country the men of the 40th wore their pistols at all times as they walked down the street in Sapporo. It was rather strange to see a Japanese come around the corner, meet a couple of them, and then run in the opposite direction.

The airfield at Sapporo was chosen as the starting point for the trip because its 8,200 foot runways were long enough for B-29s and at near sea level, the planes would get maximun lift.

It was only later that the crews learned the Japanese had planned to use almost the same flight path from Japan to America for some non-stop trips of their own. It was built by the Japanese for the purpose of sending four engine bombers on one way Kamakazi missions against west coast cities.

Just as the U.S. had been ahead of Germany in the development of an atomic bomb, the Superfortress was only about a year ahead of its Japanese counterpart.

America missed being attacked by Japanese bombers by a scant six months. The Japanese had bought the giant triple tailed DC-4E from Douglas when the airlines had demanded a smaller version, later to become the C-54. The airplane was turned over to the Japanese on September 29, 1939, who dissassembled it and shipped it by freighter to Japan. The Japanese used the DC-4E as a pattern for a four-engine bomber. It was the G5N "Liz", designed by Nakajima, both heavier and faster than a B-17. The Japanese had built six of them by the time the war ended.

The B-29s departed Hokkaido at 4:15 pm Washington time. The flight was expected to take 26 hours, ending in Washington at 7:00 pm the next day.

As the planes headed out to their destination a quarter of the way around the world the weather that had failed to cooperaate on dozens of bombing missions also turned sour on this trip. The B-29s didn't necessarily need a tail wind to make the trip a success. General LeMay would point out later, they did need something other than a head wind.

In addition to trying to set a world record for non-stop flight distance, the trip was to make use of the most direct flight path over the top of the world. The flight was designed to check out the jet stream and the 200 mph winds that the B-29 pilots had discovered flying high over Japan. The flight was supposed to determine if the winds would extend the range of planes flying over Alaska and Canada.

While the jet stream did exist, the flyers would later discover that a typhoon the week before had altered the winds along the flight path. In any case the weather officer was correct about the headwinds. The three planes were forced to cut their trip short, landing at Chicago to refuel before heading on to Washington.

When the figures were in, the three B-29s averaged 236 mph on a trip that covered 6,509 miles, almost half that against a head wind that averaged 70 miles an hour.

While the non-stop flight was still something of a success, members of the 40th Bomb Group were too busy to notice. "Most of us in the 40th knew little about the trip in September 1945 as we were busy preparing to fly our 45 B-29s home in October as part of the Sunset Project," explained Harry Changnon.

Those who did take time to notice the flight considered it something of a stunt designed to help get ranking officers as much newspaper ink as possible when they returned home. Most members of the Group were scrambling to pack up and get home as best they could without much fanfare.

While they were of questionable motive, the record breaking flights were useful. Just as the B-29 was the pioneer of long-range strategic aircraft, the flight home pioneered an air route that would later become a highway in the sky for commercial flights.

The trip demonstrated the tremendous possibilities of the air age. It was the longest non-stop flight in air force history, the first Grand Circle flight in history, (having started at Pratt, Kansas two years earlier), the first non-stop flight, and the first non-stop flight from Japan to the United States.

It was appropriate that at least a few members of the 40th Bomb Group got to participate in the flight. From their first encounter with the B-29, to their key role in perfecting it, to the flight home that explored what is now a major air route, the members of the 40th Bomb Group had helped push the use of aircraft into a new age for both military and civilian use.

In October members of the 40th Bomb Group headed home, ferrying 15 planes along with another 30 from other groups in the Wing to March Field at Riverside, California. After a month of R & R they were assigned to patrol the California coast, watching for balloon bombs and mines that may have been carried from Japan to the west coast by westerly winds. The planes were eventually equipped with radiation detection gear to monitor the coastline for radiation from the Bikini Atoll atomic tests.

Hokkaido. This hangar was the sleeping quarters for the crew of the Japan to Washington flight. (Courtesy of J. Ivan Potts, Jr.)

General LeMay's crew, Tinian, Sept. 13, 1945. Standing l to r: Capt. William W. Townes, 45th BS, 1st Lt. Stephen T. Jones, 25th BS, Major John F. Wedding, 468th BG, Lt. Col. William C. Kingsbury, 25th BS, Capt. Theodore R. Finder, 40th BG HQ, 1st Lt. John C. Eiland, 44th BS, 1st Lt. James I. Potts, Jr. 25th BS. Kneeling l to r: S/Sgt. Frank Klas, Jr. 44th BS, Sgt. Jerome A School, 25th BS, Sgt. Richard P. Fischer, 25th BS, Sgt. B.T. Freeman, 25th BS. (Courtesy of J. Ivan Potts, Jr.)

L to R: Major General Curtis E. LeMay, Brig. General Emmett O. Donnell, General Henry H. Arnold and Lt. General Barney M. Giles, shown shortly after completion of Boeing B-29 non-stop flight from Japan to Washington, D.C. Sept. 19, 1945. (U.S. Air Force photo, courtesy of J. Ivan Potts, Jr.)

There was also plenty of flying in air shows, spreading goodwill for the Air Corps in an effort that would eventually create the United States Air Force as a separate and equal part of the nation's armed forces. So many men wanted out of the Army that the 40th Bomb Group was left without enough staff to continue taking part in the shows.

The B-29s soon wore out their welcome as residents of the Riverside area complained that the huge planes made too much noise. It was more likely other considerations that prompted a move to Davis-Monthan Field near Tuscon, Arizona on 5 May 1946. Over the next six months most members of the 40th were transferred.

In September about a third went to Fort Worth, Texas to train in the new B-36 as part of the 7th Bomb Group, about a third transferred to the 43rd Bomb Group that had flown B-24s during the war, most of the remaining third were released from service. The crews who were transferred to train in the new B-36 voiced some concern about the assignment to another aircraft barely out of the experimental stage.

Turning down a chance to fly in the B-36 Harry Changnon commented, "After seeing so many of our friends lost and killed in the effort to develop the B-29, we didn't want to go through that again" Changnon, who had been with the 40th Bomb Group almost from the beginning, chose to join those who were returning to civilian life.

First Lieutenant William F. Seith was to be the last man out of the 40th Bomb Group. Special Orders Number 94 signed by Major Leslie E. Minor, Jr. (Air Corps Adjutant) officially mustered Seith out of the Group on 21 September 1946. One month later on 22 October the 40th Bomb Group was decommissioned.

BIBLIOGRAPHY

Birdsall, Steve. Saga of the Superfortress. Garden City, New York: Doubleday & Company, 198?.

Brief History of the 40th Bombardment Group, 1940-1946. Maxwell Air Force Base, Alabama: USAF Historical Division Research Institute, March 1956.

40th Bomb Group Memories. Issues 1-20 Wilmette, Illinois, 1985-87.

40th Bombardment Group (VH). San Angelo, Texas: Newsfoto Publishing Company, 1949.

LeMay, Curtis with MacKindlay Kantor. Mission with LeMay. New York: Doubleday & Company, 1965.

Morrison, Wilbur H. Point of no Return. New York: Playboy Paperbacks, 1980.

Moser, Don. China-Burma-India: World War II (V.9). Alexandria, Virginia: Time-Life Books, 1978.

Potts, Ivan. The Japan to Washington Flight. Shelbyville, Tennessee: J. Ivan Potts, Jr., 1981.

Stoumen, Lou "Round Trip to Japan" **Yank Weekly**. China-Burma-India Edition Vol. 1 No. 50, July 15, 1944.

Wheeler, Keith. Bombers Over Japan: World War II (V. 34). Alexandria, Virginia: Time-Life Books, 1982.

Wheeler, Keith. The Fall of Japan: World War II (V. 37). Alexandria, Virginia: Time-Life Books, 1983.

Wheeler, Richard. Iwo. New York: Lippencott and Crowell, 1980.

NICKNAMES AND NOSE ART

War correspondents helped keep folks back in the states interested in their reports with a liberal use of the colorful names the crews gave their planes. The colorful and sometimes risque artwork that became the rule on the noses of the huge planes also served to keep up the morale of crews. In reality, the crews did not often refer to their planes by nickname on the flight line.

Ground crews, pressed to keep each plane in good flying condition, needed to keep accurate maintenance and repair records. The effort required reams of paperwork. With dozens of planes to keep track of, most planes were referred to by the less colorful numbers emblazoned on the tail section, numbers that indicated the last three digits of the plane's serial number.

The naming of planes became complicated when plane number 574 was nicknamed the "293" (see page #63) The original number 293 was the first B-29 to be shot down over Japan. Employees of Boeing's Wichita plant who used war bonds to purchase replacements for the original 293 and the original "Eddie Allen" thought it would be appropriate to honor the crew of number 293 by nicknaming another plane after it.

BOMBIN'
BUGGY II

DING HOW!
頂好

40th Bomb Group Reunion, Anaheim, CA. 1982. (Courtesy of J. Ivan Potts, Jr.)

40th Bombardment Group (VH) Association

Reunions

No.	Location	Date
1	New Orleans, LA	Oct., 1980
2	Arlington, TX	Oct., 1981
3	Anaheim, CA	Oct., 1982
4	Dayton, OH	Sept., 1983
5	Williamsburg, VA	Oct., 1984
6	Denver, CO	Sept., 1985
7	Nashville, TN	Nov., 1986
8	St. Louis, MO	Oct., 1987
9	Philadelphia, PA	Sept., 1988
10	Omaha, NE	Sept., 1989

Ivan Potts, Ted Finder and General LeMay admire a fine cigar as they discuss the Japan to Washington flight. (Courtesy of J. Ivan Potts, Jr.)

40TH BOMB GROUP ASSOCIATION ROSTER

AARON, ELMER	BALA CYNWDY, PA
ABBOTT, JAMES W.	MESQUITE, TX
ABBOTT, ZANE L.	SALMON, ID
ABEY, NORMAN E.	GROSS POINTE, MI
ABRANOVIC, ALBERT	SCOTTSDALE, AZ
ADAMS, CLINTON S.	CAPE CORAL, FL
ADAMS, GORDON F.	SCOTTSDALE, AZ
ADAMS, JAY T.	EAST KAYSVILLE, UT
ADAMS, JOHN F.	MERILLVILLE, IN
ADAMSON, OLIVER E.	MESA, AZ
ADLER, THE REV. BARTH	LOUISVILLE, KY
AGATHER, VICTOR N.	MEXICO CITY, 10 DF MEXICO
AHERN, GEORGE I.	DENVER, CO
ALBERS, FERRIS A.	LONGVIEW, WA
ALBERT, ROBERT P.	HAMBURG, NY
ALDRICH, HERBERT	WATERVILLE, ME
ALEXANDER, C. DEXTER	GREENE, IA
ALFORD, JAMES M.	ZEBULON, NC
ALLARD, ALBERT H.	ROCHESTER, NY
ALLEN, HARLAN A.	NORTON, MA
ALLEN, LEO	MUSKEGON, MI
ALLENA, PETER	PETALUMA, CA
ALLISON, CHARLES E.	ARLINGTON, VA
ALTFELD, RICH	ELYRIA, OH
AMBROSINO, LEONARD D.	PLAINVILLE, NY
AMOROSO, JOHN J.	EAST BRUNSWICK, NJ
ANDERSON, DON	CLEAR LAKE, WI
ANDERSON, DR. PAUL S.	PITTSBURGH, PA
ANDERSON, HOWARD T.	VALPARAISO, FL
ANDERSON, MELVIN L.	KILDEER, ND
ANDERSON, PAUL A.	MIDLAND, TX
ANDERTON, DAVID A.	RIDGEWOOD, NJ
ANDREWS, HOWARD	FT. MYERS FL
ANDREWS, STAN S.	CAMERON, WI
ANFANG, WILLIAM	WOOSTER, OH
ANGOTT, DON	CEDAR RAPIDS, IA
ARCHER, E.C.	WHEATRIDGE, CO
ARCHER, MRS. LOIS A.	GRASS VALLEY, CA
ARLET, JOHN A.	PITTSBURGH, PA
ARNONE, SAM	WILLARD, OH
ARRINGTON, RICHARD V.	TULSA, OK
ATKINS, WILLIAM C.	HAMBURG, AR
AUSTIN, MRS. JOHN	ALVIN, TX
AYERS, ARTHUR M.	WICHITA, KS
BABB, ROBERT P.	CHILLICOTHE, MO
BACHMAN, GEORGE A.	CINCINNATI, OH
BACKES, JOHN	ST. LOUIS, MO
BACON, CHARLES	FT. LAUDERDALE, FL
BAETZ, WILLIAM	LIVONIA, MI
BAGLEY, CLIFFORD S.	ARLINGTON, TX
BAGLEY, WALTER S.	FAYETTEVILLE, NC
BAIAMONTE, ANTHONY B.	NEW ORLEANS, LA
BAIBA, MICHAEL S.	PHILADELPHIA, PA
BAILEY, JOHN A.	DENVER, CO
BAILEY, JOHN H.	GLENDALE, AZ
BAILEY, ROBERT T.	ALEXANDER CITY, AL
BAKER, GEORGE J.	SPRING HILL, FL
BAKER, WILLIAM E.	WALLA WALLA, WA
BAKKEN, TORVID E.	OCEANSIDE, CA
BALAGA, JACK	AUSTIN, TX
BALFOUR, LIONEL	ALBANY, GA
BALL, WALTER J.	GRAND RAPIDS, MI
BALON, JOHN S.	YORBA LINDA, CA
BALUTIS, ALBERT W.	MARSHFIELD, MA
BANKS, WILSON H.	SAN ANTONIO, TX
BANNING, RAY D.	WICHITA, KS
BARAGLIA, CAESAR	NEW BRITAIN, CT
BARBATO, JOHN F.	MIDDLE VALLEY, NY
BARG, ROBERT L.	AGUA DULCE, TX
BARNES, MRS. MAMIE	VICKBURG, MS
BARNES, WILLIAM E.	DODGE CITY, KS
BARRON, JOSEPH R.	CARMICHAEL, CA
BARRON, MRS. HAROLD E.	ST. LOUIS, MO
BARSOUM, ELIAS S.	FALLS CHURCH, VA
BARTON, DONALD W.	BRANDENTON, FL
BARTON, JOHN F.	MT. VERNON, OH
BASCH, JOHN J.	MILWAUKEE, WI
BASS, HOSKIN S.	JACKSONVILLE, NC
BASS, REUBEN G.	CENTRALIA, IL
BATASSA, DOMINICK	KENOSHA, WI
BATES, HOMER E.	MARKLE, IN
BAUGH, MRS. IRENE K.	SACRAMENTO, CA
BAUMAN, JUNIOR E.	CURTICE, OH
BAUSCH, HAROLD R.	AMITYVILLE, NY
BEABER, GLENN H.	COLUMBUS, OH
BEACH, ED	HUTCHINSON, KS
BEACHER, ALFRED R.	BALTIMORE, MD
BEAL, JESSE C.	PONCA CITY, OK
BEAN, JOHN L.	KANSAS CITY, MO
BEASLEY, EUAL	DOTHAN, AL
BEATTY, CALVIN J.	MONROE, MI
BEATY, W.R.	CARTHAGE, TX
BECK, ERNEST G.	PHOENIX, AZ
BECK, VICTOR W.	OKLAHOMA CITY, OK
BECKER, CONRAD F.	DEEP RIVER, CT
BECKLEY, CLYDE C.	MIFFLINBURG, PA
BEECHER, GEORGE J.	BALTIMORE, MD
BEHRNS, MRS. PATRICIA	FAIRPORT, NY
BEIL, LAWRENCE K.	EAST SYRACUSE, NY
BELCHER, FRANK	AMERICUS, GA
BELCHER, MILLARD E.	SPARTA, MI
BELKNAP, JEREMIAH P.	INDIANAPOLIS, IN
BELL, RAY L.	LAS CRUCES, NM
BELLOS, IRVING L.	JAMAICA, NY
BENAGER, CHARLES	OAK HARBOR, WA
BENEDICT, CAMERON, R.	ORLANDO, FL
BENNETT, CHARLES R.	WILMINGTON, DE
BENNETT, JR. W. BURR	NORTHBROOK, IL
BERG, DELBERT G.	SAUK CENTER, MN
BERG, OTTO W.	TEWKSBURG, MA
BERGH, MRS. EVELYN	MERRILL, WI
BERGSTEN, DANIEL	RED OAK, LA
BERMAN, BARNEY	SALEM, NH
BERNSTROM, CLARENCE G.	HIGH GROVE, CA
BERRY, EVERETT O.	ODESSA, TX
BERRY, MAURICE E.	ATLANTA, GA
BESEDA, JOSEPH M.	AUSTIN, TX
BESSOM, CORTLAND L.	NEWPORT NEWS, VA
BEZZEG, EMERY	PAINESVILLE, OH
BICKNELL, JACK D.	DAYTON, OH
BICKNESE, LOUIS C.	GRASONVILLE, MD
BIEHLE , MRS. CHRISTINA	NORTH VERNON, IN
BIERSTEKER, JOE	GLENDALE, CA
BILLINGS, JAMES W.	MORGANTON, NC
BILLS, HAROLD B.	BOUNTIFUL, UT
BINGHAM, JOHN F.	WALLINGFORD, CT
BISSEY, GEORGE R.	MIAMI, FL
BLACHLY, DONALD V.	CARMICHAEL, CA
BLACKARD, JOHN C.	GREENWOOD, IN
BLACKBURN, HOMER D.	SPRINGFIELD, IL
BLACKMAN, ARTHUR J.	LEWISTON, MT
BLAKELY, ROGER T. K.	ST. PAUL, MN
BLANKLEY, THOMAS S.	SOUTHOLD, NY
BLECHMAN, MARCUS (MICKEY)	ROCKVILLE CENTER, NY
BLEDSOE, OSCAR C.	LOS ANGELES, CA
BLEILER, GRAHAM L.	BOZEMAN, MT
BLEYL, GILBERT F.	HOUSTON, TX
BLICKENSTAFF, VERNON D.	BOISE, ID
BLINK, ROY E.	PELHAM, AL
BLOOM, MRS. ZANE E.	NORFOLK, VA
BLOOM, SUMNER	MEDFORD, MA
BOEVE, GERALD C.	PORT ST. LUCIE, FL
BOHM, DONALD	OAKLAND, SC
BOLES, ROB S.	RICHMOND, IN
BOLTON, ROWLAND P.	BAINBRIDGE, GA
BOMBERGER, LLOYD C.	MARTELL, NE

BONURA, FRANK	EDNA, TX
BOOGHER, FRANKLIN H.	YORK, PA
BOOTH, CLIFFORD R.	SAN ANTONIO, TX
BORDEAUX, DON	ST. CLAIR SHORES, MI
BORNHOLDT, RICHARD C.	WATKINS GLEN, NY
BOSTON, MRS. CLYDE O.	OREGON CITY, OR
BOWEN, DONALD A.	CANTON, IL
BOWEN, TRUETT	VIRGILINA, VA
BOWERS, FRED W.	EULESS, TX
BOXER, HERBERT G.	HANCOCK, MI
BOYD, EDWARD B.	CRYSTAL LAKE, IL
BOYETT, HERBERT L.	PENSACOLA, FL
BRACHA, M. FRANK	CRETE, IL
BRADDOCK, JOEL Q.	SPRING CITY, TN
BRADY, DAVID M.	TAYLORVILLE, IL
BRAEUNIG, VICTOR	CHICAGO, IL
BRANNAN, JOHN T.	TYLER, TX
BRAY, WILLIAM J.	NEW BRITAIN, CT
BREAKEY, J.G.	SEATTLE, WA
BREMER, PAUL E.	VACAVILLE, CA
BRESNOK, MICHAEL L.	SAN ANTONIO, TX
BREWER, MRS. OTIS	HUNTIGTON BEACH, CA
BREY, WARREN J.	MELBOURNE, FL
BRICE, JULIAN T.	GLEN-BURNIE, MD
BRIGGS, HAYDON G.	BLANDING, UT
BRISNEHAN, JOSEPH E.	DENVER, CO
BRITT, CHESTER O.	AUSTIN, TX
BROOKS, FRED E.	BOKOSHE, OK
BROOKS, RICHARD	LEWISTON, CA
BROUGH, CHARLES G.	VENICE, FL
BROUSSARD, FRANK L.	ORANGE, TX
BROWER, GORDON W.	DALLAS, TX
BROWN, C.A.	NILES, MI
BROWN, CALVIN	PALISADE, MN
BROWN, EARL F.	BOYNTON BEACH, FL
BROWN, FOUNTAIN L.	MERIDIAN, ID
BROWN, GEORGE R.	CARMICHAEL, CA
BROWN, IRIE L.	DECATURVILLE, TN
BROWN, JAMES	BOISE, ID
BROWN, ORVILLE O.	BAINBRIDGE-WINSLOW, WA
BROWNING, JOHN R.	GREEN VALLEY, AZ
BRUBACH, CARL H.	SYRACUSE, NY
BRUMFIELD, ROBERT M.	CINCINNATTI, OH
BRUSCO, JOHN P.	SALOME, AZ
BUCHERI, SAMUEL	SALEM, NH
BUCHOWICZ, JOSEPH M.	LAKEVIEW, AR
BUCKNER, JOE E.	AUSTIN, TX
BUDZYNSKI, EDWARD S.	ERWINNA, PA
BUECHLER, JR. W.E.	SNELLVILLE, GA
BUIS, DENNIS P.	INDIANAPOLIS, IN
BURCHETT, WADE	TUCSON, AZ
BURKE, BERNARD H.	BLACK RIVER, NY
BURKE, HAROLD J.	METAIRIE, LA
BURKE, MARION B.	SAN ANTONIO, TX
BURKHARDT, DANIEL A.	SEAGROVE, NC
BURMEISTER, GORDON R.	NEW LONDON, WI
BURNETT, WILLIAM H.	PHARR, TX
BURNOR, DONALD T.	MECHANICSVILLE, NY
BURROWS, MRS. MAXINE W.	VILAS, NC
BURTNER, MRS. JAMES E.	LEVELLAND, TX
BUSSART, DEAN	WICHITA, KS
BUTLER, ALFRED Y.	VIRGINIA BEACH, VA
BUTTERFIELD, HARRY	LIMA, OH
BUZZA, ERIC M.	ST. PETERSBURG, FL
CACKETT, JAMES	BOISE, ID
CADLE, JOHN	BARSTOW, CA
CADY, MRS. E.F.	NASHVILLE, TN
CALAMAS, BASIL	HAUPPAGE, L.I., NY
CAMERON, WILLIAM S.	NANUET, NY
CAMILLE, ALBERT J.	RIVERTON, IL
CAMPBELL, JOHN	FORTH WORTH, TX
CAMPOLO, ANTONY F.	CLEVELAND, OH
CANNAN, WILLIAM	PAYNES CREEK, CA
CAPANO, JOSEPH	NEW YORK, NY
CAPTEIN, HENRY	PORTLAND, OR
CAREY, ESMOND	GUALALA, CA
CARLTON, F.S.	FORT JONES, CA
CARMICHAEL, MARVIN E.	ALAMOGORDO, NM
CARNEY, RICHARD L.	CHESAPEAKE, VA
CARR, ALFRED W.	LOVING, NM
CARROLL, THOMAS S.	NEW CANAAN, CT
CARY, ELWES A.	SALUDA, NC
CASO, RALPH J.	HUNTINGTON ST., NY
CASSIDY, JOHN P.	SIERRA VISTA, AZ
CASTORA, WILLIAM W.	MASSILLON, OH
CATINO, PATSY	STAMFORD, CT
CATLETT, R.H.	MAYSVILLE, GA
CATTEAU, ROBERT	BRUNSWICK, OH
CAUDLE, ERNEST	ARROYO GRANDE, CA
CAUDLE, KENNETH	FRESNO, CA
CAVANAUGH, MRS. FLORENCE	RUMSON, NJ
CEBRELLI, RICHARD	VENICE, FL
CELLA, JOHN	GLEN ELLYN, IL
CHAMBERLAIN, D.J.	MASCOUTAH, IL
CHAMBERS, DONALD	SIDNEY, IA
CHANGNON, HARRY	CUPERTINO, CA
CHAPMAN, EDWARD C.	KALAMAZOO, MI
CHAPMAN, ROBERT	EDGARTOWN, MA
CHASE, PAULINE	CARLSBAD, CA
CHASE,WARREN J.	CASSADAGA, NY
CHAVEZ, R. JR.	SAN ANTONIO, TX
CHEATUM, ROBERT G.	SANTA BARBARA, CA
CHELF, HARVEY	HOUSTON, TX
CHENEY, MRS. CLINTON W.	LAPORT, CO
CHILD, JOHN	SANTA MARIA, CA
CHRISTENSEN, MRS. LAUREN	NO. SACRAMENTO, CA
CILIBRASI, JOSEPH	ARLINGTON HEIGHTS, IL
CIPRIANO, CHARLES M.	WATERBURY, CT
CLARK, EVERETT M.	DENVER, CO
CLAYTON, RUSSEL S. JR.	PORT CHARLOTTE, FL
CLAYTOR, FRED	WALLA WALLA, WA
CLEMENT, MRS. CLAUDINE	WOBURN, MA
CLENDENEN, DAVID F.	RANCHO CORDOVA, CA
CLIFTON, RHOMIE	GLEN ALLEN, MO
CLINE, CHARLIE	TRENTON, NJ
CLINTON, JAMES L.	DALLAS, TX
CLINTON, ROBERT E.	BROWNSBURG, IN
CLOSE, WINTON R.	HILTON HEAD ISLAND, SC
CLOUD, E.E.	HUNTSVILLE, AL
CLUTE, BENNETT T.	ANNANDALE, VA
COCHRAN, JULIAN C.	FORT SCOTT, KS
CODY, JOHN V.	BAY CITY, MI
COFER, HARLAN E.	AMERICUS, GA
COFFIN, L.F.	DULUTH, MN
COGGIO, THOMAS	WEST PALM BEACH, FL
COHEN, CHARLES	PITTSBURGH, PA
COIRA, LOUIS E. JR.	SAN ANTONIO, TX
COLBORN, VICTOR D. JR.	FERN PARK, FL
COLCHER, BYRON	WICHITA, KS
COLDWATER, ELLIOTT	ANACONDA, MT
COLE, EUGENE T.	BECKLEY, WV
COLE, FRANK	DEWITT, NY
COLE, M/M CLAUD	HUMBLE, TX
COLE, V.C.	PORTLAND, ME
COLEMAN, CLAYBOURNE H.	GRAHAM, KY
COLEMAN, NEIL F.	WICHITA, KS
COLLINS, D.E.	GRAVOIS MILLS, MO
COLMARK, CHARLES	SILVIS, IL
COMBS, NORMAN	MALLIE, KY
COMMON, RALPH L.	ZEPHYRHILLS, FL
CONLEY, ROBERT W.	WINDSOR, CT
CONNELLY, THOMAS J.	HOPKINTON, MA
CONRAD, HAROLD D.	BROKEN ARROW, OK
CONRATH, ALMON W.	PEORIA, IL
CONSTANDY, JOHN P.	WASHINGTON, DC
CONTI, JAMES	SPRINGFIELD GARDENS, NY
CONTZEN, JAMES W.	LOS ALTOS, CA
COOK, CLYDE	BIG FORK, MN
COOK, ROBERT I.	ANGOLA, IN
COOK, WILLIE B.	DANBURY, TX

COOLEY, NEIL W.	SILVER SPRINGS, MD
COONEY, WILBUR W.	WALTHAM, MA
COOPER, DONALD	CHATTANOOGA, TN
COPLEY, BOB	ROYAL OAK, MI
COPLEY, ROBERT E.	FORT WORTH, TX
COPPOLA, LUIGI J.	CENTERPORT, NY
CORBA, STEVE	CARNEGIE, PA
CORDOVA, NICHOLAS	ALBUQUERQUE, MN
CORE, FRANK B.	ROSWELL, MN
CORNELISON, T.B.	HUNTSVILLE, AL
CORNETT, JAMES I.	GEORGETOWN, CA
CORTINA, NORBERT R.	DETROIT, MI
COSGROVE, MRS. AGNES T.	PORTSMOUTH, RI
COSKEY, JOSEPH F.	PHILADELPHIA, PA
COSSOU, MRS. FORREST B.	ST. CHARLES, MI
COTTMAN, GEORGE J. JR.	MILFORD, NJ
COUNTS, JESSE	LANCASTER, CA
COVEY, RICHARD	MESA, AZ
COVILL, CHARLES W.	AUSTIN, TX
COWDEN, JAMES H.	GRAND JUNCTION, CO
COX, J.T.	JUNCTION, TX
COX, ORMOND E.	CANON CITY, CO
COX, OTIS	LOMBARD, IL
COX, RALPH R.	WORCESTER, MA
CRAIG, IRVING M. JR.	CHESTERFIELD, MO
CRAIGMYLE, PERRY O.	COLUMBIA, MO
CRANE, GEORGE C.	SPRINGVILLE, UT
CRAWFORD, FREDERICK W.	ARLINGTON HEIGHTS, MA
CREAGER, BOB B.	WILLIAMSPORT, MD
CREDEUR, ERNEST	CARENCO, LA
CROCOLL, RUSSELL	BUFFALO, NY
CROFT, WILLARD F.	GREENTOWN, PA
CROMER, CLIFFORD J.	GRASS VALLEY, CA
CROUGH, THOMAS F.	SANTA MARIA, CA
CROW, JOHN W.	VIOLA, IL
CROWDER, RANDOLPH J.	WAVERLY, OH
CULPEPPER, RICHARD L.	HIXSON, TN
CULVER, WARREN J.	HANNA CITY, IL
CURRY, DAVID	MERCER ISLAND, WA
CURTISS, RICHARD C.	WILLIAMSTOWN, VT
CUTTELL, DAVID W.	SPIRIT LAKE, IA
D'ANDRIOLE, JOHN J.	FT. WORTH, TX
DAHLBERG, GEORGE B.	DES MOINES, IA
DAHLGREN C. WALTER	ST. PAUL, MN
DAHMS, LESTER C.	FRANKLIN PARK, IL
DALEY, THOMAS H.	ROCHESTER, NY
DALY, PATRICK W.	MOOREHEAD, MN
DAMERY, NEOLA M.	BLUE MOUND, IL
DANKS, DAVID	HUTCHINSON, KS
DANNAN, JOHN H.	PHOENIX, AZ
DANSKIN, ALEX W.	GARY, IN
DARBY, H.C.	CHICO, CA
DAVIDSON, JASPER V.	WHITT, TX
DAVIS, ADELBERT	STERLING, CO
DAVIS, ALEX	CANOGA PARK, CA
DAVIS, ARLING W.	BETHLEHEM, PA
DAVIS, BARNEY	SEMINOLE, OK
DAVIS, DELBERT G.	OLA, ID
DAVIS, GERALD	HARTSELLE, AL
DAVIS, JAMES A.	WILSON, NC
DAVIS, LLOYD G.	NANTY GLO, PA
DAVIS, MRS. ERIS E.	PINE MOUNTAIN, GA
DAVIS, REGINALD G.	MELBOURNE, FL
DAVIS, ROBERT M.	SOUTH WINDSOR, CT
DEANE, VICTOR N.	KANE, PA
DEARBORN, E.W.	SEATTLE, WA
DEARDORFF, GORDON P.	WEATHERFORD, TX
DECKER, THOMAS J.	BRANCHVILLE, NJ
DECOSTER, MRS. JAMES V.	SACRAMENTO, CA
DEDREAUX, ALFRED F.	DAYTONA BEACH, FL
DELLACALCE, VINCENT	ORANGE, CA
DELLARIA, JAMES	BURGETTSTOWN, PA
DELONG, DAVID	ANN ARBOR, MI
DEMAYO, PHILLIP F.	HAMDEN, CT
DENNERLE, ROBERT H.	LAKEWORTH, FL
DENNISTON, RICHARD C.	KALAMAZOO, MI
DERRIG, C. MICHEAL	AKRON, OH
DERRINGTON, ROBERT	LITTLETON, CO
DESCALA, GEORGE	RIO GRANDE, NJ
DETOIA, VINCENT D.	BRONX, NY
DEUTSCH, ELMER W.	ST. ANN, MO
DEVOLL, JAMES	RANCHO PALOS VERDES, CA
DEWAY, MELVIN T.	ASHTABULA, OH
DEWITT, RICHARD S.	WINTERSET, IA
DIBONAVENTURA, GUERINO	SOUTHBRIDGE, MA
DICKERSON, H. WAYNE	ST. LOUIS, MO
DICKINSON, MRS. WM. L.	FALLBROOK, CA
DICKSON, JOHN M.	LOVINGTON, NM
DILAURENZIO, LOUIS D.	NAUGATUCK, CT
DILLON, TOM	WAKEFIELD, MA
DIMMIG, RICHARD G.	WALNUT, IL
DIMOCK, JOSEPH M.	CAMPBELL, CA
DINGLE, FREDERICK M.	HAMDEN, CT
DINGMAN, GEORGE L.	ALBUQUERQUE, NM
DINNDORF, JAMES C.	ST. CLOUD MN
DISBENNETT, MARION T.	ANAHEIM, CA
DISON, B. VICTOR JR.	SAN JOSE, CA
DIVER, DUANE I.	OROVILLE, CA
DOBROWOLSKI, EMIL	YOUNG, AZ
DODDRIDGE, RAYMOND L.	COLLINSVILLE, OK
DODGE, ROBERT L.	PORTLAND, ME
DOHERTY, THOMAS J.	MELBOURNE, FL
DONNELLY, EDWARD J.	OAK PARK, IL
DONOHUE, ELWOOD P.	BLAKESLEE, OH
DOOLEY, JOHN J.	PHILADELPHIA, PA
DORSEY, DELWIN E.	WICHITA, KS
DOTHAGE, KENNETH W.	ST. LOUIS, MO
DOTTER, JOHN E.	TOMAHAWK, WI
DOUGLAS, CURTIS	DAYTON, OR
DOUGLAS, WILLIAM	KANSAS CITY, MO
DOVER, LARRY	EAGLE POINT, OR
DOW, STANTON L.	WHEAT RIDGE, CO
DOWSE, CHARLES A.	SHERBORN, MA
DRAPEAU, RAYMOND G.	PEORIA, AZ
DRAPER, JOSEPH W.	SAN ANTONIO, TX
DRAUT, WILLIAM	WICHITA, KS
DRESNER, ROY	ST. LOUIS, MO
DREYER, DARWIN W.	CITRUS HEIGHTS, CA
DRIESBAUGH, RAYMOND	MURRELLS INLET, SC
DRISLANE, WILLIAM E.	LOUDONVILLE, NY
DRNEK, JAMES J.	BRECKSVILLE, OH
DRUMMOND, FREDERICK M.	WATERVILLE, ME
DUEMIG, JOSEPH	ROYAL PALM BEACH, FL
DUMAIS, PHILLIP A.	PONFRET, MD
DUMAS, ALTON L.	FLORENCE, AL
DUNCAN, BYRON B.	TYLER, TX
DUNSMORE, JOSEPH	CHERRY HILL, NJ
DUROSE, HARRY A.	PEQUOT LAKES, MN
DUVA, SAM J.	EVANSTON, IL
DYAR, JAMES A.	TEMECULA, CA
DYBELL, JAMES J.	CANONSBURG, PA
DYE, FRANCIS J.	GLENDORA, CA
DZEN, ANTHONY	MANCHESTER, CT
DZURIK, STEPHEN	SAN ANTONIO, TX
EADS, HERSHEY E.	KINCAID, WV
EARLEY, ARNO F.	FLATONIA, TX
EBERHARDT, WILLIAM J.	ST. LOUIS, MO
EBERLE, RAYMOND E.	BALTIMORE MD
ECKELMANN, BILL	ARLINGTON, TX
EDDLEMAN, DOLPHUS M.	CULLMAN, AL
EDWARDS, FRANCIS R.	ARCADE, NY
EDWARDS, VIRGIL B.	BURBANK, CA
EIGENMANN, JOHN C.	FORTH WORTH, TX
EILAND, MRS. JOHN C.	CLANTON, AL
EISENZIMMER, MRS. M.G.	RIVERSIDE, CA
ELLIOTT, JOHN R.	FAIRHOPE, AL
ELLIOTT, RAYMOND S. M.D.	GILBERT, AZ
ELLIS, DALE E.	BELLINGHAM, WA
ELLIS, FREDERICK W.	ANDOVER, MA
ELSNER, BURTON	ELBORT, CO

ELSTUN, MRS. CHARLES M.	CINCINNATI, OH
EMIG, ELMER B.	GREAT FALLS, MT
EMS, HAROLD S.	NEW ALBANY, IN
ENGLAND, ROBERT	TULLAHOMA, TN
ENGLER, HOWARD	SAN ANTONIO, TX
EPPLER, HOWARD W.	LINCOLN, NE
EPSTEIN, MERVIN M.D.	PALM SPRINGS, CA
ESENWEIN, DANIEL	COLUMBIANA, OH
ESPER, JOHN W.	GLOVERSVILLE, NY
ESSWEIN, MRS. SAMUEL A.	COLUMBUS, OH
ESTES, VICTOR H.	HOUSTON, TX
ESTUDILLO, CHRIS	TIGARD, OR
ETHEM, EDWIN	PARKER, CO
ETHERINGTON, GALPIN	BIRMINGHAM, AL
EUSTIS, LAWRENCE B.	NEW ORLEANS, LA
EVANS, JAMES R.	OWENSBORO, KY
EVANS, PAUL F.	GODDARD, KS
EWASKO, PAUL T.	NORTH ARLINGTON, NJ
FABAIN, ROBERT	CROMWELL HILLS, CT
FACCIOLO, JOSEPH T.	AMBRIDGE, PA
FAIR, MRS. IRENE	PERU, IN
FAIRMAN, JACK	GREENBELT, MD
FALCO, ANGELO	PEMBROKE PINES, FL
FANADAKIS, GEORGE	NORWOOD, MA
FANNIN, BILLY R.	AUXIER, KY
FARBSTEIN, STANLEY M.	ST. LOUIS, MO
FARLOW, HOWARD T.	WESTVILLE, IL
FARRAR, GEORGE B.	SHREVEPORT, LA
FARRAR, SAMUEL G.	FT. COLLINS, CO
FARRELL, MRS. SUE	RENO, NV
FAULKNER, DEAN H.	PARSIPPANY, NJ
FAYETTE, W.W.	FERNDALE, WA
FEARS, MARVIN E.	NAVASOTA, TX
FEARS, MRS. EARL	OWENSBORO, KY
FELDMAN, WALTER	TAMARAC, FL
FELLOWS, W. SCOTT	ROSWELL, GA
FERKO, ROBERT E.	GIRARD, OH
FERRAIUOLO, MRS. THERESA	WORCESTER, MA
FIELDS, SY	LOS ANGELES, CA
FILLINGER, LEO L.	BALTIMORE, MD
FINDER, THEODORE	CAREFREE, AZ
FITZPATRICK, MORRIS	ROCKFORD, IL
FLESSOR, ELIAS	ORLAND PARK, IL
FLETCHER, HAROLD	SAN DIEGO, CA
FLOYD, CLAYTON H.	LITTLETON, CO
FOLLETT, ALLAN	MADISON, WI
FONTANA, ROBERT	DAYTON, OH
FORD, CLAIR	SALT LAKE CITY, UT
FORD, JIM G.	GLENDALE, AZ
FORD, RAPHAEL	AUSTIN, TX
FORWARD, JOHN	MICHIGAN CENTER, MI
FOX, MARVIN	OMAHA, NE
FOX, RAY	MANKATO, MN
FRAME, HILDA B.	BIG FORK, MT
FRANCELL, ROBERT D.	PUEBLO, CO
FRANCKLING, DOUGLAS	PORT CHARLOTTE, FL
FRANK, JAMES A.	BLANDBURG, PA
FRANK, JOSEPH J.	HAMPTON, VA
FRANKS, C.E.	UNIVERSAL CITY, TX
FREDERICK, THOMAS M.	EVERETT, MA
FREEBORN, ROBERT M.	ALHAMBRA, CA
FREEMAN, BEETHOVEN	BC CANADA VON 3EO
FREEMAN, ROBERT E.	SEDAN, KS
FRIEDMAN, JERRY	ENCINO, CA
FRIEDMAN, THOMAS B.	SAN LUIS OBISPO, CA
FRITZ, JOSEPH C.	AMSTERDAM, NY
FUDGER, MRS. WESLEY J.	SUMTER, SC
FUERSTEIN, ALFRED	BRONX, NY
FULLER, RAY	ELDORADO, KS
FULLER, CHARLES JR.	SHERBURNE, MA
FULLERTON, RONALD C.	EDMONDS, WA
FULLMER, THOMAS F.	CIRCLEVILLE, UT
FULMER, HAROLD	LAS VEGAS, NV
FURTICK, JESSE	COLUMBIA, SC
FUSSELL, LEWIS W.	PANAMA CITY, FL
GACKE, WILLIAM H.	SONOMA, CA
GACKENHEIMER, FREDERICK W.	ROCKLEDGE, FL
GAHAGAN, JOHN J.	SEATTLE, WA
GARDNER, DAVID B.	SANDY, UT
GARDNER, WILLIAM L.	SEATTLE, WA
GARDNER, COOPER JR.	CHARLOTTE, NC
GARIFO, SALVATORE	HEMPSTEAD, NY
GARMSHAUSEN, ERIC	MARIPOSA, CA
GARRETT, HUBERT J.	FLORENCE, SC
GARRETT, OLAN	PAULS VALLEY, OK
GARRETT, VERNE M.	NORTH VERNON, IN
GASKILL, CHARLES A.	ST. LOUIS, MO
GATES, KENNETH C.	RAQUETTE LAKE, NY
GAUGH, CHESTER B.	INDIANAPOLIS, IN
GAUGHAN, ROBERT H.	ORLANDO, FL
GAULT, JOHNSON G.	GRANITE SHOAL, TX
GEISLER, ROLAND	HEBRON, NE
GELINSKIE, ANDREW C.	CINCINNATI, OH
GERBER, NELSON H.	SOUTH BEND, IN
GERECKE, EDWARD R.	ANGOLA, NY
GEROW, RICHARD J.	EGGERSVILLE, NY
GERSHONE, PAUL	ST. LOUIS PARK, MN
GIANETTI, JAMES	PITTSBURGH, PA
GIBBS, IRWIN L.	DANVILLE, IN
GIBBS, MELVIN B.	GERMANTOWN, TN
GILBERT, WILLIAM F.	BLACKWELL, OK
GIOVANNELLI, VASCO	SAN CARLOS, CA
GIVENS, EUGENE A.	BEDFORD, IN
GLASSMAN, HARRY	MEDIA, PA
GLAZE, TYLER W.	OKLAHOMA CITY, OK
GLEASON, BEAL S.	LOVINGTON, NM
GLENN, ROBERT	HARTWELL, GA
GLOVER, DELBERT	MINERAL WELLS, TX
GODING, CARL V.	SAWYER, MI
GODWIN, BILL EXEC. DIR.	HARLINGTON, TX
GOFF, JAMES H.	AUSTIN, TX
GOLDSTEIN, MORTON	REGO PARK, NY
GOLDSTEIN, WILLIAM	INDIANAPOLIS, IN
GOODE, JOSEPH,	CLIFTON, NJ
GOODMAN, WILLIAM H.	MILFORD, OH
GOODNOUGH, STEPHEN C.	BRECKENRIDGE, CO
GOODWIN, JOHN C.	SPARTANBURG, SC
GOODWIN, JOHN H.	ROANOKE, VA
GOODWYN, MARVIN	NEWPORT BEACH, CA
GORDON, ALBERT M.	PHOENIX, AZ
GORESKI, PAUL	DENVER, CO
GORMAN, MRS. DONALD	ROCKFORD, IL
GOSSAGE, THOMAS S.	GOOD HOPE, IL
GRAHAM, CHARLES	COLOMBUS, OH
GRAHAM, MRS. ROBERT W.	MELBOURNE, FL
GRAY, CLAYTON F.	NEW LONDON, NH
GRAY, JOHN W.	BOERNE, TX
GRAY, LEWIS HOWARD	CLARKSVILLE, TN
GREEN, JAMES J.	ALBANY, NY
GREEN, RALPH C.	TREMENTON, UT
GREEN, SHELLY H.	SUMTER, SC
GREENBERG, EMANUEL M. O.D.	FT. LAUDERDALE, FL
GREENE, MRS. PATRICIA	BENSON, AZ
GREENFIELD, DR. KELLER	DALLAS, TX
GREENWOOD, TOM	BELMOND, IA
GREGORIO, VICTOR A.	BUFFALO, NY
GRENOT, WARREN	LOS ANGELES, CA
GRIFFIN, MRS. ALOISE	CORPUS CHRISTI, TX
GRIM, GEORGE	LOMPOC, CA
GRISHAM, IRVING	BILOXI, MS
GROSS, CHARLES H.	KANSAS CITY, MO
GROSS, ROBERT	FOND DU LAC, WI
GROVE, CALVIN E.	HAGERSTOWN, MD
GROVE, GEORGE P.	WOOD RIVER, IL
GROVE, HAROLD W.	ROBSTOWN, TX
GUIDRY, EMICK P.	LAFAYETTE, LA
GUYTON, DEAN D.	FOSSIL, OR
GUZY, WILLIAM	GARFIELD, NJ
GWYN, HENRY H.	AMARILLO, TX
HAAK, RYNE C.	NILES, MI

HABIF, ELIAS	BOYTON BEACH, FL
HADLOCK, HARRY	REDMOND, WA
HAGERTY, ED	KANSAS CITY, MO
HAHN, JAMES O.	ALLENTOWN, PA
HALE, WILLIAM A.	KANSAS CITY, KS
HALL, ARTHUR A.	GRIFFITH, IN
HALL, CLARENCE E.	SUN CITY WEST, AZ
HALL, DURWARD W.	COWETA, OK
HALL, MRS. LEE A.	FT. WORTH, TX
HALL, ROBERT L.	ST. MICHAELS, MD
HALLETT, ROBERT J.	NORTH SYRACUSE, NY
HAMIL, LEWIS V. JR.	FORT WORTH, TX
HAMILTON, DONALD	LOCKPORT, IL
HAMILTON, EARL	BELTON, SC
HANCHETT, ROBERT M.	PEORIA, IL
HAND, SYLVAN D.	TAMPA, FL
HANSEN, BERT A. JR.	LOWELL, MI
HANSON, CARL	WATERVILLE, KS
HANSON, GEORGE J.	BLACK RIVER FALLS, WI
HANSON, MRS. HELMER C.	TUCSON, AZ
HANZLIAN, GEORGE	BUFFALO, NY
HARDEN CHARLIE	CLEMSON, SC
HARKINS, JOHN	LINCOLN, IL
HARMON, JAMES W.	IAEGER, WV
HARRIS, EDWARD A.	GLENDALE, CA
HARRISON, MILTON S.	WHITE PLAINS, NY
HART, WILLIAM D.	DOWAGAIC, MI
HARVELL, JOHN C.	HUEYTOWN, AL
HARVEY, ALVA L.	ALEXANDRIA, VA
HASH, J.S.	SHERMAN, TX
HAUEISEN, LOUIS R.	COLUMBUS, OH
HAVENS, COLLIER	NEWTON SQUARE, PA
HAVENS, GIFFORD	NEWTON, PA
HAWKINS, HAROLD	ALGER, MI
HAWKINS, LYNN	BEAUMONT, TX
HAZY, JOHN	PERRYOPOLIS, PA
HEALY, HARLEY A.	SEATTLE, WA
HEALY, ROY	HILLSBOROUGH, CA
HEARD, WILLIAM J.	BANGOR, PA
HEATH, STANLEY K.	GLEASVILLE, WI
HEBBS, JOHN W.	ROCHESTER, NY
HEBRANK, HARRY J.	LAKE CARMEL, NY
HEGAR, DANIEL T.	ARLINGTON, TX
HELFRICH, ROBERT C.	LOUISVILLE, KY
HELGESON, EUGENE	XENIA, OH
HELMS, JAMES E.	CHARLOTTE, NC
HELMS, SHERMAN A.	ELLIS GROVE, IL
HENDERSON, RALPH C.	GREENVILLE JUNCTION, ME
HENNING, CHARLES	MISHAWAKA, IN
HENRY, ADRIENE	TORRANCE, CA
HENRY, MRS. HELEN	TORRANCE, CA
HENRY, R.J.	TREVOSE, PA
HENRY, ROBERT B.	BROOKINGS, SD
HENSINGER, CLAUDE E.	SLATINGTON, PA
HERNANDEZ, RODOLFO	SAN ANTONIO, TX
HERZING, DON J.	KINGSVILLE, TX
HICKS, MRS. VIOLA L.	CAMDENTON, MO
HICKS, NATHAN T.	ORIENT, NY
HIGGINS, JOHN C.	BLOOMINGTON, MN
HILL, KENNETH L.	AMSTERDAM, MO
HILL, MRS. DWAYNE	ELLSWORTH, IA
HILLER, WILLIAM	ERIE, PA
HILLERS, CARL E.	VICTORVILLE, CA
HILT, MRS. WILLIAM H.	DAYTON, OH
HILTON, ROBERT D.	IRVING, TX
HILYARD, ERNEST	IDAHO SPRINGS, CO
HINKLE, MRS. ROBERT J.	HUACHUCA CITY, AZ
HINKLE, STANLEY A.	GLADSTONE, MO
HIRSCHFELD, HERBERT C.	YUBA CITY, CA
HITT, HARRY W.	HORSESHOE BAY, TX
HOCKEL, ALBERT F.	LONG BEACH, CA
HODGON, KENNETH G.	WESTBORO, MA
HOFF, CHARLES F. D.D.S.	WELLSVILLE, PA
HOFFMAN, ARVILLE	BALLWIN, MO
HOFFMAN, HAROLD A.	NORFOLK, NE
HOFFMAN, MRS. PHILLIP F.	S. WILLIAMSPORT, PA
HOLECEK, JOHN J.	NEW BERN, NC
HOLLEY, LAWRENCE	WATERLOO, WI
HOLLEY, VINCENT J.	BAYONET POINT, FL
HOLLOMON, HARRY L.	ATLANTA, GA
HOLLOMON, JAMES W.	HAMPTON, VA
HOLMES, ERCEL	RAVENNA, OH
HOLMES MRS. R.M.	CHARLOTTE, NC
HOMER, PHILLIP	MUNDAY, TX
HOMMERT, NORMAN O. JR.	RIDGE, NY
HONOLMICHOL, EMIL G.	TUCSON, AZ
HOOKER, KEITH G.	CEDAR RIDGE, CA
HOOKER, ROBERT J.	CAMBRIDGE, MA
HOOKER, VAN DORN	ALAMEDA, NM
HOON, JOHN	SAVAGE, MT
HOPKINS, KENNETH H.	OCEANSIDE, CA
HORLACHER, CURT	ALLENTOWN, PA
HORN, JOHN	PERKIOMENVILLE, PA
HORN, S.R.	SAN ANTONIO, TX
HORNSTEIN, EDWARD	GLENSIDE, PA
HORTON, GERALD	ROYAL OAK, MI
HORTON, JAMES P.	OAKLAND, MS
HOUGHDAHL, LLOYD	DEER PARK, WI
HOUGHTON, BRUCE R.	ELKHORN, WI
HOUSEMAN, MRS. JAMES W.	RANDALLSTOWN, MD
HOUTS, WILLIAM S.	PHOENIX, AZ
HOWE, JAMES M.	CLYDE, NC
HOWELL, JOHN D.	DALLAS, TX
HOWELL, WINIFRIED A.	BURLESON, TX
HUCKABEE, MRS. HARVEY	WACO, TX
HUDDLESTON, PHILLIP E.	CARMICHAEL, CA
HUDSPETH, ERNEST L.	CHERRY VALLEY, AR
HUG, JOHN	MERIDIAN, ID
HUGHES, ELMER	CHAPEL HILL, NC
HUIRAS, WAYNE,	MOLLALLA, OR
HULCE, JAMES C.	MARION, IN
HUMPHRIES, NED	EAGLE HARBOR, MI
HUNSUCKER, JOHN J.	POLSON, MT
HUNT, JOHN	ATWATER, CA
HUNT, WILLIAM J.	CHARLOTTE, NC
HUNTER, PAUL	PARSONS, KS
HUNTER, WILLIAM A.	ALBUQUERQUE, NM
HUNTER, MRS. ROY JR.	ROSWELL, NM
HURD, BENNIE	WARSAW, IN
HURLBURT, RONALD D. SR.	KNOXVILLE, PA
HURLEY, J.E.	BURLESON, TX
HURST, MRS. EVELYN	ARDMORE, OK
HUTCHINS, ROSS D.	MORGANTON, NC
HUTCHINSON, THOMAS	OCEAN CITY, NJ
HUTSON, RICHARD J.	CHARLESTON, SC
HUWEL, ROY	CINCINNATI, OH
HYDE, GEORGE M.	GROTON, MA
INNES, ROBERT D.	PHOENIX, AZ
IRVINE, LESLIE A.	OMAHA, NE
ISHMAN, ARTHUR L.	ST. PETERSBURG, FL
JACKSON, LEROY	FT. WORTH, TX
JACOBS, U.L.	CHECOTAH, OK
JAMES, MRS. LILLIAN D.	UNION GROVE, WI
JAMESON, GEORGE J.	ARLINGTON, VA
JEFFREY, THOMAS S.	ARVONIA, VA
JENKINS, MRS. JAMES A.	NEWPORT NEWS, VA
JENSEN, JOHN K.	DALLAS, TX
JENSON, ROY K.	EDINA, MN
JENSTROM, EINO E.	ARLINGTON, VA
JOHNSON, DALE L.	RIO, IL
JOHNSON, DELMAR A.	GREEN BAY, WI
JOHNSON, EARL E.	WETUMPKA, AL
JOHNSON, ELMER E.	LA VISTA, NE
JOHNSON, ELMER K.	PORTLAND, OR
JOHNSON, HENRY J.	DENVER, CO
JOHNSON, JIMMIE W.	ALEXANDRIA, IN
JOHNSON, JOSEPH J.	ENGLEWOOD, CO
JOHNSON, RALEIGH	TALLAHASSEE, FL
JOHNSON, WILLIAM R.	DEARBORN, MI
JONAS, RALPH B.	BOERNE, TX

JONES, BERT	SUISUN, CA
JONES, BURNELL S.	AUSTIN, TX
JONES, CARL	ANDERSON, IN
JONES, CHARLES S.	VERSAILLES, KY
JONES, CHARLES S.	WARWICK, RI
JONES, DON C.	CENTRALIA, IL
JONES, JAMES	ADRIAN, GA
JONES, LOUIS M.	NEW ORLEANS, LA
JONES, MERTON	ENGLEWOOD, FL
JONES, WILLIAM W.	LAS VEGAS, NV
JONES, LELAND G. JR.	MERIDIAN, MS
JORDAN, TULLY H.	GREEN FOREST, AR
JORDAN, WILLIAM F.	MEDINA, OH
JORGENSEN, ROBERT C.	OAK LAWN, IL
JOZWIAK, RAY	MONESSAN, PA
JUNKER, J.X. III	LONDONDERRY HILL, VT
KAISER, RANDALL J.	GRAND ISLAND, NY
KAMP, ALVIN W.	JACKSON, MO
KATZ, CHARLES I.	BRONX, NY
KATZKA, IRWIN	OLD WESTBURY, NY
KEARNEY, EARL H.	WATERTOWN, CT
KEEHAN, PAUL J.	HOCKESSIN, DE
KEENAN, JAMES	VINELAND, NJ
KEENAN, NEIL J.	JENNINGS, KS
KEENAN, R.M.	WASHINGTON, DC
KEENE, FRANCIS	SULLIVAN, IL
KELLER, EDWARD B.	PITTSBURGH, PA
KELLER, WAYNE A.	WALBRIDGE, OH
KELLY , GEORGE	MENOMONEE FALLS, WI
KELLY, JOHN J.	BOGALUSA, LA
KELVINGTON, WESLEY E.	LETART, WV
KERNER, BERNARD	OAK PARK, MI
KERSHINER, MRS. ALEX	VANCOUVER, WA
KERSTNER, OTTO	LONG BEACH, CA
KESTELOOT, FREDERICK T.	MUSKEGON HEIGHTS, MI
KETTLE, DONALD G.	PEMBERVILLE, OH
KEYES, LUTHER C.	WOODVILLE, NH
KILLIAN, JOHN	CARLSBAD, CA
KINGSBURY, MRS. WILLIAM C.	REDLANDS, CA
KINNEY, WALTER	HEALDSBURG, CA
KIRKPATRICK, DARREL L.	BAKERSFIELD, CA
KISSEL, CHARLES	LIMA, OH
KITTLE, ROBERT S.	SALT LAKE CITY, UT
KLAVER, ROYAL	MILWAUKEE, WI
KLINE, HENRY	MERTZTOWN, PA
KLINE, JOHN V.	FLINT, MI
KLING, BERNARD	PORT CHARLOTTE, FL
KLOSTER, MARION	MINNEAPOLIS, MN
KNECHT, WILLIAM A.	NEW HARTFORD, CT
KNEZEVICH, MRS. MARY L.	THIENSVILLE, WI
KNIERIM, E.L.	COLUMBIA, SC
KNODEL, RICHARD	LAFAYETTE, NY
KNOX, FORREST T.	SAN ANTONIO, TX
KOENIG, P.A.	FORT WORTH, TX
KOERWITZ, RALPH E.	HEBRON, NE
KOHUT, MRS. F. J.	SPRINGFIELD, VA
KONCAN, FRANK B.	CLEVELAND, OH
KORTIS, JOHN	WILKES BARRE, PA
KOSEL, WARREN	SOUTHOLD, NY
KOSINSKI, MRS. STEPHEN F.	SATELLITE BEACH, FL
KOTASEK, THOMAS J.	STRUTHERS, OH
KOTWICA, ANTHONY	GOLDEN, CO
KOULAS, WILLIAM G.	OVERLAND PARK, KS
KOVERT, PAUL	CROTERSVILLE, IN
KOZAK, MORRIS	DELRAY, FL
KRAUS, WALTER	PACIFIC GROVE, CA
KREIZEL, WILLIAM J.	HEWLETT HARBOR, NY
KRITZER, NATHAN	ENCINO, CA
KRUEGER, HERBERT C.	AUSTIN, TX
KRZYSKOWSKI, MRS. F.P.	NEW BERLIN, WI
KUCZYNSKI, DONALD G.	TUCSON, AZ
KUHAREK, JOHN D.	TAMPA, FL
KULICKA, FRITZ J.	VENICE, FL
KUNDINGER, HOWARD E.	SAGINAW, MI
KUNKLE, JAMES C.	MOUNT PLEASANT, PA
KUPEC, MRS. FRANK	MCALLEN, TX
KUSIAN, WALTER A.	TUCSON, AZ
KWIATOWSKI, CHARLES L.	PHILADELPHIA, PA
KYRK, DENNIS D.	OKLAHOMA CITY, OK
LABARGE, CLEMENT	PONTIAC, MI
LABRUYERE, EDWARD	METAIRIE, LA
LACY, CHARLES	BISHOP, TX
LACY, MRS. T.T.	BISHOP, TX
LADMAN, JOE	DORCHESTER, NE
LAGOY, DAVID	PLATTSBURG, NY
LAMB, EARL	OKLAHOMA CITY, OK
LAMONDS, QUENTIN H.	CANDOR, NC
LAND, MRS. WILLIAM P.	CARROLLTON, GA
LANDSMAN, IRVING	BROOKLYN, NY
LANE, H.J.	NEW ORLEANS, LA
LANGFORD, WATSON R.	LA GRANGE, GA
LANGLEY, BRUCE A.	HOLDENVILLE, OK
LARSEN, JOHN J.	LONGVIEW, WA
LARSEN, NORMAN	BALDWIN, NY
LARSON, ROBERT V.	JOLIET, IL
LASKOWSKI, ED S.	PITTSBURGH, PA
LASTON, ED	LANESBORO, MA
LAUBE, SIGMUND	SAN DIEGO, CA
LAVOIE, ALBERT	FAIRFIELD, CA
LAW, DR. ALLAN R.	ROCHESTER, NY
LAXTON, JOHN R.	PITTSBURGH, PA
LAYCAK, JOHN F.	ALPHARETTA, GA
LAYER, OTTO C.	VICTOR, NY
LAYSER, JOSEPH W.	LEBANON, PA
LAZAROS, CLARENCE J.	EAST PITTSBURGH, PA
LEAVITT, MAX V.	LAS VEGAS, NV
LECHNER, LOUIS A.	LITTLE FALLS, NJ
LECRONE, HAROLD B.	VANDALIA, OH
LEDFORD, JACK C.	TUCSON, AZ
LEE, OBED A.	CRESCO, IA
LEE, R.G. JR.	ALBUQUERQUE, NM
LEITGEB, JOSEPH	NORTHAMPTON, PA
LEMAY, GENERAL CURTIS	NEWPORT BEACH, CA
LEMOS, LOUIS D.	CARMICHAEL, CA
LENTZ, WALTER R.	HUDSON, NC
LEON, DAVID M.	DOVER PLAINS, NY
LESSIN, WILIAM	ALEXANDRIA, VA
LEVANTHAL, DAVID	NEW YORK, NY
LEVINE, JOSEPH	FARMINGTON HILLS, MI
LEWIS, JACK W.	SEAGOVILLE, TX
LEWIS, JOHN	SUN LAKES, AZ
LEYH, JOSEPH L.	NEW YORK, NY
LEZZENI, IRWIN E.	ROHNERT PARK, CA
LINCK, ROBERT	BROWN CITY, MI
LINDQUIST, CHARLES A.	CRYSTAL LAKE, IL
LINDSTROM, THEODORE E.	SO. SAN FRANCISCO, CA
LINHARD, NICHOLAS T.	LYNBROOK, NY
LINS, WILLIAM F.	OCEAN GROVE, NJ
LIPNICK, SAMUEL M.	BALTIMORE, MD
LISET, ROBERT H.	HOPKINS, MN
LISTON, MRS. GLEN E.	FAIRFIELD, IL
LLOYD, ALWYN T.	BELLEVUE, WA
LOBER, GEORGE W.	SAN JOSE, CA
LODOVICI, O.F.	VICTORIA, KS
LONG, ODELL B.	CHARLOTTE, NC
LONG, CHARLES L. JR.	SCOTTS VALLEY, CA
LONGO, EDMOND P.	BRONX, NY
LOVELESS, HERBERT R.	NORTH CHARLESTON, SC
LOW, LORIN B.	THAYNE, WY
LOWMAN, C.P.	VIRGINIA BEACH, VA
LOWRY, GEORGE E.	SANTA BARBARA, CA
LUCAS, WALTER Y.	SPRINGFIELD, LA
LUND, DONALD J.	BISMARCK, ND
LUNDQUIST, GEORGE	ALBUQUERQUE, NM
LYJAK, THADDEUS, J.	WARREN, MI
LYLE, MRS. MARIE	HAWKINS, TX
LYONS, JAMES E.	STOCKTON, CA
MACER, ARTHUR J.	WESTFIELD, NY
MACK, CHARLES	WAYNE, PA
MACK, LYLE	POYNETTE, WI

MACKEY, BILL	LUBBOCK, TX
MACLEOD, CHARLES W.	HOLIDAY, FL
MACLEOD, JOHN K.	KANSAS CITY, KS
MADSEN, HAROLD	LEADER FALLS, IA
MAJORS, FERRELL T.	FULLERTON, CA
MALAWER, LESTER	BOCA RATON, FL
MALLORY, LEROY T.	WOODSTOCK, GA
MALLORY, MRS. C.R.	TREASURE ISLAND, FL
MALLORY, WALTER E.	WOODSTOCK, GA
MALONEY, ROBERT F.	SYRACUSE, NY
MAMULA, NICHOLAS	EAST HAMPTON, NY
MANCINO, VITO R.	DANIA, FL
MANFREDO, DONALD F.	FRESNO, CA
MANFRIN, E.R.	COLORADO SPRINGS, CO
MANKE, LINCOLN R.	ST. PAUL, MN
MANNOTT, LOUIS M.	INDEPENDENCE, CA
MARCHANT, EDWARD	QUINCY, MA
MARIANI, AUGUST E.	CORAOPOLIS, PA
MARSH, WILLIAM H.	BRIDGEPORT, AL
MARSHALL, CHESTER	MEMPHIS, TN
MARTIN, ARTHUR A.	THURSTON, OH
MARTIN, CHARLES R.	STATE COLLEGE, PA
MARTIN, E.W.	RIVERSIDE, CA
MARTIN, LEONARD F.	PORT ORANGE, FL
MARTIN, ROBERT S.	WHITTIER, CA
MASON, BENTON M. JR.	LAVERGNE, TN
MASSEY, M.D.	TIPTON, IN
MASTERS, ARKLEY C.	HUEYTOWN, AL
MATHIS, EDISON E.	BIG ROCK, TN
MATTAIES, WILBERT H.	ALLEN, MI
MATTHEWS, IRA V.	MOBILE, AL
MAURER, WALTER L.	FREMONT, CA
MAUSOLF, KENNETH A.	ALPENA, MI
MAVROFRIDES, MARK	BRADFORD, MA
MAYO, ARTHUR E.	WEST SUFFIELD, CT
MAYS, ROY H. JR.	LEXINGTON, KY
MCDOWELL, FREDERICK	XENIA, OH
MCALLISTER, NORMOND B. JR.	MOBILE, AL
MCARDLE, ALPHEUS	DOTHAN, AL
MCAULEY, JAMES JR.	PHILADELPHIA, PA
MCBRIDE, THOMAS J.	MATILAND, FL
MCCLURE, GLEN E.	UNIVERSAL CITY, TX
MCCOMBIE, RUSSEL	SHEBOYGAN FALLS, WI
MCCOOL, L. FRANKLIN	LEXINGTON, KY
MCCORQUODALE, JOSEPH C.	JACKSON, AL
MCCRAW, JOSEPH C.	SHELL BEACH, CA
MCCRORY, JOHN D.	FLORENCE, AL
MCCULLOUGH, DUANE	ORANGE, TX
MCDANIEL, ELMER C.	AUGUSTUS, KS
MCDANIEL, JOSEPH L. M.D.	LOS ANGELES, CA
MCDERMOTT, MRS. VIOLET	HUNTSVILLE, AL
MCELHOM, DESMOND	LOWELL, MA
MCGINTY, FRANK J.	COTUIT, MA
MCGLAUN, ANDREW F.	LUBBOCK, TX
MCGOWAN, MRS. J.C.	BRONX, NY
MCGREGOR, CARTER JR.	WICHITA FALLS, TX
MCGROARTY, MRS. EDWARD T.	DODGE CITY, KS
MCILVAIN, MARION	ANDERSON, IN
MCINTYRE, B.A.	LONG BEACH, MS
MCKAIN, JOHN S.	ADA, OK
MCKIM, R. MERRILL	LOMPOC, CA
MCKINNEY, CHESTER M.	AUSTIN, TX
MCKINNEY, FRANK	EL PASO, TX
MCLAREN, ALAN	CAMARILLO, CA
MCLEAN, MRS. ROBERT	NORTH EAST, PA
MCLELLAND, DOUGLAS H.	CRYSTAL BEACH, TX
MCMAHON, MISS CHRISTINE	WOODBURY, NJ
MCMULLAN, KATE	NEW YORK, NY
MCNASSOR, JOHN J.	SOUTHINGTON, CT
MCNEW, DANIEL J.	MELBOURNE, FL
MCNEW, H.W.	BLOUNTVILLE, TN
MCNEW, JOHN D.	LEXINGTON, KY
MCNUTT, THOMAS	HAMPTON, VA
MCQUEEN, WILLIAM E.	BOULDER , CO
MCSWAIN, HAROLD E.	SPRINGFIELD, MO
MCWILLIAMS, MRS. JOSEPH W.	HAUGHTON, LA
MEADOR, WENDELL M.	PUYALLUP, WA
MEEK, WILLIAM L.	POWAY, CA
MEENAN, ELWYN L.	ROCKVILLE, MD
MENDOSA, ERNEST J.	CERES, CA
MERNICK, MRS. VICKI	GRANTS PASS, OR
MERRY, RUSSELL W.	DALTON, MA
MESSERSMITH, WALTER H.	WENATCHEE, WA
METZENBAUM, VICTOR H.	VAN NUYS, CA
MEWHA, JOHN	INCLINE VILLAGE, NV
MEYER, MRS. C. C.	DALLAS, TX
MICCO, MRS. MARGARET	DANVILLE, CA
MIDDLETON, JOHN L.	WYOMISSING, PA
MIEDEMA, MRS. ALICE	CROSWELL, MI
MIKULICH, JOHN R.	BURTON, MI
MILES, MRS. DOT	RIVERDALE, GA
MILLER, ALOYSIUS	PITTSBURGH, PA
MILLER, GEORGE W.	LANSING, MI
MILLER, MRS. DELBERT W.	DUPREED, SD
MILLER, NELSON	ANGOLA, IN
MILLIGAN, ROBERT F.	PRESCOTT, AZ
MILLION, NORMAN R.	COUNTRY CLUB HILLS, IL
MILLS, PERSHING F.	MADILL, OK
MIMEAU, DONALD J.	FULLERTON, CA
MINOR, LESLIE E.	NACOGDOCHES, TX
MITCHELL, LLOYD	NASHVILLE, TN
MITCHELL, THOMAS E.	PASADENA, TX
MITCHELL, VERBLE	EVANSVILLE, IN
MOCH, FRANK	ELMA, NY
MOCK, WALTER E.	CHATTANOOGA, TN
MOHEL, HAROLD	LAKEWOOD, NJ
MONK, MRS. BEN E.	SPRINGFIELD, MA
MONTEKO, JACK	PLAINVIEW, NY
MONTGOMERY, RICHARD	RIVERSIDE, CA
MOORE, CLAUD W.	ZANESFIELD, OH
MOORE, RICHARD H.	FORT WORTH, TX
MOORE, RUSSEL E.	LAFAYETTE, IN
MOORE, TOM E.	COLORADO SPRINGS, CO
MOORE, WAYNE W.	NEW LONDON, IA
MORGAN, MRS. FRANCIS B.	LEHIGH ACRES, FL
MORGAN, MRS. JAMES H.	HUNTINGTON, TN
MORIARTY, MRS. TIMOTHY R.	CHICAGO, IL
MORRIS, MERRIL	RIDGEFIELD, WA
MORRISON, WILBUR H.	FALLBROOK, CA
MORROW, B.H.	LAKEHURST, NJ
MORROW, ROBERT W.	LAWSON, MO
MOSKALIK, GEORGE	MINNEAPOLIS, MN
MOSS, ROBERT E.	STATEN ISLAND, NY
MOULTON, LLOYD E.	CIRTUS HEIGHTS, CA
MRUGALA, ROBERT	CASSADAGA, FL
MUELLER, RUSSEL	ST. LOUIS, MO
MULDOWNEY, JAMES R.	PITTSBURGH, PA
MULLIN, ROBERT E.	SPOKANE, WA
MURRAY, ANDREW B.	SHELBURNE, VT
MURRAY, JOHN J.	BUFFALO, NY
MYERS, EARL R.	LIGHTHOUSE POINT, FL
NACZEK, RICHARD A.	MILWAUKEE, WI
NAIRN, COURTNEY M.	GREENTOWN, PA
NAPOLI, MICHAEL	PEPPER PIKE, OH
NEADORFF, LOUIS	LOGANSPORT, IN
NEIL, WILLIAM	SPRING, TX
NELSON, HENRY E.	LA PORTE, CO
NELSON, MRS. NETA	GRAPELAND, TX
NELSON, ROY	PORTLAND, OR
NETT, EDWARD	CENTERVILLE, OH
NETZORG, GORDON M.	LAWRENCEVILLE, NJ
NEWMAN, ELLIS	SAUK RAPIDS, MN
NICELY, GARLAND L.	RICHARD, VA
NICHOLSON, PHIL	ELLIS, KS
NIELSON, CHARLES	SLIDELL, LA
NIERENBERG, SIDNEY S.	BROOKLYN, NY
NISITO, JOSEPH V.	LEVITTOWN, NY
NITTI, JOSEPH P.	CHICAGO, IL
NOBLE, JERRY W.	SAN ANTONIO, TX
NORAIN, HOWARD	CHICAGO, IL

NORDHAGEN, JOHN	CHOTEAU, MT
NORMAN, EDWARD R.	MANGUM, OK
NORTON, CHARLES M.	ROCKFORD, MI
NORTON, MARSHALL H.	SAN ANTONIO, TX
NOSKO, LOUIS Z.	FAIRVIEW PARK, OH
NUNNALLY, JAMES E.	MESQUITE, TX
NYE, PAUL	MULVANE, KS
NYGARD, E.J. JR.	TEMPLETON, MA
O'CONNELL, JOHN T.	LAWRENCE, MA
O'CONNOR, PHILIP C.	WESTBURY, NY
O'KEEFE, JAMES	LARKSPUR, CA
O'NEAL, MRS. BENTON	UNIVERSAL CITY, TX
O'NEIL, MRS. WILLIAM J.	OSWEGO, NY
O'SULLIVAN, FRANCIS J.	CARMICHAEL, CA
OAKES, EDWARD J.	HENDERSONVILLE, NC
OATES, MARVIN	CARMICHAEL, CA
OBLENDER, HOWARD T.	WILLOW STREET, PA
ODLE, WALTON	FORT WORTH, TX
OESTREICH, WALTER	RHINELANDER, WI
OETTINGER, HERBERT	RACINE, WI
OGLESBY, NICHOLAS P.	GREENSBORO, NC
OHR, JESSE	WAXAHACHIE, TX
OLSEN, JOHN L.	SAN FRANCISCO, CA
ORLUSKY, CHARLES L.	FRAZIER, CO
ORME, REGINALD A.	INGLEWOOD, CA
OROSZ, GILBERT A.	ELCATON, CA
ORSI, RAYMOND	NORRIDGE, IL
OSBORN, JAMES O.	LYNWOOD, WA
OTIS, HOWARD J.	AURORA, CO
OTT, ERVIN	BAY CITY, MI
OWENS, VERNARD	BANGOR, ME
PAGE, WALTER T.	FORT SCOTT, KS
PAGE, WILLIAM	SUNNYVALE, CA
PAGEL, JAMES	HUNTSVILLE, AL
PAGIOS, STEVE B.	HADLEY, MA
PALMITER, HAROLD	OXFORD, NY
PALTER, BURTON	LAWRENCE, NY
PANCAKE, FRANK	STAUNTON, VA
PAOLINI, VINCENT H.	LODI, NJ
PARADIS, JAMES L.	MONMOUTH, ME
PARENT, ALBERT H.	NEW BEDFORD, MA
PARHAM, MARION	LATTA, SC
PARK, FLOYD F.	FORT WORTH, TX
PARK, JACK	BAKERSFIELD, CA
PARKER, LEWIS, R.	SEGUIN, TX
PASCAL, STEVE C.	BRADLEY BEACH, NJ
PASLAY, MRS. W.C.	ORANGE, CA
PATCHES, RICHARD R.	TEMPE, AZ
PATERSON, PAT	ROSEBURG, OR
PAUL, CHESTER E.	NORTH HILLS, NY
PAWLUK, ALEX	POMONA, CA
PAYNE, TOM	TULSA, OK
PEARSON, CHARLES	GALESBURG, IL
PEDDER, COLIN R.	MILES CITY, MT
PEDERSON, MRS. HILDA H.	THUNDER BAY, ON
PELECKIS, ANTHONY P.	PHILADELPHIA, PA
PENASA, PETER	MILWAUKEE, WI
PENN, IRA	WICHITA, KS
PERKINS, MRS. DOROTHY	SILVER SPRING, MD
PEROZINO, DOMINIC J.	ST. PAUL, MN
PERROTTO, WILLIAM A.	GREENVALE, L.I., NY
PERRY, DONALD H.	SARASOTA, FL
PERRY, HILLARD	SAN CLEMENTE, CA
PETERSON, CARL A.	OVERLAND PARK, KS
PETERSON, JACK R.	TEXARKANA, TX
PETRAS, JOHN	PORT VUE, PA
PHALON, MRS. JOSEPH	MCLEAN, VA
PHILLIPS, OTIS C.	BAUXITE, AR
PHILLIPS, ROBERT	LANESBORO, MA
PICKARD, WALLACE	SUN PRAIRIE, WI
PIDHAYNY, DENNY	LOS ANGELES, CA
PIERCE, CHARLIE B.	COOKSVILLE, TN
PIERCE, DOC ALLEN	OKLAHOMA CITY, OK
PIERCE, JAMES B.	FAIRPORT, NY
PIERCE, ODIS	WICHITA, KS
PINSON, CLAUDE C.	ROUND ROCK, TX
PIPEK, OTTO JR.	DAYTONA BEACH, FL
PISARCIK, PAUL M.	CLEVELAND, OH
PISCIOTTA, ANGELO	ST. LOUIS, MO
PISTERZI, HENRY E.	ARVADA, CO
PITSCH, ROBERT E.	NORTH MERRICK, NY
PLEASANT, NED E.	LINDENHURST, IL
PODOLANCHUK, ANTON	LAUREL, MT
POLANSKY, HARRY	SOUTH PALM BEACH, FL
POMPONIO, NICHOLAS	ROCHESTER, NY
PONDER, J.D.	FORT WORTH, TX
POPLASKI, STANLEY	GREEN BAY, WI
PORPORA, OTTO V.	STONY BROOK, NY
PORTEGYS, JOHN E.	WAUKEGAN, IL
PORTER, CARL	LOS ANGELES, CA
PORTER, LESTER L.	SPRUCE PINE, AL
PORTER, RICHARD	BATTLE CREEK, MI
POSTON, CLIFFORD, G.	SALTVILLE, VA
POTTS, J. IVAN	SHELBYVILLE, TN
POTTS, MRS. FAYE	LOUISVILLE, KY
POWELL, LEROY L.	MEDFORD, NJ
POWERS, JACKSON JR.	BEEVILLE, TX
POWNALL, WILCO A.	ROMNEY, WV
PRATI, BENNIE	EL PASO, TX
PRESTON, WILLIAM E.	BELLEVUE, WA
PRICE, GLENN T.	SAN FRANCISCO, CA
PRIEPOT, WARREN	WINCHESTER, IL
PRIEST, STEVE B.	SPOKANE, WA
PRINCE, BRADFORD H.	ALBUQUERQUE, NM
PRITCHARD, HAROLD W.	PILOT MOUND, IA
PROSSEDA, JOSEPH A.	SHARON HILL, PA
PUDAS, CHARLES A.	BLUE ISLAND, IL
PULIDO, JOSEPH A.	NORTH MYRTLE BEACH, SC
PULIOS, VIRGIL	LONGVIEW, TX
PUNNETT, DONALD	LA BELLE, FL
PYTKO, WALT L.	ORLANDO, FL
QUALLS, PERRY L.	MIDWEST CITY, OK
QUINLAN, JOHN P.	STEPHENTOWN, NY
QUINN, MRS. JOHN D.	JEFFERSONTOWN, KY
RACILA, JOSEPH V.	ST. PETERSBURG, FL
RAINES, CLAIR E.	CANAL WINCHESTER, OH
RALSTON, GLEN D.	AUGUSTA, KS
RAMSEY, HERBERT	AVON PARK, FL
RANDALL, HUGH T.	HACIENDA HEIGHTS, CA
RANDEL, STANLEY	MCCOOK, NE
RAUSCH, WOODY	RENOLDSBURG, OH
RAWLS, HARRY	HARLINGEN, TX
RAWSON, ROBERT D.	PENDLETON, SC
RAYNO, WILLIAM J.	AMESBURY, MA
REARDON, JOSEPH A.	CHILLICOTHE, MO
REDD, WAYNE E.	LORE CITY, OH
REDFORD,WALLACE B.	WICHITA, KS
REDGATE, LEO J.	BRIDGEPORT, CT
REDLER, FRANK J.	BELLEVUE, NE
REED, LLOYD O.	VALRICO, FL
REED, WILLIAM H.	TARENTUM, PA
REGER, ROY W.	TONAWANDA, NY
REIBE, ARTHUR F. JR.	METAIRIE, LA
REID, JAMES A.	KINGMAN, KS
REIFEL, WILLIAM	RIVERHEAD, NY
REINSTEIN, HENRY	NORTHRIDGE, CA
RELLAS, STEPHEN	MADISON, CT
RENAGER, CHARLES	OAK HARBOR, WA
RENFRO, WILLIAM J.	TITUSVILLE, FL
RENZ, RICHARD	NEW SMYRNA BEACH, FL
REYNOLDS, KENNETH	DONALSONVILLE, GA
RHINER, ROGER M.	MENLO PARK, CA
RICE, GEORGE	MARYSVILLE, WA
RICHARDSON, JOHN C.	ALEX CITY, AL
RICHARDSON, WALTER L.	BREMERTON, WA
RICHEY, CECIL P.	EFFINGHAM, IL
RICHTER, WALTER W.	JERSEYVILLE, IL
RIEFEZ, WILLIAM	RIVERHEAD, NY
RIEGER, CARL	JONESBURG, MO
RIGHETTI, MAURICE G.	LOS ANGELES, CA

RINEHART, FRANK	JET, OK
RISHELL, EARL F.	GENEVA, FL
RISK, SHARON CLAY	CHEVY CHASE, MD
RITTER, ROLAND	MAHWAH, NJ
ROBERTS, DONALD W.	SAN MATEO, CA
ROBERTS, RILEA F.	CINCINNATI, OH
ROBERTS, WALTER H.	RICHMOND, VA
ROBERTSON, JAMES	POINTS, WV
ROBINSON MRS. W.H. JR.	CAMBRIDGE, MD
RODENCAL, GILBERT	PRAIRIE DU SAC,WI
RODENHOUSE, ROBERT	GRAND RAPIDS, MI
ROENICK, MRS. IRENE	CLEVELAND, OH
ROESENMANN, FRED	FARMINGTON, NM
ROGERS, DANIEL T.	NORTH MYRTLE BEACH, SC
ROHN, RALPH DAN	ALEXANDRIA, IN
ROMANOWSKI, LEONARD	PORT SAINT LUCIE, FL
ROONEY, BILL	MAXWELL AFB, AL
ROONEY, WILLIAM A.	WILMETTE, IL
ROPER, DEAN N.	LINCOLN, NE
ROSEBUSH, ROBERT W.	NEW BRAUNFELS, TX
ROSENBERGER, EDMUND F.	BALTIMORE, MD
ROTH, MORTON	COLONIA, NJ
ROWLETT, ALLEN B.	PINEHURST, NC
RUDIS, GEORGE E.	SPRINGFIELD, IL
RUDLEY, SAUL E.	BERWYN, PA
RUTLAND, WILLIAM	MERCER, TN
SABANOSH, JOHN	FAIRFIELD, NJ
SABATINO, ANDREW J.	NEW CASTLE, DE
SAFFELL, JACK T.	CLYDE, OH
SAMPLE, JOHN W. JR.	WINDSOR, MO
SAMPSEL, FREDERICK W.	MIDVALE, UT
SAMUELSON, PAUL	REDFORD, IN
SANBORN, KENNETH O.	SAN ANTONIO, TX
SANDERS, J. NELSON	AUSTIN, TX
SANDERS, ROBERT T.	FORT WAYNE, IN
SANDRICK, LOUIS L.	GARDEN CITY, MI
SANSTED, ROGER F.	FREEVILLE, NY
SARICH, MATT J.	BOISE, ID
SAUER, WILLIAM H.	DETROIT, MI
SAUNDERS, JAMES F.	LAS CRUCES, NM
SAVELA, EARL H.	ST. PAUL, MN
SAYLOR, RICHARD D.	MERCERSBURG, PA
SCADOVA, NORMAN A.	KEENE, NH
SCHACHTER, SEDWIN Z.	DENVER, CO
SCHALL, WILLIAM R.	NAPLES, FL
SCHEETZ, ROGER W.	STURGIS, MI
SCHERCK, LOUISE E.	HOUSTON, KY
SCHERMERHORN, ALFRED	BROOKLYN, NY
SCHMIDT, DAN	MT. CLEMONS, MI
SCHMITT, WILLIAM A.	TIETON, WA
SCHNEIDER, GEORGE W.	CARMEL, NY
SCHNEIDER, RAY	COLUMBUS, OH
SCHOOL, MRS. M.	SAN ANTONIO, TX
SCHUTZ, CHARLES	PLAIN, WI
SCHWARTZ, FRED W.	SOUTHGATE, KY
SCHWARTZ, PAUL	TAMPA, FL
SEBEST, JOE	TORRINGTON, CT
SEDLAK, LOUIS J.	COLUMBUS, GA
SEEBACH, RICHARD J.	SAN ANTONIO, TX
SEEBRUCK, LEONARD	BABCOCK, WI
SEIBERT, EARL M.	HUTCHINSON, KS
SEIFERT, WILLIAM F.	LAGUNA MIGUEL, CA
SEITH, WILLIAM F.	PENSACOLA, FL
SEIVERT, RICHARD L.	SIOUX FALLS, SD
SEKULA, WILLIAM S.	OSWEGO, NY
SELBIE, F.D. JR.	LITTLETON, CO
SELUZICKI, CHARLES	BALTIMORE, MD
SEMONES, MELVIN D.	WYTHEVILLE, VA
SENA, GABRIEL	WEST MEDFORD, MA
SERGEANT, C.H.	JACKSON, MI
SHADEL, CHARLES H.	SO. BURLINGTON, VT
SHAKA, NAPOLEON A.	FORT WORTH, TX
SHANKS, ROBERT C.	GRAND PRAIRIE, TX
SHAPPELL, DANIEL L.	FT. WORTH, TX
SHAUGHNESSY, RICHARD J.	ORMOND BEACH, FL
SHAW, GEORGE L.	ALTON, NH
SHEPARD P.D.	POTEAU, OK
SHERMAN, EARL E.	CUMBERLAND, KY
SHINE, ED T.	DECATUR, GA
SHOAF, C. K.	VANCOUVER, WA
SHULSKY, MR. GEORGE	SACRAMENTO, CA
SIBOLE, MRS. E. M.	NORTH PORT, FL
SIEBERT, EARL M.	KANSAS CITY, MO
SIECZKO, STANLEY J.	MISHAWAKA, IN
SILCOX, JAMES	GRAND JUNCTION, CO
SILL, SAMUEL C.	SAN BERNARDINO, CA
SILVA, CHARLES E.	ST. LOUIS, MO
SILVESTRO, THOMAS	NORTHFIELD, NJ
SIMON, HAROLD R.	LA CROSSE, WI
SIMONDS, ORVILLE C.	BRANDON, FL
SIMPSON, OSCAR L.	CINCINNATI, OH
SIMPSON, ROBERT D.	UWCHLAND, PA
SIMS, WAYNE H.	FRESNO, CA
SINGER, GEORGE J.	NEW BERLIN, WI
SINGLEY, EARL M.	SOLANA BEACH, CA
SKAER, MILTON E.	CREVE COEUR, MO
SKAER, WILLIAM K.	BOCA RATON, FL
SKEETS, ROGER	STURGIS, MI
SKORUPSKI, LEONARD	OSWEGO, NY
SKRAM, ARTHUR L.	MASON CITY, IA
SLAGLE, HARRY W.	ELYSBURG, PA
SLONINA, BERNARD	POQUOSON, VA
SLUSSER, EARL R.	NEKOOSA, WI
SMIAROWSKI, BERNARD F.	FENTON, MI
SMIETANA, WALTER	NEW BEDFORD, MA
SMITH, ALLEN	PHILADELPHIA, PA
SMITH, CHARLES G.	TALLAHASSEE, FL
SMITH, FLOYD L.	INDIANAPOLIS, IN
SMITH, HIBBARD A.	TULSA, OK
SMITH, IRVING W.	MUSKEGON, MI
SMITH, LOUIS E.	SAN ANTONIO, TX
SMITH, THOMAS S.	SAN JUAN CAPISTRANO, CA
SMITH, WILLIAM	MINNEAPOLIS, MN
SMITH, WILLIAM O.	AUSTIN, TX
SMOLA, MITCHELL	ACUSHNET, MA
SMOLE, RALPH M.	HURST, TX
SNEAD, THOMAS J.	COVINGTON, VA
SNOW, DAVID J.	BOULDER, CO
SNOWBANK, JOHN	CUMBERLAND, WI
SOKOL, PATRICK	ARVADA, CO
SOLFERT, FRED	LAKEWOOD, OH
SOMMERS, CHARLES	NEW HAVEN, CT
SOMMERS, MRS. TERESA	MARTINS FERRY, OH
SOUCY, O. FRED	MIAMI, FL
SPANNAGEL, RUSSELL E.	BOERNE, TX
SPARKS, WILLIAM E.	TOOELE, UT
SPENCER, ARTIE	COVINGTON, VA
SPENCER, JOHN C.	SARASOTA, FL
SPIVEY, WILLIAM A.	HAYS, KS
SPROULE, THOMAS	WYTHEVILLE, VA
SRYNIAWSKI, FRANK	ALLEN PARK, MI
STAHLER, KERMIT B.	ALLENTOWN, PA
STAMBAUGH, WALTER E.	BAKERSFIELD, CA
STANCZAK, SAMUEL J.	WAUKEGAN, IL
STANLEY, MRS. LUCILLE	JEFFERSON, ME
STANWORTH, ROBERT	JACKSON, TN
STARK, OTTO	FARMINGHAM, MA
STARKEY, DONALD G.	SEABROOK, TX
STARNES, ARTHUR M.	WICHITA, KS
STAUDE, HENRY A.	GLEN BURNIE, MD
STEARNS, WARREN E.	LAKE WYLIE, SC
STEBBINS, DAVID	MAYVILLE, NY
STEELE, ROBERT D.	ALBUQUERQUE, NM
STEFFENS, ALFRED G.	MILWAUKEE, WI
STEINER, FLOYD D.	NEVADA CITY, CA
STEINMAN, GEORGE W.	KALAMAZOO, MI
STEMBRIDGE, JAMES	HIGHLAND, CA
STEPHAM, MAURICE	IJAMSVILLE, MD
STEPHENSON, MRS. ELLEN	SIOUX FALLS, SD
STERN, MYRON	ROCHESTER, NY

STEVENS, DELMAR D.	CLEARWATER FL
STEVENSON, C.H. III	PINEVILLE, WY
STEWART, WALTON D.	SEATTLE, WA
STINES, ANDREW J.	GRANBY, CT
STINSON, GEORGE A.	TYRON, NC
STIVERS, E.L.	MUSTANG, OK
STOCKS, WILLIAM SR.	FINLEYVILLE, PA
STONE, ROBERT A.	GLEN ALLEN, VA
STOUT, IRBY C. JR.	TAMPA, FL
STOVAK, FRANK S.	SAYRE, PA
STRACHAN, JOHN R.	LEVITTOWN, NY
STRUCKHOFF, ED	ST. LOUIS, MO
STUCKY, HERBERT S.	MECHANICSBURG, PA
STUMPFF, DONALD D.	KEARNEY, NE
SUDEN, MELVIN W.	COUNCIL BLUFFS, IA
SUEREZ, MARVIN	ROCK HILL, NY
SULLIVAN, H. RIGGS	TUBAC, AZ
SULLIVAN, HAROLD E.	BENTON, AR
SULLIVAN, JOHN C.	NOVATO, CA
SULLIVAN, MRS. FLORENCE	CHICAGO, IL
SUNDERLAND, FRANK,	PHILADELPHIA, PA
SUTPHEN, CARL H.	RICHMOND, VA
SUWAK, ANDY	HICKORY, PA
SWALLOW, CHAD C.	KAYSVILLE, UT
SWAN, HUGO	KALAMAZOO, MI
SWANCUTT, WOODROW P.	SAN ANTONIO, TX
SWANEY, JAMES E.	HUNTINGTON, PA
SWANSON, EVERT E.	KANE, PA
SWANSON, ROBERT	LOS ANGELES, CA
SWARTZ, WILSON	INDIANAPOLIS, IN
SWEAT, W.C. JR.	CORINTH, MS
SWEENEY, DANIEL JR.	WHARTON, TX
SWEZEY, BILL	GRANBURY, TX
SWILLEY, WALLACE E.	CAMILLA, GA
SZAFRANSKI, GEORGE	LANSING, MI
TADEN, HAROLD	CRESCENT CITY, IL
TALIAFERRO, JAMES	COOLIDGE, TX
TANNER, DEAN	HURST, TX
TATE, DAVID A.	PROSPECT, KY
TATUM, CHARLES G.	WINSTON-SALEM, NC
TAYLOR, MRS. CHARLES M.	GOLDTHWAITE, TX
TAYLOR, RAYMOND L.	RICHWOOD, OH
TEAGUE, FREEMAN	MANCHESTER, NH
TELEKESI, GEZA J.	CLEVELAND, OH
TENPAS, GORDON D.	SUN LAKES, AZ
TEPLICK, NATHAN	ELKINS, PA
TEPPER, ROBERT L.	NORCROSS, PA
THE ARMY, DEPARTMENT OF	CARLISLE BARRACKS, PA
THEOPHILES, ANDREW	ETOWAH, NC
THIBODEAU, EPHRAIM J.	FORT KENT, ME
THIESS, KENNETH J.	RIVERDALE, NJ
THOMAS, ALVIN C.	N. MYRTLE BEACH, SC
THOMAS, CHARLES G.	NEWPORT, RI
THOMAS, CLARK S.	SPRINGFIELD, SD
THOMAS, DANIEL	WILKES-BARRE, PA
THOMAS, ROBERT A.	CHEROKEE, AL
THOMASIAN, KARNIG	RIVER EDGE, NJ
THOMPSON, LUKE	INGRAM, TX
THOMPSON, MRS. FRANCIS N.	SAVANNAH, GA
THOMPSON, RALPH E.	SALEM, OR
THORNE, DAN F.	LAVERNE, CA
THORNSBERRY, MRS. BETTY	ELLISVILLE, MS
THORRATT, WILLIAM	ROCKY RIVER, OH
THURBER, FOREST (HUGH)	TOPEKA, KS
TIMKO, JOSEPH	VALRICO, FL
TIPTON, JAMES D.	PEARLAND, TX
TISCHER, DONALD	FONDA, IA
TISSERAT, ROBERT A.	WARD, CO
TOFIAS, ARNOLD B.	NEWTON, MA
TOMA, RAYMOND J.	NISKAYUNA, NY
TOMES, ART	BURNSVILLE, MN
TOPOLSKI, JOHN Z.	MILWAUKEE, WI
TOPPIN, WILLIAM J.	DEARBORN HEIGHTS, MI
TOTH, ALEX S.	REDFORD, MI
TOWNES, WILILAM W.	FRESNO, CA

TOWNSEND, ORA O.	ONAWA, IA
TREANOR, MRS. WILLIAM A.	PUEBLO, CA
TREMAIN, WILLIAM	KOKOMO, IN
TREMAINE, ELLIOTT	SEATTLE, WA
TRIHAS, FOSTER G.	ELGIN, IL
TRINKNER, EDWARD F.	PEARL RIVER, NY
TROENDLE, WALTER B.	KNOXVILLE, IA
TROLL, RAYMOND C.	PAINTED POST, NY
TUCKER, EDWARD J.	MEDFORD, NJ
TUCKER, HARRY E.	MECHANICSVILLE, VA
TUCKER, RALPH	WICHITA, KS
TULLOS, VIRGIL	LONGVIEW, TX
TURESKY, WILFRED	SOUTHHAMPTON, NY
TURNER, ERNEST	GORE, OK
TURNER, LYLE	GRASS VALLEY, CA
TURNER, THOMAS E.	KANSAS CITY, MO
TURNLEY, E.W.	NASHVILLE, TN
TWEET, JOHN H.	TOLLAND, CT
TWILLEY, MRS. ELLEN	SAN ANTONIO, TX
TWILLING, JOSEPH W. JR.	COLE CAMP, MO
UEBLER, ROY A.	BERRIEN CENTER, MI
UNDERWOOD, WILLIAM S.	TUCSON, AZ
URBANIC, ALEX A.	LORAIN, OH
VALLARIO, D.A.	TEQUESTA, FL
VALLEY, JOSEPH D.	PRAIRIE DU CHIEN, WI
VAN BALEN, BERNARD F.	GAHANNA, OH
VAN CLEAVE, ROBERT T.	SIOUX CITY, IA
VAN DOORN, WILLIAM	HOBOKEN, NJ
VAN HOGENDORF, MRS. F.	BALTIMORE, MD
VAN ORMER, MRS. RUTH	ELIZABETHTOWN, PA
VANDERLOOVEN, GUSTAVE R.	ESSEXVILLE, MI
VANWINKLE, JOSEPH F.	ORLANDO, FL
VAROFF, GEORGE E.	SAN ANTONIO, TX
VAUCHER, T. ROBERT	BRIDGEWATER, NJ
VEACH, RICHARD A.	OMAHA, NE
VELIE, JOHN J.	MINNEAPOLIS, MN
VELTHOUSE, GERRIT	GRAND RAPIDS, MI
VELTRIE, LEE T.	SPOKANE, WA
VERTRIEST, ALFONS C.	MT. CLEMONS, MI
VETVICK, HARRY A.	GRAND RAPIDS, MI
VICKERY, EDWIN H.	MELROSE, MA
VICKERY, MRS. HAZEL	PEMBROKE PINE, FL
VOLK, JAMES P.	CAPE CORAL, FL
VOLK, MRS.	OLD GREENWICH, CT
WAGNER, FRANCIS J.	ST. PAUL, MN
WAGNER, MELVIN F.	WICHITA FALLS, TX
WALKER, GERALD R.	SANTA BARBARA, CA
WALKER, ROBERT T.	RHINEBECK, NY
WALLING, JACK	CEDAR KEY, FL
WALSH, JOSEPH	WARRENSVILLE HEIGHTS, OH
WALTER, GEORGE H.	WAYNESBORO, PA
WALTERS, WARREN H.	GREENSBORO, NC
WANCHIK, JOHN JR.	LIVONIA, MI
WANDREI, ALFRED E.	OXFORD, MA
WARD, DON	BLOOMINGTON, MN
WARDELL, CLARENCE E.	HADDON HEIGHTS, NJ
WASILEWSKI, VINCENT T.	FALLS CHURCH, VA
WASMUND, HARRY W.	EUSTIS, FL
WATKINS, PAUL R.	PITTSBURGH, PA
WATKINS, WALTER A.	TINTON FALLS, NJ
WATSON, ROBERT E.	TUCSON, AZ
WEAVER, WILBUR	MARIETTA, GA
WEBB, MELVIN O.	BROWNFIELD, TX
WEBER, RALPH	SKOKIE, IL
WEBER, ROLAND H.	MORRISVILLE, PA
WEBER, MRS. CHARLES JR.	REDONDO BEACH, CA
WEBSTER, DAVID F.	FINDLAY, OH
WEEDEN, CHARLES	SYCAMORE, IL
WEHMAS, RICHARD S.	NORWOOD, MA
WEILBACHER, CLEBURN	SAN ANTONIO, TX
WEINBERG, MILTON	DIX HILLS, NY
WEINBERG, RALPH	PHILADELPHIA, PA
WEITLAUF, LARRY STEPHEN	PADUCAH, KY
WEMPLE, NEIL W.	TUCSON, AZ
WERBANETH, LOUIS A.	ALLISON PARK, PA

WERNET, JOHN K.	WEST ISLIP, NY
WESCHLER, GEORGE T.	MOSCOW, ID
WEST, BYRON W.	PUNTA GORDA, FL
WEST, GEORGE R.	CHRISTIANSBURG, VA
WESTBERG, CARL N.	ERICK, OK
WETZELL, CARLTON K.	LONG BEACH, CA
WHARTON, FORREST E.	LONGVIEW, TX
WHITAKER, JOHN T.	W. CHATHAM, MA
WHITE, BENNIE	CORNING, AR
WHITE, JOSEPH D.	KERRVILLE, TX
WHITE, LINN R.	MARYLAND, NY
WHITE, RICHARD H.	TOLEDO, IL
WHITEHOUSE, FRANK JR.	ANN ARBOR, MI
WILCOX, PAUL I.	FT. MYERS, FL
WILDE, HAROLD A.	MIDWEST CITY, OK
WILKENING, VERNON	WASECA, MN
WILKERSON, R. WARREN	TULSA, OK
WILKERSON, WILMER R.	HAYWARD, CA
WILKINS, RAYMOND M.	ROSSVILLE, GA
WILKINSON, HERMAN G.	BRISTOL, VA
WILLIAM, ELIJAH	BLAKELY, GA
WILLIAMS, IRA	ECTOR, TX
WILLIAMS, JAMES	STEELTON, PA
WILLIAMS, JOHN	LONGWOOD, FL
WILLIAMS, LLEWELYN T.	RACINE, WI
WILLIAMS, ROBERT E.	OAK PARK, MI
WILLIAMS, WILLIE C.	BIVINS, TX
WILLIERS, RAY T.	TAMPA, FL
WILLINS, RAYMOND M.	ROSSVILLE, GA
WILSON, CLARK	LAGRANGE, IL
WILSON, TAYLOR W.	ROCHESTER, IN
WINBORNE, SAMUEL P.	ATLANTIC, NC
WINDER, WILLIAM L.	YARDLEY, PA
WINGFIELD, WILLIAM R.	ROSWELL, NM
WINSHIP, J. MERRICK	LAKE SAN MARCOS, CA
WINTERS, ROBERT A.	WICHITA, KS
WISEMAN, HAROLD D.	COOPERSTOWN, ND
WISEMAN, MRS. WAYNE	ADEL, GA
WISSEMAN, FRED J.	WOODHAVEN, NY
WITTE, ELMER H.	BURT LAKE, MI
WIX, ROBERT A.	MERRILL, WI
WOJCIK, ROMAN J.	MILWAUKEE, WI
WOJICK, EDMOND	NORWICH, CT
WOJTUSIK, FRANK J.	TUCSON, AZ
WOLFERT, FRED G.	LAKEWOOD, OH
WOLFSON, EVERETT	STONY BROOK, NY
WOOD, BURTON L.	PLACERVILLE, CA
WOOD, FORREST G.	SAN DIEGO, CA
WOOD, MRS. RAYMOND V	DALLAS, TX
WOOD, ROBERT L.	MILWAUKEE, WI
WOODRUFF, JASPER W.	LAFAYETTE, CA
WOODRUM, LOUIE E.	PHOENIX, AZ
WOOLFSON, WILLIAM	LOS ANGELES, CA
WOOLSEY, CHESTER A.	FORT WORTH, TX
WORTHLEY, LEIGHTON E.	KAILUA, HI
WOTIPKA, BARNEY F.	FLATONIA, TX
WOTUS, FRANK	BUTLER, PA
WRIGHT, HAROLD V.	SOLANA BEACH, CA
WRIGHT, HERBERT W.	BAY CITY, MI
WRIGHT, WESLEY	DETROIT, TX
WRIGHT, WILLIAM T.	SILSBEE, TX
WYANT, THEORDORE	TRACY, CA
WYATT, BERNIE	CANADA L7L 3Y2
YAGOS, MRS. J.T.	AURORA, CO
YODER, WALTER J.	MARSHALL, AR
YONKERS, KENNETH S.	KALAMAZOO, MI
YOSCO, ANTHONY J.	POMPTON PLAINS, NJ
YOUNG, MAYO W.	BELLINGHAM, WA
YOUNG, WILLIAM	GOLIAD, TX
YOUNGBLOOD, CHARLES	WARNER ROBINS, GA
ZALABAK, WILLIAM H.	AUBURN, CA
ZEBART, ANTHONY F.	BOCA RATON, FL
ZEIGLER, CLARENCE	RYERSFORD, PA
ZEIGLER, GRANT N.	WASHINGTON, DC
ZELL, WILLIAM A.	SALUGA, PA
ZEMBAL, HARRY	DOWNEY, CA
ZIEGLER, OSCAR K.	CARSONVILLE, MI
ZIMA, JOSEPH J.	PITTSBURGH, PA
ZIMMERMAN, WILLIAM G.	LOCH SHELDRAKE, NY
ZINK, W.G.	SAN FRANCISCO, CA
ZINKAN, ROBERT	INDIANAPOLIS, IN
ZINN, MARTIN H.	MERRICK, NY
ZONARS, ATHANS C.	TIPP CITY, OH
ZWEIG, SHELDON S.	PLAINVIEW, NY

Left to Right: Ed Whitney, Art Blackman, unknown, Major Lamb, unknown and Flecker.

Ground grew in Chakulia, India on Aircraft #319-"Himalaya Hussy". Back row, left to right: Crew chief "Doby", unknown, Norm Huber, Ray Toma, Elias Flessor, unknown. Front row, left to right: John Arlet, John Bergen, unknown, Angelo Crivelli, Earl R. Slusser. Of the original B-29s in the 44th, Aircraft #319, the "Himalaya Hussy", was one of the few surviving aircraft left at the end of our C.B.I. tour, and flew back to the states.

POW's rescued from Rangoon prison-four 40th Bomb Veterans pictured, they are sitting on left Nicholas P. Oglesby and standing from left bare chested are Julian C. Cochran, G.M. (Bud) Etherington, and Harold E. Fletcher.

Crew No. 95, Clovis, NM, Aug. 1944. Standing L to R: 1st Lt. Stacy Hall, 1st Lt. J. Ivan Potts, Jr. 2nd Lt. Wm. E. McQueen, 1st Lt. Rudolph C. Zubach, Zane E. Bloom. Front row L to R: Cpl. George E. Kelly, Cpl. Robert Mrugala, Capl. Irving M. Craig, Jr., Cpl. Reginald A. Manning, Sg.t Leslie F. Savage, and Cpl. Donald C. Jones. (Courtesy of J. Ivans Potts, Jr.)

Veterans of The 40th Bombardment Group (VH)

Dress Parade, Chakulia, India (Courtesy of J. Brusco)

Standing l to r: Capt. William "Bill" Renfro, 1st Lt. Robert "Con" Conley, 2nd Lt. Robert "Shorty" Pollard, 2nd Lt. John P. Brusco, "Joe" Herbert. Kneeling l to r: Sgt. Leo "Pops" Gainey, S/Sgt. Frank "Hut" Hentmaker, S/Sgt. Rolph "Tuck" Tucker, S/Sgt. William "Bill" Schrage, and S/Sgt. "Al" Ebert.

ZANE L. ABBOTT, born Mar. 29, 1914 in Farmington, UT. Attended schools in the Tremonton, UT area, went to Utah State University and University of New Mexico. Enlisted in Flying Cadet program in February 1940 Class 40-F. Commissioned 2nd Lieutenant at Kelly Field, TX. Was a basic instructor at Randolph Field and San Angelo, TX.

Zane L. Abbott

Completed B-24 transition at Ft. Worth, TX and assigned to 302nd Bomb Gp. (H), Clovis, NM. Requested transfer to B-29 program. Completed B-29 combat crew training Alamogordo, NM. Crew arrived Tinian May 1945 and assigned to 40th Bomb Gp., 45th Sq. Completed 17 combat missions, 13 in #47 "Eddie Allen II." Served as 45th Sq. Ops. O. and Sq. CO.

Returned to U.S. October 1945 unassigned. Reassigned to 40th Bomb Gp. March Field, CA, and appointed 45th Sq. CO. November 1946 transferred, separated and advanced to Lieutenant Colonel Air Reserve.

Enlisted as M Sergeant February 1947. Retired March 1970 in grade of SM Sergeant advanced to Major USAF Ret.

In 1942 married Helen Allen, results three sons, ten grandchildren. Is now living with his wife near Salmon, ID.

CLINTON S. ADAMS, was born in Adair Co., KY and at an early age moved to Kokomo, IN. Except for a three year stay in Florida he remained there through high school. The family moved to Lexington, KY in 1936 where he attended the University of Kentucky.

Clinton S. Adams

He obtained a commission in armament in the Aviation Cadet program. He was sent from the West Coast Training Command to Lowry AFB to be assigned to the B-29 program. Moving his wife and small son into a basement apartment in Pratt, KS, he joined the 40th Gp. in the hectic preparations to go overseas. His part of the 40th went on the USS Mt. Vernon around Australia to India. Another sea voyage moved the 40th Gp. to Tinian. When V-J Day came he was in Hawaii.

Released from active duty he returned to the University of Kentucky for a master's degree and three years toward a PhD. After serving as a Park Historian in Vicksburg, MS, he returned to active duty in 1952 and retired in 1968. Assignments were to: Wright-Patterson AFB; Office of the Air Attache, London, England; Robins AFB, GA; and Little Rock AFB, AR. Twelve more years as a civil service employee completed his career. He and his wife now reside in Cape Coral, FL.

GORDON F. ADAMS, born June 15, 1925, in Shenandoah, IA. Entered service in June, 1943, and commissioned June, 1944. Navigation training at Hondo, TX; radar training at Boca Raton, FL; combat crew training at Clovis, NM; received new Wichita plane and orders at Herington, KS; flew to Chakulia, India, in January 1945.

Gordon F. Adams

Hospital confinement prevented moving to Tinian with the rest of the group, but followed later via ATC. While in hospital, his crew bailed out (Pat Donelan crew) and only the co-pilot Dale Ellis survived. Flew missions out of Tinian with several different crews. After war ended, was transferred to North Field and served on the Standardization Board.

After separation, received B.S. degree in business from University of Colorado, and received photography certificate from Brooks Institute of Photography. Married 1949, widowed 1985. Has worked for The IOWAN Magazine, W.A. Krueger, Motorola Semiconductor, and is now print production manager at corporate headquarters of The Dial Corporation in Phoenix, AZ.

FR. BARTHOLOMEW ADLER, born St. Louis, Mo. Sept. 3, 1908. Ordained a Roman Catholic priest, May 18, 1940 at Louisville, KY. Member of a religious order known as the Congregation of the Passion. Enlisted in the Army on Feb. 16, 1942 at Chicago, IL. Assigned Chaplain of the 40th Bomb Gp., Rio Hato, Panama, May 25, 1942. Remained with Group as it moved to Pratt, KS, Chakulia, India and the island of Tinian. Separated from the Service, Mar. 20, 1946 at Camp Grant, IL.

Bartholomew Adler

Awards received during time of Service apart from usual Theater Ribbons were: Soldier's Medal and Air Medal.

Presently resides as a member of the Passionist Community, Sacred Heart Monastery, 1924 Newburg Rd., Louisville, KY 40205.

GEORGE IRVING AHERN, born Jan. 30, 1920, at Denver, CO. Attended school at Cathederal and then University of Colorado a short time; worked for AT&T two years; worked for Continental Airlines as station manager for ATC Branch. Enlisted in the Army Air Corps Nov. 18, 1943. After boot camp, gunnery and radar school beginning in St. Louis, was assigned to the 40th Bomb Gp. in Clovis, NM and remained with the group throughout my service tenure and went to India then to Tinian. Served as radar operator on two B29 crews, completing 21 missions with the highest rank of S/Sergeant. Awards received other than the usual Good Conduct Medal were the Asiatic-Pacific Theater Ribbon with four Bronze Stars and Air Medal with two Oak Leaf Clusters. Discharged Oct. 30, 1945.

George Irving Ahern

Married June 14, 1944. Employed by Continental Airlines and enrolled at University of Denver for accounting major. My career as an accountant has been varied and am now retired with a private income tax practice. In 1987, celebrated my 43rd wedding anniversary. Have one son, one granddaughter and three step-grandsons. Interests are traveling, bird hunting and Model A cars. I joined the 40th Bomb Gp. Assn. in 1982 and was one of the hosts for the Denver reunion in 1985. In 1986 I joined the Lowry Heritage Museum Foundation, Inc. to assist in the restoration of B-29 #729, T Square 54.

RICHARD L. ALTFELD, S/Sgt., 39th Air Force Sdn. was born in Elyria, OH Feb. 16, 1918. Drafted into Army Air Corps June 1941 and sent to Bowman Field, Louisville, KY for basic training.

Richard L. Altfeld

After training was placed in machine shop where repair parts were made for airplanes.

Dec. 7, 1941 was declared, knew my one year of draft would be extended but never realized it would be almost four and a half years. From Kentucky to Shreveport, LA to live on a pier for six weeks.

On to Blythe, CA, the temperature went to 120°. Could fry an egg on an airplane wing. Married in Blythe to girl friend from home whom I sent for.

On to Riverside, CA for a short rest, then to Great Falls, MT 40° below 0° then to Ft. Dix, NJ.

Left for Chakulia, India to be the first B-29 Gp. overseas. Next to Tinian Island. Discharged October 1945.

Went into family business next. Retired in 1984. Have two children and four grandchildren. Spend summers in Ohio and winters in Florida.

MARK ALSTON ARMSTRONG, born Jan. 6, 1920 in Whipple, WV. Graduated from high school in Mt. Hope, WV. Joined the U.S. Army Air Corps Sept. 8, 1939 at Langley Field, VA. Stationed at Borinquen Field, Puerto Rico; France Field, Panama Canal; Guatemala City; The Rock, Galapagos Islands; Pratt Air Force Base, Pratt, KS; India; Tinian. Discharged from the 44th Bomb Gp. as S/Sergeant Sept. 4, 1945.

Mark Alston Armstrong

Awards included: WWII Victory, National Defense Service Medal, Good Conduct Medal, Asiatic-Pacific Campaign, American Campaign, and Air Force Good Conduct Medal.

On Sept. 7, 1945 he married Julie Kuretich and they have three children and five grandchildren. For 28 years Mark worked as a Tool Room Foreman with Cessna Aircraft Co. in Wichita, KS, retiring in January 1982. Mark passed away Sept. 15, 1987.

JOHN BACKES, enlisted November 1942 and trained at Coffeyville, KS. Then to A & M School at Amarillo, TX and B-29 School at Boeing in Seattle, WA. Joined the 44th Bomb Sdn. at Pratt, KS in August 1943. Crewed B-26 and B-29 aircraft as they became available. Attended R3350 school and fuel injection school at Wright Engine Factory in Patterson, NJ.

John Backes

The 44th had left for India when I returned from New Jersey and became part of the 40th pool. Pool was broken up after a 2-1/2 month wait and was assigned to Ground School as engine instructor in the old 40th Gp. Hq. building until December 1945. Discharged in February 1946 after a short stay in Roswell, NM.

Worked for McDonnell Aircraft 1946 thru 1979. Married Ona Dupay in 1951 and have two children.

JOHN A. BAILEY, born, reared, and educated in Ohio. After college, Engineer on Curtis SOB2C a year, then Engineering cadets, Class 43-11, Chanute Field and Yale University. Commissioned, volunteered for first Boeing B-29 Flight Engineers class. Aeronautical rated at Salina, KS, assigned as instructor. Volunteered for Pratt, assigned 395th on Lowry's crew. Moved to 44th in Chakulia, appointed Sdn. Flight Engineer, completed tour on Tinian. Awarded DFC, four Air Medals, Commendation Medal, Philippine Liberation Medal, A-P Medal with nine Battle Stars.

John A. Bailey

After my around-the-world tour, married Evelyn Moore, Air Force Day at Peterson Field, CO. Assigned IG, March Field, CA. Air Officer the day Gen. Ramey and Col. Skaer arrived to reassemble the 40th. VOCG was 40th Gp. Flight Engineer. Worked on Bikini A-Bomb Blue Streak Mission at Davis-Montham. Assigned by Gen. Arnold as Very Heavy Flight Test Engineer at Eglin Field, FL. Left service in 1947.

Worked for Chick Pitts, Boeing Wichita Superintendent, on Boeing 202. Returned to college for Degree in Business. Managed Weyerhaeuser and Independent Lumber Company operations, ten years. Started as Construction Contracting Officer for Department of Interior agencies in western states and Alaska. Commendation by Secretary of Interior for Alaskan pipeline work. Presently responsible for facilities maintenance and communications (radio, telephones, microwave, satellite) in eight states for Wildlife Service. Also Communications Officer for Colorado Civil Air Patrol Sdn., Fly 200 hours/year, Search and Rescue. Member Board of Directors, 40th Assn., promoting its historical significance every opportunity possible.

GEORGE J. BAKER, born Jan. 29, 1920 in New Jersey. Enlisted in 1942-basic at Ft. Dix, Keesler Technical School, Mississippi-B26 Technical training, Glenn L. Martin, Baltimore - Jefferson Barracks, MO then to Panama. On "The Rock" off the coast of Ecuador, patrolled the approach to Canal Zone.

George J. Baker

1943 assigned to Marvin Goodwin's crew, 20th Bomber Command, 40th Gp., 45th Sdn. as mechanic-gunner at Pratt, KS. March 1944 Chakulia, India via Newfoundland, Morocco and Egypt. Developed oil leak landed at Agra for repairs and had opportunity to tour Taj Mahal.

Twenty combat missions from China. 25 missions over the "Hump" including the longest bombing flight in history of aviation.

Awards received: Distinguished Flying Cross, Air Medal with two Oak Leaf Clusters, American Theater Medal, Asiatic-Pacific Theater Medal and Good Conduct Medal.

Separated from service August 1945 - married Jacqueline Griffin. Had four children, nine grandchildren, and one great-grandchild. Worked as gear cutter, retired in 1982. Now raising Polled Herefords.

ROBERT L. BARG, born in San Benito, TX on Nov. 20, 1918. Enlisted at Chanute Field,

IL on June 20, 1940 to attend mechanic's school. After graduating was kept as an Instructor. Was later sent to March Field, CA for Crew Chief training on B-17s. After three years as an enlisted man and holding the rank of T/Sergeant was commissioned at Yale as Maintenance Engineering Officer. Then to B-29 school at Seattle, and Flight Engineer school at Denver.

Robert L. Barg

Joined the 44th Sdn., 40th Bomb Gp. at Pratt, KS in December 1943; then to Chakulia, India, and on to Tinian. Was Flight Engineer for E.O. Berry and L.A. Thomas on "Sleepy Time Gal." After thirty-five missions and earning the Unit Citation with two Clusters, D.F.C., Air Medal with three Clusters and seven Battle Stars, returned to civilian life in January 1947.

Was employed by Tenneco Corp. for 34 years, retiring July 1981. Have a wife and two children.

JEREMIAH P. BELKNAP, (Jake) born on Aug. 22, 1917, in Napoleon, OH. Attended grade and secondary schools in Napoleon, followed by attendance and graduation from University of Michigan.

Jeremiah P. Belknap

Admitted to the bar in Ohio and Indiana and practiced law briefly in Indianapolis, IN. Entered the Army of the U.S. on Apr. 11, 1942, and discharged in October 1945. After Tech School training at Chanute Field, IL, was assigned to 44th Bomb Sdn. in Guatemala and remained with the 44th for the duration through Pratt, Chakulia and Tinian. After progression through the ranks, wound up as Crew Chief and Master Sergeant, thanks to a good crew.

Received the usual ribbons and citations, plus the Bronze Star and Air Medal.

After leaving the Service, returned to the practice of law in Indianapolis and ultimately became a senior partner and now of Counsel to the firm of Barnes & Thornburg. Married in 1945 after discharge from the Service and in due course had five children and now into grandchildren.

BARNEY BERMAN, born Apr. 7, 1911 Boston, MA SS. Graduated Winthrop High School, Winthrop, MA. Entered service Oct. 9, 1943. Basic training, Miami Beach, FL. Joined 40th Bomb Gp. at Pratt, KS 1943. Sheet Metal Specialist at Chanute.

Barney Berman

U.S. Rubber School Detroit, MI self-sealing tank specialist was in 25th, 45th, 40th Bomb Hq. in charge of Group Oxygen Service at Chakulia, Tinian. Discharged Oct. 22, 1945. Married Ione Schlossberg 1966.

In New Hampshire from May to October. Address: Box 43, Salem, NH 03079, Tel. No. (603) 898-5615. In Florida from October to May. Address: 313 Center Island, Golden Beach, FL 33160, (305) 931-7449. If any of my old buddies are visiting New Hampshire or Florida would like to see you. Retired.

EVERETT O. BERRY, graduated from Dallas Technical High School in 1937. Four years at the University of Texas at Austin with a major in physics. Entered the Cadet Flying Program in 1941 at Kelly Field in Texas. Commissioned in 1942. After B-17 training at Sebring, FL joined the 40th Bomb Gp. in the Panama Canal Zone and assigned to 44th Bomb Sdn. Returned to U.S. in 1943 and assigned to Pratt, KS for B-29 training, later serving in India and China. Selected for regular commission in 1946 served 28 years, last assignment as Base Commander.

Everett O. Berry

Awarded Air Medal with Oak Leaf Cluster, Air Offensive Japan, Asiatic Pacific Campaign with four Battle Stars, Philippine Liberation Medal, Vietnam Service Medal, Air Force Commendation Medal with Cluster and Legion of Merit.

Since retiring have been active in civic and community affairs serving on several boards and as president of the Odessa Rotary Club. Received award for excellence in community service.

Wife: Mary Evelyn (married in 1945) daughter and two sons, five grandchildren.

Highlight of Military Career was service in 40th Bomb Gp.

JOSEPH M. BESEDA, Lt. Col., USAF, born Port Lavaca, TX, 1914. Received BBA, Texas Tech University, 1941. Commissioned and awarded Bombardier wings at Midland AAF, TX, June 1942. Served as bombardier instructor and then short tour 5th AF, New Guinea, in B-17s and B-24s. Joined 40th Bomb Gp. (B-29) at Pratt, KS. Went to India as 40th Gp. Bombardier.

Joseph M. Beseda

Went on first B-29 combat mission, June 5, 1944, Bangkok, Thailand. Went on first B-29 mission over Japan, June 15, 1944, Yawata, Japan. Went on longest combat mission WWII from Ceylon to Sumatra.

Served short time Hq. 20th AF and then went with advance staff to Hq. 58th Bomb Wing, at Tinian Island, as Wing Bombardier. Went on one of the last combat missions over Japan after atomic bombs were dropped.

Awarded Bronze Star, Air Medal with four Oak Leaf Clusters, two Air Force Commendation Medals, Asiatic-Pacific Theater Medal with five Battle Stars, etc.

Separated after war and then recalled for Korea conflict. Flew combat missions out of Okinawa. Then to James Connally AFB, Waco, TX, and upgraded to Navigator. Served there as Squadron Commander, Training Group Commander, and Base Provost Marshal. Finished tour at Hq. Pacific Air Force, Hawaii, with Air Inspector General. Retired 1967 and reside at Austin, TX. Worked several years with Internal Revenue Service as tax auditor.

CHARLES E. BIEHLE, born July 28, 1919, Jennings Co., IN, graduated Vernon High School 1937. Drafted into the Army June 1941, transferred to Air Corps Cadet Training August 1942. Failed Pilot Training December 1942. Graduated Bombardier School July 1943 and Navigation School December 1943.

At Pratt, KS became a Bombardier-Navigator on B-29s. Saw combat with the 40th Bomb Gp. and was Bombardier-Navigator on the third B-29 to bomb the mainland of

Charles E. Biehle

Japan, also had 14 bombing missions plus Hump trips. Left active duty October 1945 joining AF Reserves, 434th Troop Carrier Wing in 1954 as Navigator and remained active until retired as Lieutenant Colonel in 1971 with 30 years active and reserve time receiving 14 awards.

Farmed and worked for Cummins Engine Co., Columbus, IN until I retired in 1983. My wife and I raised six children, all married and have 14 grandchildren. Deceased June 16, 1987.

GEORGE R. BISSEY, "Dutch" born March 1920 at Springfield, OH. Moved to central Illinois 1929 following death of father. Grew up in country type atmosphere attending one-room school house utilizing one teacher for eight grades. Total enrollment of high school was less than fifty students. My class had seventeen, the largest of the four classes.

George R. Bissey

Enlisted in "Brown Shoe Corps" July 1941 requesting overseas duty. Two weeks later was assigned to Hq. Sdn., 40th Bomb Gp., Borinquen Field, Puerto Rico. Took basic training with nine other recruits in the streets of "Tent City," supervised by S/Sgt. "Tiny" Marchinson.

First duty assignment Clerk Typist in Gp. Sgt. Major's office. Transferred to Motor Pool and from there to 45th Sdn. and armament section. Remained in armament until retirement.

Was mustered out of Service October 1945. Re-enlisted September 1950 and finally retired July 1966. Enjoying retirement doing woodworking and fishing.

Married Angie Vansickle of Pratt, KS in November 1943. We have three children and six grandchildren.

My duty in the 40th was neither heroic nor illustrious. Probably the most noteworthy experience was surviving "The Battle of Borinquen." As anyone connected with this engagement can attest, this was no small feat.

DONALD V. BLACHLY, was in Sdn. 45 of 40th Bomb Gp. I was APC, airplane number was 39 (old and slow, but dependable).

My engineer was James J. Rowan, now deceased. Radar operator was Frank Kascher—last I heard living in Boyonton Springs, FL, other exec. Herbert F. Drake accounted for.

I entered Army Air Corps in June 1942. After preflight at Santa Ana, CA went to Mather Field near Sacramento in a special class, 43-A-1, and through primary, basic, advanced, plus instructor training in BT-13s. Spent a few months at Las Vegas, NV training co-pilots in B-17s and also gunners. Trained in B-29 at Alamogordo, went overseas to join 40th in Tinian late June 1945. Went on about ten missions.

Returned to Sacramento area and worked for construction companies mostly as controller or contRact administrator. Now retired in the suburbs. Had five children and now seven grandchildren. Still do some occasional administrative work for employer of the last 20 years.

ARTHUR J. BLACKMAN, born Oct. 31, 1914 - Hobson, MT. Schooled through high school at Moccasin, MT. Heating & Refrigeration School by correspondence. Drafted from Douglas Aircraft.

Arthur J. Blackman

Joined Army Air Corps in September 1942. Discharged October 1945. Went to Boot Camp in Utah. AM school Wichita Falls, TX. Electric school at Chanute Field - B-29 in Seattle. More training at Marietta, GA. Supercharger school at Minn. Honeywell-Minneapolis. After 13 months of schooling was assigned to 45th Sdn., 40th Bomb Gp. at Pratt.

Overseas from Newport News, VA through Mediterranean. Were bombed at Naples - on through Suez Canal - Red Sea to Bombay. Across India by train to Chakulia. Flew the hump from India to China several times and to Tinian and back to U.S. by B-29.

Received Air Medal and highest rank was Technical Sergeant. Married in 1948 and have two sons. Have owned and operated a Heating & Refrigeration business in Lewistown, MT since 1950.

GRAHAM L. BLEILER, born in Brownsville, PA, Sept. 25, 1914. Graduated as a pilot class of 41-H and sent to Puerto Rico in November 1941 where I joined the 44th Sdn., 40th Bomb Gp. Remained with the same outfit during the war. From Caribbean to Guatemala, anti-submarine and patrol work, to Pratt for B-29 training, to Chakulia, India then to Tinian. Completed 35 missions being awarded D.F.C., six Air Medals and five Battle Stars.

Graham L. Bleiler

Returned to the states late summer of 1945. Remained in the service and was one of the original members of Strategic Air Command. Saw action during Korean War as a SAC Combat Operations Officer stationed in Japan. Retired from the Air Force 1962 with rank of Lieutenant Colonel.

Moved to Bozeman, MT and was on the faculty of Montana State University with the Dept. of Continuing Education. Retired from the University and now in Real Estate. Married Ruth Davidson in 1942 and have one daughter Cheryl.

ROY E. BLINK, born Oct. 24, 1920 in Grand Rapids, MI. Drafted into Armed Service December 1942. Took basic training with 44th Amphibian Engineers. Transferred to Air Corp in fall 1943. Was sent to Grove City College and then to Armament and Central Fire Control School at Lowery Field, Denver, CO and Aerial Gunnery School at Buckingham Field, Ft. Meyers, FL. Was assigned to crew of Alan McClaren at Clovis, NM. After training, we picked up a B-29 at Topeka, KS. Flew to Chakula, India by the way of Brazil, Gold Coast West Africa and assigned to the 44th Bomb Sdn.

Roy E. Blink

Flew 20 missions from India and Tinian Island. Received the Air Medal with four Clusters and three Battle Ribbons. Separated as a Sergeant, December 1945.

Spent most of my civilian life in manufacturing management with three corporations in four different states. Presently reside in Birmingham, AL. Have two sons. Married to Marjorie Smith Blink. Retiring December 1987.

RICHARD C. BORNHOLDT, born Feb. 20, 1920, Dayton, NY. Graduated from Cattaraugus High School in 1937. Attended Cornell University prior to entering the service. Enlisted in the Army Air Corps May 1942, and was discharged November 1945.

Richard C. Bornholdt

Joined the 45th Sdn., 40th Bomb Gp. in Pratt, KS as Central Fire Control Maintenance Specialist. Remained with the group at Chakulia, India and Tinian Island.

Married Ada Parshall in 1946. Have one son. Returned to Cornell University and received B.S. in Agricultural Economics in 1947. After six years as a Marketing Specialist with an Agricultural Cooperative, he became a Cooperative Extension Agricultural Agent. In 1964 received M.S. in Agronomy from Cornell University. Served as an Extension Agent for 25 years. Retired in 1978. Awarded USDA Superior Service Award for his Rural Community Development program in Schuyler Co., NY (Watkins Glen) in 1976.

Remains active in retirement as Chairman of the Schuyler County Industrial Development Agency, the County Planning Commission, and a member of several quasi-governmental agencies, as well as Planning Consultant for the County Office for the Aging.

CHARLES G. BROUGH, born, attended schools in Methuen, MA. Graduated Phillips Andover Academy 1939. Enlisted October 1942. Honorably discharged as S/Sergeant November 1945.

Charles G. Brough

Attended A/C Mechanics School Keesler Field, MI; A/C Electrical Chanute Field; B-29 Electrical/Mechanical at Seattle; assigned Great Bend, KS. Shipped Casablanca March 1944, then flew Crescent route to Karachi and Chakulia. Assigned 45th Sdn. Electrical Chakulia and Tsinching. On USS Callan early 1945 to Tinian. Declined OCS Australia August and flew B-29 Guam, Kwajelein, Oahu to Mather's Field, CA. Awarded Good Conduct, China Medals; Presidential Unit Citation; earned Asiatic Pacific Ribbon w/five Battle Stars, American Theatre and Victory Ribbons.

Received B.S. Harvard 1949; Plant Engineer, Supervisor, and Manager Plant Engineering in Virginia, Massachusetts, and at Kollsman Instrument Corp., New Hampshire. Registered Professional Engineer Massachusetts and New Hampshire. Married Rosamond Redpath of No. Andover, MA December 1945 (d. 1960), raised two sons; remarried Elaine 1962. Two stepsons in 'Nam. Now retired in Venice, FL.

FOUNTAIN L. BROWN, born May 3, 1921 in Lock Haven, PA. Graduated from high school in 1939. Commissioned and rated pilot in July 1943, and assigned to the 44th Bomb Sdn., Pratt, KS. Flew six missions in CBI as Capt. William Hunter's co-pilot before checking out as aircraft commander. Completed 35 missions at Tinian in August 1945.

Fountain L. Brown

Married Audett Bond in Wichita. Discharged as a Captain in November 1945, reenlisted as T/Sergeant in 1946 and was recalled as Captain in 1948. Instructor pilot for Korean War B-29 replacement crews. Flew 22 Korean combat missions as B-29 sdn. commander at Yokota, Japan. Three years at Hq. SAC, then B-52 aircrew duty.

Retired in 1965 as Lieutenant Colonel with 23 years service. Five years at Beech Aircraft Corp., two years in college and nine years teaching school in Idaho. Three daughters and seven grandchildren.

JOHN P. BRUSCO, born Nov. 15, 1918 at Alexandria, LA. Education: Lower grades and high school in the Napa, CA area. Enlisted in the Army Air Corps in Phoenix, AZ, November 1941. Radio Tech School training at Scott Field, IL. Then an instructor at Scott Field, IL. Then extensive radar training at Boca Raton, FL. Attended Officer's Training School, receiving a commission as a Second Lieutenant at Yale University in New Haven, CT. Assigned to the 40th Bomb Gp. at Pratt, KS, then overseas to Chakulia, India.

John P. Brusco

Awards received during the service, other than the usual Good Conduct Medal, Battle Ribbons, etc., were the Distinguished Flying Cross and the Air Medal with two Oak Leaf Clusters.

After separation, married Olga Shainoff of Alhambria, CA. Have one son.

After the war went into Mining, Real Estate and Business Management. It was a distinct honor to be a member of the 40th Bomb Gp. At present, I live in Salome, AZ 85348.

ERIC M. BUZZA, Lt./Col. Retired. Born Cornwall, England and immigrated to the United States with my parents and brother in 1931.

Educated: Public schools in Brownville, Jct. Maine. Attended Worcester Jr. College and Boston University.

Eric M. Buzza

Military: Commissioned 2nd Lieutenant Army Air Corps. Flew 30 combat missions as a Bombardier on a B-29 Aircraft Bomb Sdn. , 40th Bomb Gp.with the 45th Bomb Gp. while stationed in India and Tinian in the Mariannas. Received the Distinguished Flying Cross, the Air Medal with three Oak Leaf Clusters, the Presidential Unit Citation with Three Oak Leaf Clusters, and other medals. Remained in the Active Reserve retiring with 28 accredited years as a Lieutenant Colonel. The major part of my reserve activity was an assignment in the counseling Service for the Air Force Academy as Liaison Officer Coordinator for the state of New Hampshire.

Just completed a career in the Insurance Business, retiring December 1986. However, I still remain active with an office I opened in St. Petersburg.

Moved here to Florida in 1979 with my wife (the former Muriel Feeney of Worcester, MA) who I married in 1944, leaving my son and daughter and their families including three grandchildren, in New Hampshire.

BASIL CALAMAS, born June 7, 1917 in New York City. Attended University of Alabama before joining Air Force in 1943. Assigned to the 40th Bomb Gp. and served on a B-29 as left gunner, stationed on Tinian.

Basil Calamas

One of the most memorable and terrifying moments occurred when pilot Lt. Jack Oakes asked me to sit at the bombardier's seat on take off - an all-out mission to Japan prior to the bombing of Hiroshima. The plane was loaded heavily with extra bombs and we had trouble getting airborne. The quick thinking of Lt. Oakes and co-pilot, Lt. Bennet Clute as we were nearing the end of the runway and still hitting the ground (and I with a bird's-eye view from the bombardier's seat), lifted the landing gears at the right moment. The plane dropped many, many feet over the cliff and skimmed the ocean waters and righted itself, and we took off for Japan. The first thing Lt. Oakes said later was, "Calamas, don't ever come up front again!" ARE PILOTS SUPERSTITIOUS?

Discharged in 1946, joined the U.S. Post Office and served 35 years. After retiring, worked at the Suffolk County Health Service Dept. on Long Island. Now fully retired. Married 41 years - two children and five grandchildren.

ORVAL WADE BURCHETT, CAPT., A-0771289, U.S.A.F. Res., retired was born and raised on a cattle ranch in Decatur Co., IA. I enlisted in the Army Air Corps in October 1942. I went to (C.T.D.) college training detachment, Central State Teachers College, Stevens Point, WI and then to classification, at Santa Ana, CA.

Orval Wade Burchett

My primary flight training in Stearman biplanes was at Rankin Aeronautical Academy, Tulare, CA. I attended basic flight training at Marana Army Air Base, Marana, AZ, flying BT-13's. I graduated from flight training in the class of 44-C at Marfa Army Air Base, Marfa, TX, where I flew twin engine Cessna AT-17's.

Transition was at Hobbs Army Air Base, Hubbs, NM, flying B-17 "Flying Fortresses". After graduating from four engine transition, I went to Lincoln, NB, where I was assigned co-pilot of Lt. William Buechler's B-29 crew.

I reported to Clovis Army Air Base, Clovis, NM, for combat training in the "Super Fortress", B-29. During my stay at Clovis, I married Yvonne Roth, Junction City, WI. At completion of my training, we reported to Kearney Army Air Base, Kearney, NB, where I was assigned a new B-29 combat equipped to fly to India.

The crew reported to the 44th Bomb Sdn., 40th Bomb Gp., 58th Wing, on Oct. 16, 1944 in Chakulia, India. We were one of the first replacement crews there.

We flew C-109's across the "Hump" to China, carrying fuel. Back in the B-29's, we carried out bombing missions to Singapore, etc. Soon I was assigned co-pilot for Fountain L. Brown's crew where we continued bombing and then to Tinian Island with the 40th.

I was made aircraft commander and stayed in this capacity until the end of the war; returning to Sacramento with our plane Oct. 16, 1945; 579:10 combat time later. I then stayed in the U.S.A.F. reserves for 15 years before retirement. Since WWII I have been a highway contractor in asphalt and bridging, living in Harlan, IA.

MARVIN E. CARMICHAEL,"Red", born Oct. 4, 1919, at Maxwell, OK. Attended lower grades and high school in that rural area. Enlisted in the Army Air Corps in November 1940, and was discharged in August 1945.

Marvin E. Carmichael

After "boot" camp and Tech School training at Chanute Field, he was assigned to the 40th Bomb Gp. at Borinquen Field, Puerto Rico. He remained with the group throughout its odyssey from Puerto Rico; Panama; Guatemala; Pratt, Kansas, Chakulia, India and Tinian Island.

At the time he was a mechanic, engine specialist, Flight Engineer and Crew Chief. Lowest rank held was "yard bird"; highest rank, M/Sergeant.

Awards received during service, other than the usual Good Conduct medal, Battle Ribbons, etc. were: Air Medal and Bronze Star.

After separation from the service, he attended and received a B.S. degree in Mechanical Engineering from the University of Oklahoma. Upon graduation, he was employed by the Boeing Company at Wichita, KS in July 1950, where he remained until his retirement in October 1976. Then he worked as an engineer, engineering supervisor and engineering manager in the Experimental Engineering Flight Test Section. He rejoined the 40th Bomb Gp. in 1982, and was elected treasurer of the association, a position he still retains.

DARL J. CHAMBERLAIN, born Liberal, KS Aug. 28, 1921. Graduated high school South Bend, IN 1939. Joined Army September 1940. Graduated Radio Operator/Mechanic school Scott Field August 1941. Joined 45th Bomb Sdn., 40th Bomb Gp. October 1941 in Puerto Rico. Stayed with the 40th through Panama; Gallapegos; Pratt, KS; Chakulia, India; Hsinching, China; and Tinian Island. Completed 35 missions June 1945 with DFC, Air Medal w/four Clusters.

Darl J. Chamberlain

Stayed in service. Was radio/operator on "Voice" B-29 during Able/Baker A-bomb tests, Bikini Atoll 1946. Retired from Air Force as Chief Master Sergeant in April 1967 with over 26 years.

Married Dorothy Rasmussen of Beatrice, NB in December 1946 and we have two sons and six grandchildren now. After the Air Force, worked for 19 years as computer programmer and retired again January 1986. Now living in Mascoutah, IL and enjoying trailer camping and spending winters "Down South".

HARRY M. CHANGNON, born Feb. 13, 1918 in Idaho Falls, ID where he attended local schools, graduating from IFHS in 1936. Business major at Idaho State University, Pocatello, ID, and Univiversity North Carolina (Chapel Hill). Took CPT flight course at UNC and received Private pilots License. Enlisted in the USAAC in early 1942 and went through Pilot Training schools at Santa Ana and Mather Fields in California; Ft. Stockton and Pecos, TX; and received Pilot Wings June 22, 1943 at Roswell, NM where he also graduated from B-17 4-Engine school there.

Joined the 40th Bomb Gp. and 45th Sdn. of original 58th Wing, 20th Air Force in October 1943 at Pratt, KS. Flew YB-29s as CP in training for overseas duty. Arrived at Chakulia, India on Apr. 10, 1944. Flew B-24, B-25, L-5, C-46 and C-109s in addition to 18 B-29 missions in CBI (and received credit for 33 HUMP trips). Flew to Tinian Apr. 20,

Harry M. Changnon

1945, where 15 more combat missions were flown on Lead and Pathfinder Crews (Tokyo and other Fire Raids). Became A/C with own crew. Received DFC, PH, AM/Clusters, in addition to 40th Bomb Gp. awards/decorations. Flew "SHAG'N home" back to U.S.A., October 1945. Served as 45th Sdn. and 40th Bomb Gp. Athletic, Mess, Historian, PRO, and S-2 Officer at March and Davis-Monthan AFB until leaving Military Service in late 1946.

Returned to Idaho in 1947 to operate family resort near Yellowstone Park and Jackson Hole, WY, with wife, Jane (McCaffery) after Tucson, AZ marriage. Received BS Business Admin. degree from ISU in 1948 and taken many additional college courses since. Was construction contractor on dams, forests and commercial sites. Worked on missile and engineering jobs in Arizona and California. Spent last 25 years as Contract Admin. at Stanford Univ. prior to retirement in 1985. Have two children; four grandones. Keeps busy writing about B-29 and 40th History when not playing tennis/sports.

LEWIS L. CHASE, entered Army Air Corps Feb. 1, 1943. After completing radio school at Scott Field, IL, advanced radio at Philadelphia and Madison, WI; received flight training at Walker, KS.

Lewis L. Chase

Assigned as Radio Operator to B-29 crew at Clovis, NM - Lt. W.S. Markham - trained and sent to Chakulia, India via West Palm Beach, FL; British Guyana; Brazil; Africa and Egypt.

Temporary duty at Dacca, India on C-109 tankers flying gas over "The Hump" to Chengtu, China.

Crew transferred to Tinian - 44th Bomb Sdn., 40th Gp. 58th Wing.

Honorably discharged Nov. 21, 1945.

Returned to hometown - Carlsbad, CA - and married wonderful wife, Polly. We have two sons who have provided us with a fine family.

Retired from Building Contractor business in 1986.

WARREN J. CHASE, born in Arkwright, NY, Jan. 3, 1926. Joined U.S. Army Air Force Cadet program upon graduation from high school. Sworn in February 1944 and discharged Dec. 7, 1945.

Warren J. Chase

Basic training in Greensboro, NC; Gunnery School Tyndall Field, FL. Assigned to B-29 school at Pyote, TX. Sent to Chakulia, India, as replacement crew in February 1945, and assigned to 44th Sdn. Flew on crew of Lt. George Hoppus. Sent to Tinian in May 1945, and flew total of 18 missions plus 3 P.O.W. missions. Our airplane #20, at end of war, was flown by Gen. LeMay on flight from Tokyo to Washington.

After separation from service graduated from business school and went into insurance and tax consulting business. Retired end of 1987. Father of three children; we have a daughter and two sons. Have attended both the 40th Bomb Gp. and 58th wing reunions at various times.

JOHN E. CHILD, Col. USAF Ret., born Baltimore, MD. Left Maryland in fall 1935 to attend Colorado College. Joined Army Air Corps, Flying Cadets, at Ft. Logan, CO-1940. Commissioned Class 41-F, Stockton, CA-August 1941. BT-13 Flight Instructor until June 1943. Flew bombardiers (AT-11) at Victorville, CA; then B-17's at Hobbs, NM. B-29 crew training at Clovis, NM. Arrived 25th Bomb Sdn. (Chakulia, India)-December 1944. Moved to Tinian (Mariannas Island), lead crew and squadron operations officer. 33 combat missions. Home on Sunset Project October 1945.

John E. Child

After R&R, re-joined 40th Bomb Gp. at March Field, CA. Attended USAF Institut of Technology, 1947-49. In Strategic Ai Command 1949 on B36/B47/B52 operation in England, 1952-54. On Gen. LeMay's staf Hq. SAC, 1955-58. Commanded first Titar ICBM Sdn. (395th). Wing Deputy Commander-90th SMW (Minuteman). Last assignment-Hq. 15th AF Director/Missile Maintenance. Retired in grade of Colonel at March AFB, CA-1970.

DFC/OLC, Meritorious Service Medal, Air Medal w/three Oak Leaf Clusters, Commendation Medal, Presidential Citation w/two Oak Leaf Clusters, Asiatic-Pacific Theater w/five Battle Stars. Command Pilot. Command Missileman.

Married Dalcie London, Bakersfield, CA-1943. Son-John. Daughter-Diane. After AF retirement, tax consultant and property appraisal work through 1977. Residing in Santa Maria, CA since 1971.

JULIAN C. COCHRAN, born Sept. 2, 1918, Ft. Scott, KS. Joined army June 24, 1943; in December 1943 assigned Aviation Cadet Center, San Antonio. Classified Bombardier, assigned Ellington Field, TX for preflight. Bombardier training San Angelo, TX; Navigation training Monroe, LA. Joined 40th Bomb Gp., 45th Sdn., Pratt, KS Nov. 13, 1943. Position was Navigator on Bob Shanks crew the whole time. Ended overseas duty as POW for five and one-half months, Rangoon, Burma. Awarded Air Medal w/Cluster, Purple Heart, four Campaign Stars on Pacific Ribbon. Discharged Nov. 19, 1945.

Julian C. Cochran

Married Leona Callahan, Little Rock, AR, Mar. 16, 1941. Have one daughter, Judy and one granddaughter, Katie. Leona accompanied me on my military journeys which made it much more bearable. We had many "good" times.

Employed by Corps of Engineers total of one and one-half years. While in Manila, P.I. in 1946 part of duties was assigning Japanese POW's to work parties. Employed by Western Ins. Co., Ft. Scott, KS for 34 years in claim dept. as supervisor of Illinois claims.

Retired in 1982; we have attended all 40th reunions. I served two years as Association Secretary.

LIONAL F. COFFIN, born Aug. 21, 1919, graduated from high school in 1937. Entered Army Air Corps in May of 1942. Attended Curtiss-Wright Technical Institute, Glendale, CA. Upon graduation was accepted for Aviation Cadet program at Santa Anna,

Visalia, Taft, CA and Marfa, TX where I received my Pilot Wings and commission, class of 1943 G, in July 1943. Graduated from B-17 school and volunteered for B-29 program at Pratt, KS, 25th Bomb Sdn., 40th Gp. Arrived Chakulia, India, in April 1944. Flew 26 Hump trips and eight combat missions to Manchuria, Formosa, Palembang, Sumatra. Bailed out over central China in October 1944. POW with Japanese after A/C was blown up over Rangoon, Burma, on Dec. 14, 1944. Released May 1945.

Lional F. Coffin

Returned to U.S.A. for Pilot Instructor Duty, Denver, CO. Separated from service in February 1946. Served with 9703rd Troop Carrier till retirement as Lieutenant Colonel in August 1979. Campaigns: AP Theater w/six Battle Stars, Air Offensive Japan, Air Combat Palembang, Western Pacific, India Burma, Central China. Decorations: Purple Heart, Air Medal w/three Oak Leaf Clusters, China Defense, Distinguished Unit Badge, ATO and Victory Medals.

Civilian occupations include: Furniture business, School Teacher and University Professor, with retirement in 1984. Education includes: Business Educ. Degree, BS Degree in Industrial Educ. and Masters Degree in Education. Married, five children. It was a privilege to serve with the men of the 40th Bomb Gp.

VICTOR D. COLBORN, JR., "Dave" enlisted in USAAF Aviation Cadet Program Feb. 15, 1943 CTD Fenn College, Cleveland, OH. Classified a Bombardier. Aerial Gunnery at Laredo, TX. B-29 Gunnery at BAAFB, Ft. Myers, FL. B-29 transition at Alamogordo, NM. Crew picked up a new B-29 at Kearney and flew four hours acceptance flight, then headed for Tinian. Blew a tire being turned around by tug on strip at Kwajalein. Arrived at Guam right on schedule. Gave up new B-29 (666) whose digits we weren't too happy about anyway. Assigned to 25th Bomb Sdn., 40th Bomb Gp., 58th Bomb Wing, B-29 #8 "Monsoon II." Separated from active Air Force Mar. 4, 1946.

Indiana University two years, major in Graphic Arts; Stetson University, major in Art Education; graduated Meinzinger Commercial Art, Detroit. Enlisted in USAFR; retired Apr. 16, 1978 CM Sergeant; Sr. Adviser Civil Engineering Wing.

Back to Michigan, married Joyce Hummel; one son, 24 years Navy, one son 21 years AF (Ret), one son ex-Marine BS BM, one daughter BS Soc., BS Psy.

Victor D. Colborn, Jr.

Employed by Martin Marietta Aerospace, Orlando, Aug. 5, 1957; retired Aug. 31, 1987 a Sr. Graphics Illustrator.

VERANUS C. COLE, born May 27, 1916 at Machiasport, ME. Graduated from Portland High School and Hemphill Diesel Engineering School in Boston.

Veranus C. Cole

Enlisted December 1939 - discharged October 1945. Completed basic training at Langley Field, VA and assigned to 40th Bomb Gp. there. Then to Puerto Rico; Panama; Guatemala; Galapagos and Pratt, KS. He completed R3350 Engine School in Texas. Navigational School in Puerto Rico and Survival School in Panama. He was airplane mechanic, Inspector, Aerial Engineer and Crew Chief. Highest rank held was T/Sergeant.

Awards received were Good Conduct Medal and Air Medal.

After separation from the Service, he worked for New England Tel. and Tel. 31 years. He was President of the Portland Council of Telephone Pioneers, President of the Pioneer Life Member Club, member of the Keller Chapter of Pioneers, Vice President of Portland Hammond Organ Society and charter member of Amateur Organists Association International.

Married Carolyn L. Libbey of Gray, ME in 1949.

CLAYBOURN H. COLEMAN, born June 13, 1922 in Graham, KY. Graduated from high school in 1941. Was inducted into service January 1943. Discharged November 1945. After basic training in Miami, FL attended Amarillo Technical School, Amarillo, TX, B-29 School, Seattle, WA and was assigned to 45th Sdn. at Pratt Air Force Base, Pratt, KS. Left Pratt for New Port News, VA, there I boarded a Liberty ship and was sent to Oran, Africa. From there we were sent to British troop ship around Italy, back through the Suez Canal and unloaded at Bombay, India. I was S/Sergeant and in charge of electrical work on the line in Chakulia, India. I made a couple mission repair trips over the Hump. Left Chakulia for Tinian Island, and after the bomb was dropped was sent back to the States and discharged.

Claybourn H. Coleman

I am married and the father of one daughter. Retired in 1986 after 29-1/2 years as Asst. Manager of Farm Supply Store. I live on a small farm at Graham, KY 42344.

NEIL F. COLEMAN, presently single, no children, 505 N. Rock Road #1428, Wichita, KS 67206, 316-686-7616. Born Dec. 29, 1923 at Jamestown, NY. Graduated from Sherman Central, Sherman, NY 1942, United Aircraft Tech School-Detroit, MI, 1943. Computer programming, University of Hawaii, 1968.

Neil F. Coleman

Entered Service Feb. 9, 1943, Ft. Niagara, took Basic at St. Petersburg, FL. Armament and Central Fire control School at Lowry. Assigned to Graham Bleilers Crew in the 44th Bomb Sdn. at Pratt October 1943. Departed Miami Mar. 16, 1943, flew ATC southern route to Chakulia, arriving Mar. 23, 1944. First B-29 Crew to arrive in India. Due to engine problem at Agra, we saw the Taj Mahal at 2:00 A.M. under a full moon. To Tinian. Left Tinian Aug. 1, 1945 after 31 Combat and Operational Missions and 514 hours. Discharged October 1945. Recalled into Air Force July 1951. Assigned to SAC 2nd BW, Hunter AFB, 54th WRS, Guam, Eglin AFB, Flight Test Center, Edwards AFB, 6th MAS, Hickam AFB. Retired as M/Sergeant with 22 years service in October 1968. 13 Awards including DFC, Air Medal w/three Oak Leaf Clusters and AF Commendation.

Between 1946 and 1951 worked as tool designer for G.E. at Erie. Owned bowling business Sherman, NY. After retiring from the AF, was General Manager of 24 lane bowling center in Ocala, FL and 50 lane center in Tampa, Director of Training for electronics firm Orlando, business manager for video store and law firm, owner Central Florida Chlorotron, Winter Haven, FL. Fully retired 1986 and moved to Wichita.

JOHN P. CONSTANDY, born June 11, 1924, in New York City. Joined U.S. Army in March 1943 and was assigned to the 49th Armd. Inf. Reg., 8th Armd. Div. Transferred to U.S.A.A.F. and completed navigator training at Hondo AAF Base in class 44-11-4B, was rated and commissioned 2nd Lieutenant, August 1944. Assigned to 25th Bomb Sdn., 40th Bomb Gp. in May 1945 on Tinian. Was proud to fly with A/C Capt. Thomas Turner and crew in "Genie", #455, (Sdn. #10).

John P. Constandy

Returned to active duty in April 1951 for the Korean Conflict serving with the U.S.A.F. as 1st Lieutenant until November 1952.

Schools: Oklahoma A & M (aviation cadet), Univ. of Bridgeport, Univ. of Miami, Northeastern Univ. (LLB).

Past activities: trial attorney; Assistant District Attorney (New York City); 14 years counsel to various U.S. House of Representatives and U.S. Senate congressional committees, last as Chief Counsel, U.S. Senate Permanent Subcommittee on Investigations; Foreign Service Officer (FSR-1); Assistant Secretary of State.

Current activities: attorney (admitted D.C. and New York bars); officer and director of petroleum and trading (helicopter) corporations (both in China); and director and officer of domestic insurance company.

Married to Arlette Nicole Constandy (nee Schmitt) of Nice, France.

ROBERT E. COPLEY, born in Inavale, NB. Travels amounted to being in two states prior to joining the Aviation Cadet Program at Omaha the day after Christmas, 1940. Spent two years at Las Vegas aerial gunnery school watching students firing at and around targets we pulled in B-10s. My new bride and I joined the 40th Bomb Gp., 25th Sdn. in Pratt, KS the fall of 1943. Had many memorable experiences with as fine a crew that was ever assembled at Chakulia. Crew was decorated after a sensational photo

Robert E. Copley

mission the day after the daylight Yawata mission in August 1944.

Took up instructor duties in B-29s at Randolph Field upon rotation. With acceptance of a regular commission was privileged to fly the Aleutian Chain for three years followed by fifteen years in SAC. Retired from the Air Force in 1968. While working with FEMA (Federal Emergency Management Association) endured greeting 20,000 Cubans at Ft. Chaffee, AR during their infamous exodus. This mentioned because it was there I very nearly qualified for the Purple Heart. Spent an interesting year chasing and taking soundings on the Concorde aircraft as it traversed along the New Jersey coastline.

Now enjoying complete retirement and in particular associating with the comrades in the 40th Bomb Gp. The greatest!!

LUIGI J. COPPOLA, was born June 5, 1914 in Brooklyn, NY. Both my parents and sister passed away in 1918 due to Spanish Influenza. My brother and I were placed in an orphanage, and my grandmother, who had 13 children of her own, raised us. I was enrolled in high school for one year. I drove a taxi in New York City, was married in 1940, had my first son in 1942 and was drafted in August of 1943.

Luigi J. Coppola

I was in the Airborn Eng. at Westover Field, MA, and, after basic training, I was transferred to Pratt, KS. I was in the 25th Bomb Squad Motor Pool as a truck driver in Chakulia, India. I made many trips to Calcutta for supplies, booze, and beer for the officers. On Tinian, the 25th mail clerk had to return home. I, then became the 25th mail clerk. I was known as; (No Mail Today Luigi). I flew home on a B-29, and was discharged on Oct. 30, 1945. I returned to driving a taxi, and then joined the painters union. I retired in 1975.

I have two sons and six grandchildren, and will be married 48 years in February. I am a Legioner and avid in volunteer work for the V.A. Hospital. I am also an amateur boxing coach for the P.A.L., and an a boxing historian.

I've attended three reunions, but missed the one in St. Louis because I was in Europe. I will make the next one in Philly.

J.T. COX, "Corky" born at Mertzon, TX on Oct. 11, 1919. After finishing school there, attended Airplane and Mechanics School at Love Field, Dallas, TX.

J.T. Cox

Enlisted in Air Corps fall of 1940. Was sent to Puerto Rico, assigned to 44th Sdn. Worked on the line there. Was sent to Guatemala, flew as crew member on B-17s and B-24s to the "Rock" and back chasing submarines. Went to Pratt with squadron. Was Tech. Sergeant. At Pratt was sent to Flight Engineer school along with Elmo Gray, Stumpy Ramsey and Richard V. Arrington. On graduation was promoted to F/O. Was assigned to crew of Joseph V. McWilliams. Went to India and China on A.C. #297. After about a year was rotated back to U.S. going to Muroc Air Base, CA. Total time in service four and a half.

After discharge in 1945 was in ranching business till 1980. Married 43 years; one son one daughter, four grandchildren. Now retired near Junction, TX.

OTIS M. COX, "Wynn" born Jan. 28, 1920 at Hudson, IL. Attended high school at Normal IL. Enlisted in the Army Air Corps December 1939 and was separated July 1945.

Otis M. Cox

Attended Radio Communication School at Chanute Field and then Scott Field. Assigned to a Langley Field Sdn. that moved to Borinquen Field, Puerto Rico and went there after completing Radio Tech School. As signed to 40th Bomb Gp., 44th Sdn. when it was formed and remained with it from Puerto Rico, Panama, Guatemala, Pratt, KS, and Chakulia.

Started as a Private and advanced in rank to Technical Sergeant on flying status as a Radio Operator trained as an alternate Gunner. Flew ten combat missions and a dozen Hump trips before Rotation to U.S. in December 1944.

Awards received were Good Conduct Medal, American Defense Medal, Asiatic-Pacific Medal, American Theater Medal, and Air Medal with two Oak Leaf Clusters.

After separation from the service, employed at Hallicrafters Radio factory and then by Ryerson Steel Service Center, a wholly owned subsidiary of Inland Steel Company, working with a large IBM computer national network as a senior programmer and systems analyst for 39 years.

Hobbies are gardening, grandfather clock kit building, and clock repairing.

IRVING M. CRAIG, (Jack), born Aug. 6, 1925 in Alexandria, VA. Entered army in 1943 following high school, and assigned to Army Air Corp. Received basic training at Miami Beach, FL, Gunnery School at Tyndel Field, FL and combat crew training at Clovis, NM before assignment to the 40th Bomb Gp.

Completed 30 combat missions from CBI and Tinian. Award DFC and Air Medal, both with clusters.

Discharged fall of 1945 with the rank of Staff Sergeant. Awarded a BS degree in Mining Engineering from Virginia Polytechnic Institute in 1949. Married Lucille Cope of Matewan, WV and have a son, Alan. Worked in various engineering positions with coal mining companies, cement producers and engineering firms in West Virginia, Ohio, Pennsylvania and Missouri.

WILLARD CROFT, born July 4, 1918 in Greentown, PA. Enlisted in the Army Air Corps in 1943. Attended Bombardier school at Carlsbad, NM.

Willard Croft

Joined Capt. Wilber Shockley's crew at Davis Monthan Field, Tucson, AZ. After training together, we flew to Tinian Island and joined the 40th Gp. in the 44th Sdn. in the spring of 1945.

Photos were taken from our plane as the Missouri went into the harbor for the surrender ceremonies.

I was separated from the service in December 1945 as a 1st Lieutenant.

I dairy farmed with my father until 1972. Since then until the present time am working as a Draftsman for a fireplace door factory.

I am married to Marion Cross. Have three children to my first wife Jacqueline.

I am proud to have been a member of such a fine group as the 40th, and also to have had a part in our Country's History.

RANDOLPH J. CROWDER, "Randy" a native of the Shenandoah Valley of Virginia - born at Fincastle and attended all grades of schooling at Waynesboro.

Randolph J. Crowder

Enlisted in the Army Ordnance Department in March 1941 and initially trained at Ft. Slocum, NY. Assigned to the 485th Aviation Ord. Co. (which was attached to the 40th Gp. and later assigned to the 45th Sdn.) at Borinquen Field later in 1941.

Remained with the 40th Gp. (Puerto Rico, Panama, Galapagos, Pratt, Chakulia, Tinian) as Assistant Ordnance Chief, 45th Sdn., until September 1945.

Stayed in service until retirement in August 1962, mostly in security, law enforcement and corrections.

Worked for U.S. Department of Justice, Bureau of Prisons, from September 1962 through October 1974.

Served as a member of the Board of Directors of the 40th Bomb Gp. Assn. for several terms.

Enjoying complete retirement with wife (Edie) in Bristol Village, a retirement community, in Waverly, OH.

RICHARD L. CULPEPPER, born Oct. 30, 1919, Manchester, GA. Graduated from Georgia Tech June 1941. ROTC Commissioned July 30, 1941. Ordered active duty Aug. 4, 1941. Aviation Ordnance Officer. Joined 40th Bomb Gp. May 27, 1943 in Panama. Stationed at Pratt, KS and then to Chakulia. Transferred to Hq. 20th Bomber Command February 1945 Karagaphur. Transferred to Hq. 8th Air Force, Okinawa July 1945. Separated from Service October 1945. Major.

Richard L. Culpepper

Accepted a job in Engineering Dept., Combustion Engineering, Inc. January 1946. Retired as Director, Projects Dept., January 1982.

Married Ann Toehl, July 14, 1943, Savannah, GA. Two children-Lee, born June 1947, Beth born April 1951. Two grandchildren.

LESTER C. DAHMS, born Aug. 17, 1917 in Chicago, IL. Drafted into the Army Air Corp in 1942. Was at the Army Air base at Ft. Dix, NJ. I was in the 28th service Gp. Transferred to the 40th Bomb Gp. We were sent to Chakulia India.

Lester C. Dahms

I was a sheet metal man. From there we went to Tinian Island. I was discharged in 1945. I went to work as a pressman in a printing plant. Married and have one son.

(Battles and Citations) India-Burman air offensive-Japan China Central Burma air combat. (Decorations and Citations) Distinguished Unit Citation Gp. #8 Hq. 20af 45, and Good Conduct Medal 43. Asiatic Pacific Theater Service Medal. Three Overseas Service Bars.

LLOYD G. DAVIS, born Feb. 13, 1918 in Ebensburg, PA. Graduated from high school. Branch of Service - U.S. Army, joined Feb. 10, 1942; U.S. Army, joined Nov. 29, 1942.

Stationed at Camp Crowder, MO; Ellington Field, TX; Childress, TX; Selman Field, LA; Pratt, KS; Chakulia, India; and Tinian. Joined 40th Bomb Gp. on Nov. 30, 1943 as Bombardier/Navigator.

Bailed out interior of China - photo mission to Singapore, two Tokyo firebomb missions 35 missions.

Received the DFC with Cluster, Air Medal with five cluster and the Presidential Unit Citation. Discharged as a 1st Lieutenant. on Oct. 29, 1945.

Married Mary on Oct. 16, 1943 and has two children and three grandchildren. Worked as a sales representative in insurance and retired Sept. 1, 1981.

JAMES V. DeCOSTER, Colonel USAF, Retired, born Dec. 22, 1922 Independence, OR. In October 1943 joined 40th Bomb Gp. (VHB) 45th Bomb Sdn. (VHB) at Pratt, KS. Trained as Co-Pilot with Brigadier General (Retired)

Ledford's crew in U.S. and departed Pratt AAF, KS for India via Miami, FL, Belem, Brazil, Azores, Accra, Gold Coast, Egypt, Krachi and final destination, Chakulia, India.

James V. DeCoster

Flew combat and hump missions and on Oct. 25, 1944, our B-29 was badly shot up over Omura, Japan, killing the engineer, M/Sgt. Harry C. Miller, and seriously wounding then Capt. Ledford. WWII over, I remained in Army Air Force later to become USAF, instructed Aviation Cadets in AT-6 and T-33 Aircraft at Randolph AFB, TX. Instructed U.S. Army Officers in liaison and Helicopter Aircraft at Ft. Sill, OK.

Attended various service schools and graduated from University of Maryland in 1956 under USAF program for regular officers. Married Frances Cooper at Pratt, KS December 1943. Two children: Daughter Terry, son James Keith. Retired as Colonel (Commander) 1st Aero Space Communications Group Headquarters Strategic Air Command, Offutt AFB, NB, September 1969.

GORDON P. DEARDORFF, born Aug. 30, 1920, Lafayette, IN. Attended school in Chicago, Il. After schooling worked in Salem, IL and Abilene, TX. Enlisted in 1939. Did duty at Kelly Field, TX and Borinquen Field, Puerto Rico (B-18 aircraft). Transferred from Air Base Gp. to 44th Bomb Sq. in 40th Bomb Gp. Shipped out to Panama Canal Zone. I went to Guatemala, CA with 44th Bomb Sq. Col. Cornett was C.O. and Sgt. Wright was 1st Sergeant. Squadron did sub patrol to Galapagos with a mixture of B-17 and B-24 aircraft. The 40th Gp. regrouped and went to Pratt, AAB, KS to a new mission and training with the first B-29s.

Gordon P. Deardorff

I married Tippie Christine Hawk while in Pratt, KS and have two daughters, three grandchildren and one great grandchild.

I was one of the bunch that went to India by ship via Oran Africa, Naples Italy (underwent German bombing while in harbor), Suez Canal, Indian Ocean, Bombay India. A train ride to Chakulia (Wow!). I was NCOIC of flight line supply 1st Bomb Maint. Sdn. and 25th Bomb Sdn

After the war I continued military service until 1960. Was stationed at March Field, CA, Davis-Monthan AFB, Tucson, AZ, Carswell AFB and Naknek, AK. Air Force retirement as M/Sergeant. in 1960. Worked at General Dynamics on B-58 and B-36 programs, then to the A-7A, D and E programs at L.T.V. Then to Postal Service and retirement in December 1985.

THOMAS J. DECKER, 395th-44th Sdn. Pilot, born July 12, 1918 Branchville, NJ. Graduated Newton, NJ. High School 1935. Employed by Selected Risks Insurance Co. 1935 until entering military service Jan. 12, 1942. Ft. Dix, NJ. After basic training in Alabama entered Aviation Cadet training. Primary flight school Visalia, CA. Basic Gardner Field, Taft, CA. Advanced Marfa, TX. Graduated Pilot 2nd Lieutenant July 28, 1943. Assigned B-17 Transition Roswell, NM. October 9 assigned to 40th Bomb Gp. Pratt, KS. After tour in CBI returned to U.S.

Thomas J. Decker

Instructed four engine school, Columbus, OH. Discharged Nov. 11,1945. Returned to Selected Risks Insurance Co. as Claims investigator, promoted to company officer and claims examiner handling serious bodily injury litigation; Retired Aug. 1, 1983; after 42 years with the company. Also flew Co-pilot part time for Scripps Howard Newspapers on converted B-23 Executive aircraft. Still fly a Cherokee for recreation. Enjoy golf, fishing and hunting. Have two sons, one granddaughter and one grandson.

Received Distinguished Flying Cross, Air Medal and Oak Cluster, four Bronze Stars, Presidential Unit Citation.

RICHARD DENNISTON, born June 8, 1924 at Kalamazoo, MI. Attended school ten and a half years. Enlisted in Army Air Corps Sept. 5, 1941, discharged June 25, 1945.

After basic training at Ft. Slocum, NY, was assigned to the 40th Bomb Gp., 44th Ordnance at Borinquen Field, Puerto Rico, and remained with the group throughout its odyssey from Puerto Rico; Panama; Guatemala; Pratt, KS; Chakulia, India; A-1 Advance Base, China; and Tinian Island.

Richard Denniston

I was a Crew Chief Buck Sergeant. (several times). Awards received were Asiatic Pacific Theater Ribbon with three Bronze Battle Stars. (I received notice of Silver Star after I was discharged for participation in Nagasaki A Bomb attack.) I serviced the Enola Gay's guns and bombs through her full career up to my discharge time. I had five Overseas Service Bars.

After discharge had couple of jobs, then went into own business of Heating and Air Conditioning, of which I closed out in 1983.

GUERINO DIBONAVENTURA, (BONNIE), born July 13, 1919 in Southbridge, MA, attended lower grades and high school in Southbridge. Graduated from High School the class of 1937. After graduation was employed by the American Optical Company until the break of WWII. Enlisted in Army Air Corps Jan. 13, 1942.

Guerino Dibonaventura

Attended Basic Training at Jefferson Barracks, St. Louis, MO. Was then assigned to the 112th Observation Sdn. in Dover, DE as an Air-Craft maintenance mechanic. From Dover, we were assigned to the East Coast for observation duty in Georgetown, SC, Lantana, FL and Key West, FL. We later were sent to San Antonio, Cuba for patrol duty there.

On return trip from Cuba we were sent to Alamogardo, NM to train on B 24's. Which took us to Tucson, AZ and Briggs Field, TX. Upon completing our training we were sent to Pratt, KS, to join the 40th Bomb Gp. Remained with the 40th Gp. thru Chakulia, India to China territory to complete my overseas duty to the Island of Tinian. Was discharged Nov. 5, 1945 with the rank of S/Sergeant.

After discharged returned to American Optical Company, also joined the Air Force Reserve Program. Spent 14 years in the Air Reserve, the program was discontinued to complete my tour. I enlisted with the Combat Engineers, retired as Sergeant. First Class in 1975. Retired from all duties in 1980, and I am at this time enjoying retirement life.

MARION DISBENNETT, born Dec. 5, 1919 in Bellflower, IL. Graduated from high school in 1937in Orange, CA. Enlisted in Army Air Corps in March 1942.

Marion Disbennett

Received radio operator training in Scott Field, IL, Truax Field, Madison, WI and Philco Plant in Philadelphia. Joined 40th Bomb Gp., 44th Sdn. in Pratt, KS and on to Chakulia, India. Flew as radio operator on Maj. John C. Eigenmann's crew. Returned to Scott Field as an instructor just prior to group's move to Tinian. Discharged September 1945.

Worked at a variety of jobs until joining the Post Office Department, as a mail carrier. Retired as Supt. of Mails at Orange, CA after 23 years of service.

Margaret Mills and I were married in St. Louis while I was in radio school. We have two sons, Don and Jim. We enjoyed visiting the church where we were married, during the 40th Gp. reunion in that city.

EMIL DOBROWOLSKI, "Doby", born July 10, 1921 in Buffalo, NY. Moved to Detroit and attended schools there. Enlisted Army Air Corps March 1942, Boot Camp at Jefferson Barracks, MO. Attended Casey Jones School for Aeronautics.

Emil Dobrowolski

Shipped out to the 44th at Guatamala, then to Panama Air Depot at Albrook Field. Still had some B-18s but mostly worked on B-17's and LB-30's. Went back with the 40th to Kansas and did transition on B-26's. Went on the 29s as they came on the scene.

Left for overseas as Crew Chief on #319 for Chakulia, with stints to China; then to Tinia. Discharged in September 1945. Got recalled for Korea, then back to civilian life. But I stayed in Guard and Reserve outfits for a total of 35 years.

Was General Foreman on building the C-119 Flying Boxcar. Retired from Airesearch after 28 years and at present living in the mountains of Arizona.

RAYMOND DRIESBAUGH JR., born Apr. 26, 1920 in Mogadore, OH. Graduated from high school in 1938. Enlisted in the Army Air Corps in 1941. After completion of Airplane Mechanics School was assigned to the 29th Bomb Gp., Gowen Field, ID. In December,1942 was a crew chief on B-17 aircraft, when I was reassigned to Boeing Airplane Company, Seattle, WA to attend the first airplane mechanics course on the B-29 airplane. After three months training, the class was reassigned to Smoky Hill Army Air Field, Salina, KS to establish the first B-29 Flight Engineer School.

Raymond Driesbaugh Jr.

After completion of training, a Flight Officers appointment, and a stint at being a Flight Engineer instructor, was reassigned to the 44th Bomb Sdn., 40th Bomb Gp., Pratt Field, KS, in September, 1943. Assigned to Capt. Graham Blielers Crew. Departed Pratt Field March, 1944 with advanced party to Chakulia, India. Completed 35 combat missions with the 44th Bomb Sdn. out of Chakulia, Hsingching and Tinia. Departed the 44th Bomb Sdn. in July 1945.

Retired from the USAF as Chief Master Sergeant. Spent entire career in bombers in the Aircraft Maintenance field. Was assigned to Strategic Air Command B-29, B-50, B-36, KC-97, KC-135 and B-52 aircraft.

After military retirement worked for the U.S. Civil Service. Performed duty as Quality Assurance Representative with the USAF and Defense Logistics Agency. At time of retirement from Civil Service was Chief, Quality Assurance Division, Cincinnati, OH.

Medals and awards include the DFC, Air Medal with Silver Cluster, Asiatic-Pacific Theater Ribbon w/5 Battle Stars, American Defense Medal, Good Conduct Medal w/Silver Loop, Air Force Longevity Ribbon with four Loops and Presidential Unit Citation.

Married to the former Doris Ann Chase of Grand Rapids, MI for 45 years. Have four sons and one daughter and blessed with eight grandchildren. Presently retired, residing in Murrells Inlet, SC.

RAYMOND ELLIOTT, MD, born Sept. 15, 1920 in Warren, PA, and attended public schools. Graduated from Washington Jefferson College with a Bachelor of Science Degree and was accepted in Medical School at the University of Pennsylvania. However, Pearl Harbor was attacked and Ray enlisted in the Aviation Cadet Program, Jan. 8, 1942.

Raymond Elliott

Graduating from the Southeast Training Command in Columbus, MS. He was commissioned a 2nd Lieutenant in the United States Army Air Corp and attended instructors school in Maxwell Field, AL. After instructing twin engine advanced flying at Blytheville, AR. For one year, Ray volunteered for four engine flight training at Lockburn Air Base in Ohio and then joined the 58th Wing, 40th Bomb Gp. of B-29's at Pratt, KS. He accompanied the 40th Gp. through Chakulia, Cheng Tu, and Tinian, completing 35 missions as Aircraft Commander.

On Friday, July 13, 1945, Captain Elliott returned to the states and resigned from the Air Force on V.J. Day. He continued his education and graduated from the School of Medicine, University of Pennsylvania in 1950 and completed internship and residency in Obstetrics and Gynecology at the Hospital University of Pennsylvania in 1955. Dr. Elliott practiced Obstetrics and Gynecology in Mesa, AZ for 32 years. He retired in 1986 and resides at 15433 East Elliott Road, Gilbert, AZ.

HOWARD W. EPPLER, born K.C. Kansas, attended public schools, enlisted in AAF October 1942. Graduated B-24 A.M. school, Keesler Field March 1943 and Adv. Instrument School, Chanute Field, May '43. Assigned to 491st Bomb Gp. Biggs Field, TX.

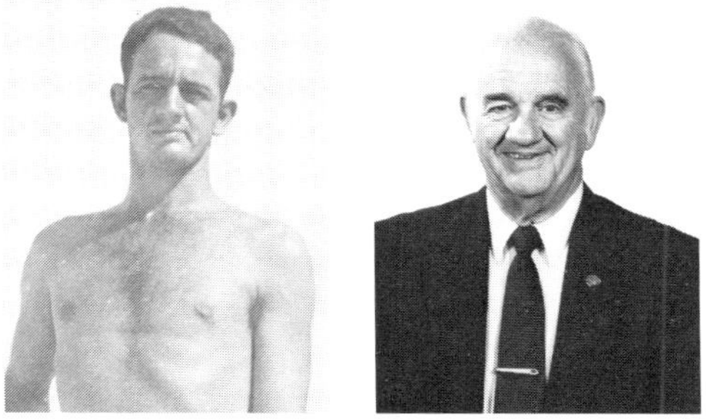

Howard W. Eppler

Joined 40th Bomb Gp. Pratt, KS Dec. 10, 1943, deployed to India February 1944 arriving Chakulia Apr. 8, 1944. Made three flights to A-1, China in ground support of combat missions.

Redeployed by ship to Tinian, February-March 1945, arrived Apr. 7, 1945. Served as Inst. Specialist in 44th Bomb Sdn. December 1943 to September 1945, working on at least 41 B-29s assigned to the 44th Sdn. of the 40th Bomb Gp.

Discharged December 1945 as S/Sergeant., returned to civilian employment while attending missionary course at K.C. Bible College, was ordained as Minister, 1950. Married Virginia Lee July 5, 1946 and served with her in Philippines as missionaries, 1951-70. Their son and two daughters were born in Manila.

Howard is serving on the Counselling Staff of Back to the Bible, Lincoln, NE.

CHRIS F. ESTUDILLO, born May 25, 1919 at Goodyear, AZ. Graduated from Long Beach Poly High, Long Beach, CA 1937. Graduated from University of Southern California 1949.

Enlisted in Army Air Corps Oct. 15, 1940. Aircraft Armament School, Lowry Field, Denver, CO 1941. Gunnery and Turret School, Davis-Monthan Field, Tucson, AZ. T/Sergeant. October 1942.

Appointed W/O JG July 1943. Gunnery Range Officer, Davis Monthan Field, Tucson, AZ.

Chris F. Estudillo

Assigned to 40th Bomb Gp., Pratt, KS, 1943. Armament Officer with Clinton Adams in 4th Bomb Maintenance Sdn. Then in 44th Bomb Sdn. with Melvin Gibbs and Frank Redler.

One trip over the Hump to China with George Lowry and his crew at the time of the explosion of #582 of the 44th.

On R&R in Hawaii with Clinton Adams when Enola Gay dropped the Atomic Bomb on Hiroshima.

Separated from service December 1945.

Married Alma Anderberg May 1961. Retired from Bank of America in Los Angeles, CA in 1979 with 30 years service, last 20 in the Data Processing Department.

Moved in 1979 from Covina, CA where we lived for 16 years to Tigard, OR to be with Alma's daughter and grandchildren

GALPIN M. ETHERINGTON, (Bud), born in Owosso, MI in 1921. Graduated from Worcester Polytechnic Institute with Degree in Mechanical Engineering in January 1943 after having enlisted in the Army Air Corps. As Aviation Cadet, attended Maintenance Engineering School at Yale University. As Second Lieutenant attended B-29 School then Flight Engineer School. Joined the 40th Bomb Gp. in Pratt, KS in December 1943 as Flight Engineer on combat crew.

Married Margo Beck from Normanna, TX in February 1944 at the Base Chapel.

Galpin M. Etherington

Left for overseas in March 1944. Based in Chakulia, India. Flew many trips over the Hump and several bombing missions before going down on the disastrous mission over Rangoon on Dec. 14, 1944. Was Prisoner of War until escape in 1945.

After WWII, earned Master Degree in Metallurgy from Massachusetts Institute of Technology. Have one son and one daughter and three grandchildren. Worked primarily in the Foundry Industry, particularly in the areas of research, process development and management. Was the recipient of the American Foundrymen's Society Award of Scientific Merit in 1976.

Retired in January 1985 and reside in Birmingham, AL. Still work part time as consultant in the Foundry Industry.

GEORGE FANANDAKIS, born June 28, 1922, Boston, MA. I enlisted in the Army Air Force on July 9, 1942 after graduating high school. Upon completing several training programs, I was sent to Clovis, NM where I was assigned to Lt. Derrington's crew as a radar operator. On Nov. 25, 1944 our crew flew out of Miami headed for Chakulia arriving on December 11.

George Fanandakis

Three days later my pilot went as an observer on a mission over Rangoon. The plane was hit and he was forced to bail out. After the loss of my pilot and several crew changes, I was placed in R.C.M. where I flew 18 missions. I was awarded the Air Medal with one O.L.C., four Battle Stars and a Presidential Citation.

In October 1945 I went from active duty to the reserves. September 1950, during the Korean War, I was called back to active duty for an additional year and was stationed at Hunter A.F.B. Savannah, GA.

After leaving the service, I entered the restaurant business. I have been married to Helen Marinakis for 35 years. I have a daughter, a doctor; and a son, a business executive; both of whom I am very proud.

THEODORE R. FINDER, born New York City, Oct. 28, 1914. Enlisted 1942. Graduated Airplane Mechanics School, Goldsboro; Aviation Cadets (Engineering), Boca Raton and Yale. Commissioned June 1943. Detached service Boeing Renton B-29 Factory; graduated Flight Engineer School, Lowry January 1944. Detached service Wichita B-29 factory.

Theodore R. Finder

Arrived Chakulia on Lt. Bob Williams' crew, June 1944. Transferred to Major John Sanders' crew after his Flight Engineer was lost on ditching. Assigned to Headquarters as Group Flight Engineer early 1945 and promoted to Captain in May 1945. Flew 28 missions from Chakulia, Hsinching and Tinian. Was Flight Engineer on Gen. LeMay's crew on first nonstop flight from Japan to U.S. on Sept. 19, 1945. Received DFC twice, Air Medal with cluster, Bronze Star Medal, Presidential Unit Citation with cluster, five campaign ribbons with battle stars.

Practicing law with the same firm since December 1945. Married to former Maxine Allen Merrill. Live in Carefree, AZ.

THOMAS MILTON FREDERICK, TSG, Retired, USAF, 6148055. Born in Everett, MA, Apr. 24, 1921. Attended Horace Mann Grammar School, Fairfield Whitney & Albert N. Parlin Jr. High School, graduated in 1939 from Everett Senior High School. Enlisted in U.S. Army Air Corps at Boston, MA July 19, 1939. Was assigned to Ft. Slocum, NY for recruit training and prior to shipping to overseas assignment of enlistment, Republic of Panama, Canal Zone. Left from Brooklyn Army Base and Navy Yard on the U.S. Army Transport Leonard Wood. Arrived in the Canal Zone approximately Aug. 5, 1939 and was assigned to the 15th A.B. Sdn. Albrook Field Canal Zone for further recruit training and when finished was reassigned to the 24th Pursuit Sdn. 16th Pursuit

Gp. Albrook Field. During which period, received training in Radio Mechanics and Radio Operation at the Albrook Field Radio School in Engineering Hangar. After working on the line for several months I took the Air Medhanics Examinations in Radio, and passed it being then rated an air Mechanic 2nd Classs, and was made PFC. During this time, there was need of voluteers for a Radio Weather Observers School, so I volunteered as a candidate and graduated as a Radio Weather Observer, which entailed plotting balloon runs, and making observation through a transit with stints at copying radio weather reports from weather station transmission through the South American Region, including the Carribean. Since they were building a new pier and Air Field at Rio Hato. During this time I was upgraded to Corporal, and then finally to Buck Sergeant. Although I never received the Air Mechanic 1st Class Rating. I was engaged operating from the Radio Trailer similar to the one employed by the 40th at David R.de P. Also a teletype operator, and radio mechanic, jack of all trades. Being passed over, although senior in rank for Staff Sgt., I decided that promotion lay in getting a transfer to an observation or bomb sqaudron. Since I was eager to fly, and had flown by myself by begging rides at Alb rook with the 44th Recon. Sdn. and had learned to operate the BC-191 that was installed in those aircraft that they had which were B18A's.

Thomas Milton Frederick

I recall most of the time training some pilots to learn to send and receive International Morse at more than 6 words a minute, which they were required by regulations to do, either with key or light. Also, we were given a course in emergency situations which concerned wounds, etc., a very interesting part (thought) each radio operator was taken the dispensary and performed a minor operations on living patient there under a surgeon's supervision. We also had the nice experience of going through the Altitude Chamber, to show us what happens when we might lose our oxygen supply. That was a very, very good experience.

Also during the Pratt Days, besides the routine flying in B-26's and night bombing in B-17's we had the opportunity to have assigned to our group, the left-overs of the famous B-17, which was piloted by Maj. Morgan in the 8th Air Force, who were supposed to give of their expertise on the problems of avoiding flak, and shooting down enemy aircraft.

I went home on a B-17, with Sgt. Telemachus Mavofrides who lived in a town close to mine in Massachusetts. I managed to oversleep in Washington, DC after visiting my cousin because we made an overnight stop there, and had to hitch-hike a ride back to Salinas, KS in a B-25. When I got there and phoned in so I would not be declared AWOL, I could get no transportation and they told me to get back to Pratt immediately. I got back to the base and reported in, and they accepted my excuse of oversleeping with no bad time lost. I retired from the Air Force in 1962, from March AFB, CA. Unable to work, because I had to take care of aged relatives for quite a few years, married first wife in 1955, who died of brain tumor, remarried in 1966, no children. Active in Masonic Lodges, PM, etc. Enjoy the memories and the up-to-date info on members of the group, filled in many a question I had about things that happened.

ROBERT M. FREEBORN, Lieutenant, was assigned to the 40th Gp. (44th Sdn.) in July 1944. He remained in that assignment until October 1944 when he was transferred to the 505th Gp. and then to the 6th Gp. Hdq. (13th AF) at Clark Field, Philippines. He served as a pilot (and operations officer with the 6th Gp.). When the living quarters and area of the 40th Gp. on Tinian was closed down, Freeborn was assigned as "liaison" officer. His job was to supervise the closure and secure the unit area. He spent his last night with the 40th as the only (and very lonely) person to sleep in the officers section.

Robert M. Freeborn

Bob Freeborn was born in Alhambra, CA on May 4, 1925. He enlisted in the Reserve, in the Aviation Cadet program, in December 1943. He completed junior college when called to active duty. He became a B-25 pilot, then B-17 and then B-29. He served briefly as a B-29 instructor at Pyote, TX before being assigned to the 40th Gp. He remained in the A.F. Reserve and served in a variety of programs until retired in 1985 (Lieutenant Colonel).

He was married before going overseas. He and his wife, Miriam, have two sons and two daughters and sixteen grandchildren. After the war he received degrees from Whittier College and the University of Southern California. He earned his Ph.D. degree at Claremont Graduate School. He became a high school math and science teacher in the Alhambra School District in 1949. He retired in 1984, after 35 years as a teacher, counselor and administrator.

Special Note: In 1948 Freeborn spent two weeks on a duty tour at Davis-Monthan A.F.B. There he flew the B-50. Basically, it was a B-29 with Pratt-Whitney engines. These had reversible pitch props. On take off the plane could immediately start to climb. It would have been a great improvement during WWII, but by 1948 the jet age was here.

LEWIS W. FUSSELL, born Oct. 22, 1916 Grand Rapids, MI. Graduated high school Washington, DC. Mar. 18, 1941 drafted and assigned 265th Coast Artillery. July 1, 1941 re-enlisted in the Army Air Corp and sent to Chanute Field Aircraft Mechanics School. Jan. 19 1942 assigned to Moody Field, GA and then to George Field, IL. April 1944 to Lowry Field to Flight Engineer's School. July 1944 to Clovis Field, NM B-29 Combat Crew Training and TABOOMA Crew was formed.

Lewis W. Fussell

Dec. 10, 1944 flew TABOOMA I to 40th Gp. in India and assigned to the 25th Sdn. Flew seven missions India and 25 missions Tinian in TABOOMA I, II, III, and IV. Returned to the states in TABOOMA IV as a Flight Officer with a DFC and Air Medal with three clusters. January 1946 rejoined 40th at March Field. Separated as F.O. July 1946. Re-enlisted as M/Sergeant. at Chanute September 1946. January 1947 assigned to 22nd Bomb Gp., Okinawa. July 1948 returned to Smokey Hill AFB as Squadron Flight Engineer 2nd BS, 22nd BG. Three months TDY to Lakenheath, England with the 22nd returning February 1949.

Separated May 1949. Hired at Chanute AFB as Civilian Instructor Flight Engineer. January 1958 transferred to Tyndall AFB 306th FTD, ATC. I instructed Aircraft Maintenance Systems F-104, F-102, F-101, T-33, T-38 and F-106. March 1967 transferred to ADC F-106 Aircraft Technician.

Retired July 1, 1973 with total AF service of 32 years, two months.

PAUL B. GERSHONE, born in Minneapolis, MN on May 5, 1919. Drafted Sept. 10, 1941. Infantry training Camp Roberts, CA. Guarded railroad tunnels in Utah and also guarded ships in San Francisco in M.P. Battalion.

Then went into Air Corps and had B-24 training March Field, Riverside, CA. Flew eight bombing missions over Kiska in the Aleutian Islands. Sent back and went to Radar School. Sent to India with Skousan's crew. Flew on Frank's and Brigg's crew for 35

Paul B. Gershone

missions. Was on the Rangoon "catastrophe." Bailed out at 400 feet with four others in China.

Received three Air Medals and one DFC. Discharged as Staff Sergeant Oct. 12, 1945.

Married to Millie for 40 years. Met her one week after discharge. Have son and daughter and two grandsons.

Co-owner of Box Factory making wooden and corrugated shipping containers. Retired in 1986.

Have attended five 40th Bomb Gp. Reunions.

HARRY GLASSMAN, 33478070, born Aug. 14, 1916, Philadelphia, PA. Enlisted 1943-trained A.M. Lincoln, NE, P.P. Spec. Chanute Field, IL, Arm, Lowery Field, CO, 234th CCTS (V.H.) Clovis NM combat duty 395th Bombardment Sdn., 40th Bombardment Gp. from Aug. 6, 1944.

Harry Glassman

Combat Stations: Chakula, India: China; Tinian; Mauapas. Thirty-two combat sorties from Kure May 5, 1945 to Hachioji Aug. 1, 1945. Total 491.05 combat flying hours.

Awards: Distinguished Flying Cross-Air Medal two OLC. Married Evelyn Swift Dec. 28, 1941. Discharged Aug. 14, 1945. Three children; son Richard and twin daughters Jayne and Carol.

Opened retail business 1951, Richard's Housewares. Founded Richard's Travels with son-in-law Jeff Kaplow 1971. Traveled extensively throughout the world revisiting many wartime stations and targets.

Six grandchildren: Andrea and Jonathan Kaplow, Leah, Diana and Justin Smith, Jacob Glassman.

(Died June 6, 1987).

WILLIAM GOLDSTEIN, born Nov. 10, 1916, Indianapolis, IN. Graduated Indiana University 1939.

Enlisted as Flying Cadet November 1940. "Washed out", but drafted four months later. Disillusioned with sloughing through the mud of Texas, Louisiana and Carolina maneuvers with the First Armored Corp, returned to Air Force and to Bombardier school at Midland.

William Goldstein

Joined the 40th in Panama (the 45th Sdn.) with Lt. Bill Hunter and crew. Pulled anti-submarine patrol with the 25th, 45th and 44th sdns. Tours on the "Rock" as well as fought the "Battle of Guatemala City".

Skipped back to States and Pratt, KS for cadre for B-29s. Did the Chakulia, India scene with Col. Wilkinson and crew.

Flew 24 "Hump" trips. Participated in first aerial attack over Japan (after Doolittle)—the night mission over Yawata. Completed 15 missions including Nagasaki, Anshan, Singapore, the ill-fatted Rangoon one.

Led formation over Rangoon (secondary target) and although the release was especially effective, the bomb explosion blew our formation apart. Ours was the only plane to get back to the base that day. We lost Hal Soules, our navigator, on that mission and I "dead reckoned" back.

Back to the States and to Muroc Dry Lake (now Edwards) as part of "Project Tiger" to train for B-52s. Never materialized at that time.

Discharged in November 1945 and back to Indiana.

Self-employed until 1968 when I lost my first wife. Happily remarried now with five kids to call me "Dad" and four grandchildren.

Reoccurrence of a cancer has kept me from making the last several reunions, but looking forward to seeing the old gang at the next.

JOHN C. GOODWIN, born Nov. 16, 1914 in Columbia, SC. He joined the Air Force October 1942 at Shaw, Goldsboro, NC. Also stationed at Chanute Field, IL; Tucson, AZ; El Paso, TX; Pratt, KS; and India, China, Tinian.

John received the Bronze Star and was discharged as a T/Sergeant. in December 1945.

He married Janie L. Goodwin and they have three children and seven grandchildren. He was the owner of Goodwin Auto Service and retired in 1972 due to bad health.

MARVIN W. GOODWYN, born Bessemer, AL. Graduated Bessemer High in 1935; University of Alabama Law School 1940. Commissioned 2nd Lieutenant Pilot 1941. From Puerto Rico to Panama with 45th Sdn. mid 1942. Flew Caribbean anti-sub patrol (B-18s), then Pacific patrol (B-17s, 24s) from Galapagos. To Kansas mid 1943 to "break in" first B-29s. To India April 1944. Staged missions from there and China one year. Was 45th Operations Officer three years (Also lead crew.) Then Sdn. C.O. To Tinian for six months maximum effort. against Japan. (45th suffered no combat fatality while I was C.O.) At war's end was Lieutenant Colonel with three DFC's, six Air Medals, one Bronze Star. Also 29 combat missions.

Returned home to practice law. Recalled to Pentagon three years later as Judge Advocate. Promoted to Colonel in 1953. Retired in 1964. Have one 33 year old son and one two year old granddaughter.

PAUL M. GORESKI, born Mar. 26, 1919, Mead, Co. All my schooling was in Denver, Co. Caddied in National Open 1938 at Cherry Hills Country Club. Enlisted at Ft. Logan, CO Jan. 16, 1941.

As a Yarbird I was assigned to 40th Bomb Gp. June 1942 at Borinquen Field. O.J.T.'d as a photographer, clerk, dog robber, transp. driver and mechanic and aircraft mechanic. (Slonina was my first C/C).

Paul M. Goreski

Made a single engine (B-18) landing at Boringquen. (I think the pilot was Gianetti.) Helped Speedy Miller get his B-29 at Pratt ready for India. Was dropped back into 73rd WG. I went to Saipan in 1944.

Finished 20 years in the Air Force in 1961. (14 years at Lowry.) Had 14 more years in Civil Service. I combined the two for a 34 year Civil Service Retirement. Spent one year at Fairbanks, AK (1955-56).

Married a Hoosier, R.N., Virginia Hart, in 1947. Have a son, John, and a daughter, Jane. Made the 1985 and 1987 reunions and both were great. Rebuilding (B-29) T square 54 at Lowry was a fine experience this past year.

CLAYTON F. GRAY, after graduation from Dartmouth College (1941), entered Army Air Corps receiving wings and commission at Kelly Field, TX, February 1942.

Following service as single and multi-engine instructor, joined the 40th Bomb Gp. at Pratt, KS, November 1943.

Participated in 40th Bomb Gp. (44th Sdn.) Combat operations from April 1944 - August

Clayton F. Gray

1945 in India, China and the Mariana's (Tinian) as Aircraft Commander and Flight Commander with 35 combat missions.

Returned to active duty as a regular officer January 1952 and had various command/staff/operations assignments at Randolph AFB; Command and Staff School, Maxwell AFB; 41st AD, Japan; 4th TAC Fighter WG., Seymour Johnson AFB; AF Advisory Gp., MACV, Vietnam; Defense Nuclear Agency, Kirtland AFB.

Awards and Decorations include The Distinguished Flying Cross, Bronze Star and the Air Medal with three OLC.

Retired in 1973, Lieutenant Colonel USAF, and living with wife Evelyn and family in New London, NH.

LEWIS HOWARD GRAY, born June 21, 1920, Clarksville, TN. Entered military September 1941. 2nd Lieutenant Army Air Corps, rated Bombardier Apr. 17, 1943. Rated Navigator August 1943. To 40th Bomb Gp. 45th Bomb Sdn., Pratt, KS, September 1943, as Navigator on Capt. Charles R. (Dick) Mallory's crew. Flew 30 "Hump" and 27 combat missions with Dick's crew: in 45th, 395th and 25th sdns., finishing June 1945. Returned to States July 1945. Retired as Regular Air Force Lieutenant Colonel July 1964. Assignments included two tours in Japan and one in Korea; four years, AFROTC.

(A.B. University of Southern California, 1953) Command and Staff School 1956-1957; Air Staff 1957-1960; Purdue University, M.S. Human Factors Engineering 1961; three years Electronic Systems Division Staff.

Lewis Howard Gray

Awards include: Distinguished Flying Cross, Air Medal (three OLC), AF Commendation Medal, plus service ribbons.

After AF retirement spent five years with Boeing; seven years consultant to U.S. Army Night Vision Laboratory; one year at Idaho National Engineering Laboratory; three years at Oak Ridge National Laboratory, retiring July 1985.

Married Mary Winters July 1945; four sons (two are USAF Lieutenant Colonels), three grandchildren. Currently managing Gray-Winters Vineyard, Clarksville, TN.

LEE AKER HALL, born Feb. 18, 1914 in St. Louis, MO. Graduated from St. Louis University Medical School in 1940 and joined the Army Air Corp as a flight surgeon in July 1942. Immediately assigned to Alconbury, England with the 93rd Bombardment Gp. From there to Algeria and Libya against Rommel's Africa Corps.

Lee Aker Hall

Later, assigned to the 45th Bombardment Sdn, Pratt, AAF, KS with the brand new B-29 Superfortress crews. Went overseas again to Chakulia, India for a year and then on to Tinian where Lee was promoted to Group Flight Surgeon. He was discharged in October, 1945 with the rank of Major and returned to St. Louis to practice obstetrics and gynecology.

Lee married Kay Huey in 1943 and had one daughter. Kay died in 1974, and Lee married Eleecia Kleuser of Ft. Worth, TX in 1976, a widow with six adult children. Retired from practice in 1979 and moved to Ft. Worth where he volunteered his time as the medical director of the first Hospice for terminally ill cancer patients in Ft. Worth. Lee died Jan. 15, 1987 of a sudden heart attack.

ROBERT L. HALL, born Feb. 25, 1924, at Atlanta, GA. Moved to Connecticut, 1928. Attended Yale University, 1941-42. Entered the Army Air Corps in January, 1943 and attended Armament School and CFC school at Lowry Field, Denver. Joined 44th Sdn., 40th Gp., in Pratt, KS, in October, 1943, as CFC specialist and gunner. Flew overseas and on six missions with William Hunter's crew; then completed combat tour with Fountain Brown's crew. Left 40th Gp. at Tinian late in July, 1945, as T/Sergeant., and was discharged Oct. 25, 1945.

Returned to college on the GI Bill. Received the B.A. from Yale (1947); the M.A. (1950) and Ph.D (1953) from University of Minnesota. With the Air Force Personnel and Training Research Center, 1952-57, as a civilian research social psychologist, conducting research on training, performance and evaluation of combat crews.

Robert L. Hall

Married 1957 to Joy Engleking; raised two daughters and one son. On Faculty of the University of Minnesota, 1957-62. Program Director at National Science Foundation, 1962-65. Professor (and various administrative jobs) at University of Illinois at Chicago, 1965-87. Retired 1987 as Professor Emeritus.

Attended all 40th Gp. reunions from 1982 to 1987 and served as co-editor of the 40th Gp.'s Memories.

ROBERT HANCHETT, "Bob", born Apr. 23, 1924 in Peoria, IL. Went into Army Air Corps March 1943 and discharged November 1945.

Robert Hanchett

Tech School training at Kearns, UT, Lowry Field, CO and Detroit, MI.

Joined the 40th Bomb Gp. at Pratt, KS; on to Chakulia, India. Next was Tinian Island.

Highest rank S/Sergeant. Central Fire Control CFC 960 Ground Crew.

After discharge returned to Peoria, IL and Bradley University. Joined the family business. Had a heart attack June 1980, retired. After that try to stay active enjoying golf and fishing.

EDWARD A. HARRIS, born Dec. 16, 1920, Marietta, GA; raised in Athens, GA. Completed high school 1940; Aircraft School, Nashville, TN, 1941 and began work at Lockheed Burbank. Entered USAF February 1944. Completed Basic, Miami Beach, Gunnery School, Ft. Myers, FL (B-29s) Lincoln, NB to Clovis, NM for O.T.U. Staging, Kearney, NE, West Palm Beach to C.B.I. Chakulia, India. Then Tinian via Perth Australia. Assigned Tail Gunner, A.C. John H. Hug crew ship 33. Fourteen missions, Presidential Unit Citation, five Battle Stars, Air Medal with Clusters, Good Conduct.

In January 1946 returned to Lockheed,

then to Georgia. Obtained L.L.B and L.L.M., a Certified Manager (CM) in 1977, Reg. in L.A. County. Continued Lockheed Management and Engineering positions. Retired February 1986.

Wife, Martha M. Harris; son, John E., two grandsons, Brad and Matt, Marty is mother, one daughter Marsha E. and Robert MacDuff, La Canada, CA, one son Douglas. Reside with wife Mildred in Glendale, CA.

FREDERICK D. HENRY, born Oct. 15, 1921, at Oswego, NY. Graduated from Oswego High School, then from Ryan School of Aeronautics in June, 1941. Worked in flight test at Ryan Aeronautical Co. until enlisting, October, 1942, in the Army Air Corps at Ft. Rosecrans. Following Basic Training at Ft. McArthur, served at George Army Air Force Base as Crew Chief on two AT 11 Bombardier Trainers. Became Propeller Specialist at Chanute Field, Winter 1943. Assigned to 40th Bomb Gp., Pratt, KS, May 1943. Remained with group through Chakulia, India, Hsinching, China, and Tinian, Mariana Islands. Achieved rank of S/Sergeant and awarded Bronze Star, five Battle Stars, and Group Citation.

Frederick D. Henry

After service separation in October 1945, earned a Bachelor of Aeronautical Engineering Degree from Rensselaer Polytechnic Institute. Stress Engineer five years, North American Aviation on F-86's and F-100's. Stress Engineer 30 years, Northrop Corp., Aircraft Division, on Col. J.P. Stapp's Rocket Sled Runs at Holloman AFB, NM, T-38's, F-5's, YF-17's, F-18's plus various classified projects. Retired January, 1987.

RODOLFO HERNANDEZ, born Mar. 24, 1919 at Laredo, TX. Graduated from Martin High School and worked for the City until November 1940, when he enlisted in the Army Air Corps. Had Basic Training at Barksdale, LA, and Jefferson Barracks, St. Louis, MO. Attended Tech School at Chanute Field and in August 1941, joined the 45th Sdn., 40th Bomb Gp. at Borinquen Field, Puerto Rico. Remained with this wonderful Group through France Field, Chiriqui (David), Albrook, and Galapagos Islands. Returned to the U.S. in June 1943, and married the former Maria Consuelo Pierce of Brownsville, TX. Left Pratt, KS in January 1944 for India and China. Next area was the Mariana Islands, where that lovely little paper said, "WAR IS OVER GO HOME".

Rodolfo Hernandez

The rest of his military career was mostly on special assignments. Retired in December 1963, as Senior Master Sergeant. Entered Civil Service and 20 years later December 1983, retired as U.S. Customs Inspector.

NATHAN HICKS, "Nate", born in Melrose, MA July, 1924. Enlisted in February 1943 after attending Northeastern University. Served as the Radar Navigator Bombardier on Capt. Tom Turner's crew (some of the "new boys') with the 25th Sdn.

Nathan Hicks

Separated in January 1946 and attended University of Miami (FL) until additional active duty from January 1949 to March 1953. Served as an instructor at Air Intelligence School and as Observer and Navigator with the 449th Fighter Sdn. (AW) based at Fairbanks, AK.

Married in 1951 to Mary Jane McDonnell. Three children-Michael, Eugene, and Mary Louise. Self employed as a consultant in the development of non-profit, subsidized senior citizens housing primarily under the DHUD Sec. 202 Program. Retired in September 1986 and now residing at Orient (Long Island), NY.

WILLIAM M. HILT, born in Lafayette, IN on July 8, 1918. Graduated Purdue University 1936 B.S. EE; graduated Purdue University 1951 M.S. EE. Radar Schools: Harvard, MIT, Bell Labs and Signal Corps.

Joined 40th Bomb Gp. at Guatemala City, CA 1942 as Radar Officer, 44th and 74th Bomb Sdns.

Was transferred to Hq. 40th Bomb Radar Officer at Albrook Field, Panama Canal Zone, then to Pratt, KS, where we received our first B-29s. Received Air Medal with Oak Leaf Cluster. Was stationed in Chakulia, India, Sin Ching, China, West Field, Tinian. Was later transferred to Hq. 58th Bomb

William M. Hilt

Wing as Communication and Radar Officer.

Served as Chief, Strategic Bombing Branch, Armament Laboratory, Wright Air Development Center, Dayton, OH.

With his wife "Markie" have three children, Bill, Jim and Jane. Two grandsons, Jeremy and Zachary.

Retired from Control Data Corporation as General Manager, Research and Development Marketing in December 1983.

STANLEY A. HINKLE, born Jan. 23, 1925 at Garden City, MO. Enlisted in Army Air Corp June 1943. Joined 40th Bomb Gp. January 1945 at Chakulia, India. Was transferred to Tinian Island March 1945. Flew as CFC Gunner with 45th Sdn. Received Air Medal with one Oak Leaf Cluster. Was discharged from Army Air Corp. December 1945.

Stanley A. Hinckle

Graduated from Kansas University June 1954 with Mechanical Engineer's Degree. Worked for Various Companies and retired March 1986. Presently am operating my own business (Good Buy Specialty Co.) in Kansas City, MO area.

HERBERT C. HIRSCHFELD, born Aug. 9, 1921 in Chicago, IL. Received an A.B. at the University of Chicago; M. Div. Pacific School of Religion; Doctorate, San Francisco Theology Seminary; graduate Air War College; graduate Command and Staff College. He joined the Army Air Corps on Mar. 13, 1942, joining the 40th Bomb Gp. in Pratt, KS. Flew with Goodwyn, Matthews and Lanzoni in Kansas, India, China and Tinian. Also flew combat in the Korean War. Retired as a Lieutenant Colonel after 28 years (active and reserve).

Married Ivy Whitcomb on Aug. 12, 1945 and has two daughters and four granddaughters. Herb entered the seminary after

Herbert C. Hirschfeld

the Korean War and was ordained a Methodist Minister in 1955. He is a Senior Pastor in the Methodist Church.

ALBERT F. HOCKEL, born Oct. 10, 1921 in Romania. Emigrated with family to U.S. in 1923, settling in Philadelphia, PA. Graduated from high school in 1939, enlisted in Army Air Corps July 1942. After basic training, was transferred to Denver for tech courses in Aircraft Armament and B-29 Central Fire Control. Then assigned for flight crew training in Pratt, KS to 44th Bomb Sdn., Capt. William Mueller as Aircraft Commander.

Albert F. Hockel

After intensive training our crew was selected to take A/C #26322 to Chakulia, India in early 1944, arriving without any serious mishap. I flew but three missions with this crew until a takeoff disaster in China took the lives of most of them. Recovering from injuries, I was reassigned to other crews, flew as CFC Gunner until relieved in August, 1945, having completed 33 missions from India, China, and Tinian. Awards include Air Medal with four OLC's, DFC, Soldiers Medal, Campaign and battle ribbons. Attained rank of Tech Sergeant.

Graduated from Drexel University in 1948 with B.S. Degree in Electrical Engineering. Married in 1948 to Florence Schrott, have two sons. Moved to Long Beach, CA in 1960, retired in October, 1984.

LAWRENCE H. HOLLEY, "Hank", born May 8, 1924 in Blue Mounds, WI, moved to Madison, WI at age four. Attended grade school, high school and college in Madison, WI. Entered service Apr. 10, 1943. Basic training at Greensboro, NC, attended Air Force technical school at Greeley, CO and was assigned to the 40th Bomb Gp. in Pratt, KS in the Fall of 1943. Assigned to 45th Sdn. and put on special duty to Headquarters Sdn. working in the Statistical Section. Continued in the capacity with the 40th in Chakulia and on Tinian until sent home for discharge in November 1945.

Lawrence H. Holley

After returning home continued education at the University of Wisconsin, graduating in June 1949. In January 1953 became associated with the McKay Nursery Company and have continued with them since that time with retirement a couple of years away. Served under Lt. Conrad Seipp and Canio Decheka and was discharged with rank of T/Sergeant.

VINCENT J. HOLLEY, born Oct. 31, 1919 in Wallington, NJ. Moved to Passaic, NJ and attended Passaic, NJ schools. Drafted August 1942 and discharged September 1945. Boot camp, Ft. Dix, NJ and Atlantic City, NJ. Stationed at: Lincoln, NE; Seattle, WA; Chanute Field, IL; Marietta, GA; Pratt, KS. Promoted to S/Sergeant. prior to leaving Pratt, KS for overseas.

Vincent J. Holley

Shipped to Chakulia, India as Left Waist Gunner and Assistant Flight Engineer on "Devilish Snooks" with Capt. Pilot Graham "Jug" Blieler. Also stationed on Tinian Island prior to leaving for discharge. Received DFC, Air Medal and Clusters and two Battle Stars.

Married June 26, 1943 while on furlough from Marietta, GA to Carolyn Ward from hometown of Passaic, NJ. We have two children, Joanne and James, along with four grandchildren.

After separation from service joined Clifton, NJ Police Department and retired in 1975. Now residing in Florida.

S. R. HORN, Sergeant, 1st Lt. USAF, Retired. Born Oct. 17, 1917 in Post, TX. Moved to Oregon 1920. Received amateur radio license, enlisted United States Naval Communication Reserve, and graduated from high school in Salem, OR May-June 1936. Enrolled in CCC July 1937. Radio operator on two Oregon forest fires. March 1938 was transferred to Vancouver Barracks, Washington as chief operator of the CCC District Radio Net. First station was located directly above Brig. Gen. George C. Marshall's office.

Enlisted U.S. Army Air Corps on Jan. 11, 1940. Operator at Post Radio Station, Moffett Field, CA. Attended Radio Operator and Mechanics School at Chanute Field. Instructor in radio schools at Scott Field and Chicago. Commissioned as a Communication Officer, June 1943, and then finished Radar Maintenance Officers course.

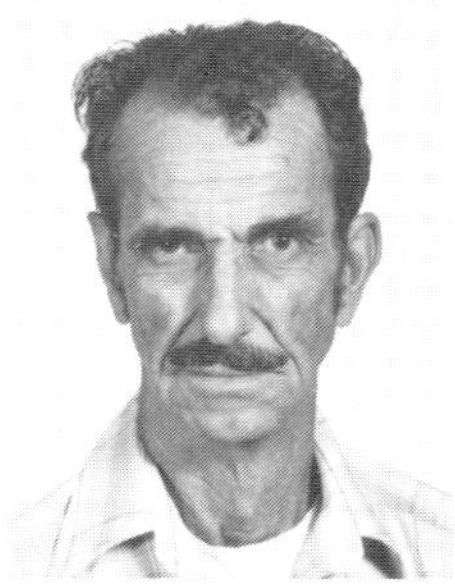

S. R. Horn

Assigned to 45th Bomb Sdn. in March 1944. Flew as a radio operator on first B-29 mission in "Monsoon Minnie". Finished missions on a lead crew, Aug. 6, 1945, with over 600 combat hours. Without an aeronautical rating, I returned to enlisted status in April 1946. Overseas tours in Germany, Libya, Crete, Turkey, and two in Japan. Met an American school teacher in Tripoli, married her in Japan, and son born in Tokyo 1957.

Retired at Kelly AFB Aug. 1, 1969. Worked as a senior electronics technician at Southwest Research Institute 1972-1977. I now operate my amateur radio station, W5IB, and keep my lawn mowed in San Antonio, TX.

WILLIAM S. HOUTS, born in Craig, MO, on Nov. 14, 1915. Enlisted in Signal Corp at Ft. Bliss in 1940. Transferred to Air Corp and went to Aircraft Mechanics school, 409th Tech School Sdn. at Amarillo Army Airfield, then to Boeing, Seattle. From there to Pratt, from Pratt via Liberty Ship and Atlantic Convoy thru Mediterranean Sea, Suez Canal, to India.

William S. Houts

Train across India to Chakulia, India, where assigned as a B-29 Crew Chief in the 25th Bomb Sdn. Flew from Chakulia to Tinian. Tinian via Siapian, Aircraft carrier, Honolulu, San Francisco to Ft. McArthur. Discharged October, 1945. After discharge, learned watchmakers trade, but gave it up for electronics field. Retired from large Electronics firm in 1979. Married in 1943, my wife and I have two daughters. Present home is Phoenix, AZ.

JOHN H. HUG, received commission and wings Class 43-B at Roswell, NM. Flew as Bombardier Pilot for about 18 months then to Clovis AFB for B-29 training. Arrived in Chakulia January 1945 as one of the first replacement crews. Completed 18 combat missions - most of them with #33 "MISS DONNA LEE", named after my first daughter, born while I was in India.

John H. Hug

Instructed B-29 Combat Crews at Randolph AFB during the Korean War. Went into Weather Recon in 1952, flying Hurricanes and Typhoons in WB-29s, WB-50s and WB-47s. Racked up over 6,000 hours in B-29s and B-50s.

Commanded a WB-47 WX Recon unit at Clark AFB PI for two years. Wrapped up 30 years service after flying a combat tour in C-130s in Vietnam. I am still flying (Cessna 206) but only enough to be dangerous!!

Took up motorcycling in 1980 and do a lot of touring. Pull a tent trailer and camp out alot - it's made me feel 20 years younger! Crew #33 have their own reunion about every other year. There are nine of us still going strong and we look forward to our next reunion in Wyoming in 1988.

I am proud to have been part of the 40th Bomb Gp. History and look forward to their news letters and reunions.

PAUL W. HUNTER, born near Parsons, KS Aug. 14, 1921. Attended schools there through junior college. Entered the air force in August 1942. Went through airplane mechanics school at Lincoln, then to cadet school and was commissioned at Yale in June 1943. Went through B-29 school and flight engineer's school, then joined the 40th (45th Sdn.) in December 1943, assigned to Woodruff's crew.

Went overseas by boat to Casablanca and ATC to Chakulia. Completed 35 missions in July 1945. Awarded DFC, Air Medal with three clusters and five battle stars. Left the service effective in January, 1946.

Paul W. Hunter

Returned to the farm in Kansas and semi-retired in 1987. Married Helen Thomas in 1949. Have five children and three grandchildren. Have been active in church and have served on many farm related boards and committees, especially those related to soil conservation. Helen and I received the Kansas Master Farmer-Master Farm Homemaker Award in 1983.

WILLIAM A. HUNTER, born Aug. 26, 1919 - Paris, TX, graduated Gainesville High 1938, attended North Texas State for three years where I met my future wife, for which my B-29 was named "Bombin Buggy". Entered Army Aviation Cadet Program September 1941, graduated 2nd Lieutenant Pilot, Class 42D Williams Field, AZ. Joined the 45th Bomb Sdn. Gp. June 1942 France Field, Panama, transferred to 44th Guatamala December 1942. Remained with the 44th until December 1944. Assigned to such scenic places as The "Rock", Pratt, and CBI, completed 22 hump trips and eight combat missions. Received regular commission 1946.

William A. Hunter

Graduated Texas Christian University 1948 with degree in Chemistry. From 1948 until retirement in 1969, served in various staff and command positions, including Air Force Academy Planning Board, Plans, Pentagon, Special Weapons Center, Kirtland AFB, NM. Commander 4930th Support Gp. for Operations "Redwing" - Pacific, United States European Command - Special Weapons. Promoted Brigadier General August 1966. Service schools completed - Air Command and Staff and Industrial College of Armed Forces. Awards - Legion of Merit - two Oak Leaf Clusters, Air Medal - one Oak Leaf Cluster.

Married Ethel Marie "Bug" McDaniel June 25, 1942 - four children of this marriage - two deceased. After retirement from the USAF, served as a commercial loan officer for local bank for 11 years.

The highlight of my military career was my association with the great people of the 40th Bomb Gp.

Particularly with my B-29 crew, crew chief, and ground support personnel. In brief many men of the 40th owe their lives to the professional and dedicated efforts of these men. Marvin E. "Red" Carmichael, crew chief for "Bombin Buggy" not only led the way for my crew, but set the standard and trained others by his expertise and example. A Great Man! A Great Organization!

DELMAR JOHNSON, born June 22, 1919, Beechwood, MI. Joined military January 1942 (enlisted) Anti aircraft Bn. - Texas. Assigned to 40 mm Bofors Gun Crew. Attended pre OCS school until accepted by Air Force for flight training. Pre-Cadet School - Texas, CTD, Oklahoma. Primary flight training - Oklahoma. Bomb Navigator, Midland, TX. Gunnery School, Laredo, TX. Requested B-29 duty. Assigned a Bombardier, Clovis, NM. Joined John Hug Crew for OTC - shipped to Kearney, NB for new aircraft - destination: India.

Assigned to 40th Gp. 45th Sdn. at Chakulia, India, but lost our new plane at Kharagpure. Flew at least one mission over Rangoon and several practice missions in the "Eddie Allen II" and the rest in another aircraft. Then on to Tinian to fly another approximately 20 missions.

Medals: Air Medal with two clusters Seven Oak Leaves. Presidential Citation.

At war's end, I was assigned as Executive Officer Quartermaster Corp to finish clothing allocation to remaining EM and disposition of equipment and destruction of some returning, several months later by ship to U.S. and reassigned to Randolph Field Air Base, getting out November 1946. Top rank as Air Force Officer, Captain. Joined local National Guard Chapter - four years Executive Officer - Captain.

Post War - 1947-49, Auto Sales; 1950-59 Kraft Foods: Sales, Supervision, Management; 1959-63 On Loan by Kraft to IGA - Director of Perishable Division International; 1963-68 Vice President - International Sales Manager Director, Marketing, Procurement Independent Grocer's Alliance, U.S. and Canada; 1968-73 Senior VP and President - Farm House Food Service Corporation, Director of Purchasing, Transportation, Label and Design; 1974-Present VP and Owner, Wholesale Pallet Distribution, Inc. Executive VP, Wisconsin Sports Car Company.

Awards and Achievements: 1954, Kraft Caramel Sales Promotion - National Winner - World Series Trip; 1955, Winner-Woman's Home Companion National Merchandising Contest-Kraft Foods; 1962, Winner - "Jade Ring" - Kraft Foods Co.; 1965, Senior Executive Member Independent Retailers of America (Nixon Program-Washington); 1967, Consultant-Hossman Refrig. Company, Dairy Department and Sales Development Film.

ELMER K. JOHNSON, (Al), born Feb. 12, 1918 at Minneapolis, MN. Family moved to the West Coast and he was raised in Portland, OR where he still resides. Took exams for Air Cadet at Seattle, WA in March of 1942 and was sworn in.

Elmer K. Johnson

Graduated and Commissioned on Apr. 17, 1943 at Albuquerque, NM and then completed Navigation course at San Marcos, TX. Joined the 40th Bomb Gp. at Pratt, KS and assigned to the 44th Bomb Sdn. as Navigator on crew of Ronald A. Harte on Sept. 28, 1944. He flew on first mission to Yawata, Japan and many others from CBI and then moved on to Tinian to complete missions just before the war ended. Awarded the D.F.C., Air Medal with three OLC's, Army Commendation Medal, Unit Citation with OLC and Campaign Medals.

He was recalled during the Korean conflict and was stationed at Bordeaux and then Leon, France to train French pilots for B-26 missions in French Indo-China.

He was an active partner with his father in the construction industry as General Contractors. He later accepted a position as Associate with a larger company where he acted as Estimator and Supervisor for more than twenty years.

Since retiring, he has done some traveling with wife Phyllis and daughter Irene and also enjoys fishing the great Northwest. His love of philately has led him to many auctions and shows here and abroad.

JAMES L. JONES, born Apr. 4, 1922 at Adrian, GA. Raised on a farm and went to school at Adrian, GA. Was drafted into Service Dec. 16, 1942. After basic training at Kearns, UT was stationed at Great Bend, KS and later sent to Pratt, KS where I joined the 45th Bomb Sdn. When the 40th went overseas I was left at Pratt for awhile.

James L. Jones

Later went overseas to rejoin the 40th Bomb Gp. and was assigned to the 44th Bomb Sdn. Worked as an engine mechanic. After we left India and went to Tinian, Red Carmichael was my Crew Chief.

Was discharged Nov. 22, 1945 with the rank of S/Sergeant. Came home and went back to farming.

LOUIS M. JONES, born July 21, 1918, Dallas, TX. Newman High School, 1935. Bachelor of Business Administration and Juris Doctorate degrees from Tulane University, 1941.

Louis M. Jones

Drafted Feb. 4, 1941. Discharged as a sergeant in October 1942 upon graduation as a 2nd Lieutenant from Army Air Force Administrative School, Miami, FL the same month. Graduated from Army Air Force Combat Intelligence School, Harrisburg, PA in January, 1943.

Joined 45th Bombardment Sdn. of the 40th Gp. stationed in Galapagos Islands in January, 1943. Graduated from Evasion and Escape School in Washington, DC in February, 1944.

Remained with the 40th Gp. during the India and China operations. Invented a survival vest that was used on the first B-29 bombardment mission over Bankok, Thailand, June 5, 1944. Awarded the Bronze Star.

Assigned as Army Air Force representative to the American Military Mission to Yenan, Communist China in June, 1944 to assist in rescue operations of Army Air Force personnel down in communist controlled territory in China.

Discharged as a Captain from the Army Air Force in November 1945. Returned to New Orleans, LA where I have been engaged in the private practice of law as well as serving on the staff of the Attorney General of Louisiana.

STEPHEN TISDAL JONES, born Cordell, OK Sept. 10, 1917. Graduated Cordell High School 1934, Central State College 1938, Oklahoma University School of Medicine 1952. Taught school and was officer in bank before WWII. Enlisted Army Air Corps February 1942.

Pilot training until broke collar bone and separated shoulder. Returned to Aerial Gunnery, Las Vegas, NV. Graduated 2nd in Class of 500 Navigation School Hondo, TX. Commissioned May, 1944. Radar Bombardier School, Boca Raton, FL. Flew as naviga-

Stephen Tisdal Jones

tor on R.E. Derrington crew Kearney, NB to Chakulia, India. 34 combat missions and hump. CBI and Pacific on Tinian. Lead crew and pathfinder 17 missions. Sdn. navigator 25th Sdn., 40th Bomb Gp. Navigator on Gen. Lemay's crew from Japan to Washington, DC 27 hours 30 min. Non-stop, non-refueling.

Air medal with four Oak Leaf Cluster. Distinguished Flying Cross with four OLC, Asiatic Pacific four Battlestars, Personal Citation from Gen. H. H. Arnold for Japan - Washington flight. Was navigator for Bob Derrington, Bob Dale, Bill Kingsbury and Delmar Stevens. Discharged October 1945.

Married Ellen Daniel 1949. Have two daughters and three granddaughters all in Monte Vista, CO. Family physician Cordell, OK and Creede, CO 1952-1982. Retired Sun City, AZ.

TULLY H. JORDAN, born July 14, 1923, McAlester, OK. Reared at Fayetteville and Harrison, AR. High School: Harrison, Arkansas, Freshman at SMSU, Springfield when Pearl Harbor occurred. University of Arkansas for a semester before entering basic training, Keesler Field, MS.

Tully H. Jordan

Radio Operator and Mechanic School, Scott Field, IL, Philco Radio School, Philadelphia, PA. Special courses at Truax Field, Madison, WS for intensive First Aid Battle Wound Training and VHF equipment. Eventually assigned to 45th Sdn., 40th Bomb Gp., Pratt, KS. Veteran Operators from the "Rock", Lyle, Klaver, Stockton, Miller, Thompson, Trayor, and Strausser, were great to us (the Neophytes), like big brothers. I served on Robert Haley's crew, "Duces Wild,", Carter McGregor's "The Eddie Allen", and Charles Thornsberry's "Virginia Tech". McGregor, Nordhagen, Kryzkowski and I flew two months in C109's while in India, learning a lot about each other's capabilities. Always felt our crew was as capable as any in the 45th, 40th Bomb Gp., 20th Bomb Command. Received same decorations as did other crewmen. Finished 35th Mission on July 21, 1945.

Entered St. Louis College of Pharmacy and graduated June 1948 with a B.S. in Pharmacy and Allied Sciences. Owned Pharmacy 25 years before selling and retiring. Have practiced Pharmacy 40 years. Shirley is my wife of 16 years. Two children and two step-children. Six grandchildren. I'M VERY PROUD TO HAVE BEEN A PART OF THE 45TH SDN., 40TH BOMB GP., 20TH BOMB COMMAND.

ALVIN W. KAMP, born Mar. 8, 1918 near Jackson, MO. Attended lower grades and graduated Jackson High School. Enlisted in Army Air Corps in November, 1942 and had basic training at Miami Beach, FL. Airplane Mechanics School at Gulfport, MS, Airplane Engine Specialist School at Chanute Field, Rantoul, IL and Aircraft Armament School, Lowry Field, Denver, CO. Joined 40th Bomb Gp. at Pratt, KS and served at Chakulia and Tinian Island as a ground mechanic. Highest rank attained was Buck Sergeant.

Alvin W. Kamp

For separation from service flew from Tinian to Sacramento, CA and then by train to St. Louis, MO. Separated from service at Scott Airforce Base, Belleville, IL, October 1945. Returned to old job as mechanic at Jackson Hosiery Plant. In 1977 started working for LENCO, INC. and ELECTRONICS who manufacture 85 different products for the electric welding trade and electronic devices for T.V. Stations. Married and have a son and daughter. Retired: 1987.

JOHN J. KELLY, born Sept. 16, 1917 in Evanston, IL. Joined the Army Air Corps July 10, 1942. Graduate Navigation School, Hondo, TX, Sept. 16, 1943; graduate Bombardier School December 1943. Joined 40th Bomb Gp. March 1944. In September 1944 crew flew photo recon to Okinawa for Navy. Received the Distinguished Flying Cross, Air Medal with Oak Leaf Cluster and the Air Force Commendation.

John J. Kelly

Married Georgie Gahn Kelly and has two children and two grandchildren. Separated from Active Service Jan. 2, 1946. Started work for the U.S. Army Engineers after separation and still employed as a Chief Dredge Operator. Also active in U.S. Air Force Reserve until retired as a Colonel in August 1976.

OTTO KERSTNER, born in Lorain, OH 1916. After high school graduation joined the CCC camp and later worked for U.S. Steel. January 1941 drafted into president Roosevelts' one year draft (166 infantry). After Pearl Harbor joined cadets, class 42-X (Hap Arnolds' Guinea Pigs), then became a basic flying instructor at Randolph Field and Garden City, KS. In 1944 attended B-29 school, Clovis, NM.

Otto Kerstner

As a pilot of a B-29 flew to Chakulia, India in latter part of 1944. Assigned to 25th Bomb Sdn., 40th Bomb Gp. Flew a number of missions in CBI, several trips to China, then to Tinian. After several missions over Japan bailed out into Pacific. The crew was split up, became co-pilot for Maj. John Child's lead crew. Total 29 missions. Awarded DFC, Air Medal with two OLC's, Asiatic Medal with three Battle Stars. After discharge attended Indiana Tech, received BSME degree. Worked for Hughes, Northrup and Rockwell International. Retired in 1982. Married 1963, two stepsons.

MARION J. KLOSTER, born July 27, 1918 at Nevada, IA. Attended schools in Des Moines, IA. BS in General Engineering June 1942 at Iowa State College, Ames, IA. ROTC Field Artillery.

Commissioned in Air Force August 1942. Sdn. Engineer Cadet Course in Grande, March 1943, Yale University. Boeing B-29 Factory Course June 1943. B-29 Flight Engineer Course.

Joined 40th Bomb Gp., 25th Bomb Sdn., September 1943. Chakulia, India March 1944. Served as Flight Engineer, Lead Crew, Maj. Garth Doyle. Entered inactive service August 1945.

Graduate School September 1945, Institute of Technology, University of Minnesota.

Married Feb. 12, 1959 to Dorothy Irene Clemmings. Have two daughters, Mimi and Mary, and four grandchildren.

Marion J. Kloster

Career: General Mills, Inc. September 1945; Minneapolis Milling Co. President and Founder February 1963; General Mills Inc., Minneapolis, 1969; Conkey and Associates Inc. Consulting Engineers; Peavey Co., Minneapolis, February 1974, Director Corporate Engineering; Conkey and Associates Inc. Consulting Engineers; Fegles Power Service Inc., Minneapolis, 1981; Consulting Engineer, Minneapolis, 1984; Minnesota Department of Public Service, to date, Energy Specialist. At present have no plans for retirement.

WALTER KRAUS, 40th Bomb Gp.- Aug. 17, 1987. born May 22, 1925, Bronx, NY. Entered Army Air Corp Cadet program, August 1943. Classified for Navigator training, Nashville, TN; on-the-line trainee, Bainbridge, GA; gunnery school at Tyndal AFB, Panama City, FL; pre-flight school, Maxwell AFB, Mont., AL; Navigator training, Hondo, TX; Radar navigator/bomb training, San Bernadino, CA; assigned to the Eino Jenstrom B-29 crew at Clovis, NM; joined the 40th Bomb Gp. on Tinian, May 9, 1945, as a new crew. Flew last two missions of the EDDIE ALLEN, and it got us home from Tokyo alive, both times. Completed 20 combat missions, the last one flown on V-J Day, Aug. 14, 1945. Separated from service, March 1946.

Walter Kraus

Graduated teacher-training program, UCLA, June, 1950. English teacher, Madera Union High School, Madera, CA, and San Jose High School, San Jose, CA. English Supervisor and senior high school Vice-Principal, San Jose Unified School District. Retired from public education, June, 1987. Glad to be alive and member of a crew that has had three reunions since we found ourselves again in 1982. The fiery forge of combat welded us together forever.

NATHAN W. KRITZER, born Jan. 14, 1920 in Poland and arrived in the United States in 1929. Attended school in Cleveland, OH, and enlisted in the United States Air Corps February of 1941. I was married on Pearl Harbor Day while I was on furlough. I attended service school at Langley Field, VA, Army Air Force School of Applied Tactics at Eglund AFB and B24 School in San Diego. Assigned to the 44th Bomb Sdn. October of 1943 in Pratt, KS, where I served as Squadron Inspector until I was assigned as crew chief on Aircraft 394, known as "The Last Resort".

Nathan W. Kritzer

On my 25th birthday, Jan. 14, 1945, the accident on 582 took place at Chakulia, India. After that period, I was assigned a new aircraft, 542, which we named "The Kritzer Blitzer", and this remained my airplane until the end of the war.

I returned to civilian life in October of 1945. In addition to being the parents of three daughters and one son, we have six grandchildren. Florence and I have just celebrated our 46th Anniversary together. I am now retired and enjoying life.

SIGMUND LAUBE, drafted in January, 1943 from New York City, and under 20 years of age, was inducted in the Army Air Corps. He achieved the rank of Staff Sergeant and was a Radio Operator on the B-29's.

Sigmund Laube

Total missions flown were 35 in the Burma Theatre and Pacific zone of which 17 of these were over the Hump.

By order of China's General Chiang Kai-shek, the China Burma Medal was struck to honor the 5000 men who helped China during their wartime siege. Laube was awarded this medal.

Other medals earned were: The Distinguished Flying Cross; Air Medal with two Oak Leaf Clusters; Asiatic Pacific Campaign; Victory Medal and Good Conduct.

Discharged in September, 1945 he began his lifetime career in the jewelry industry. Retirement since 1981, is enjoyed in San Diego, CA with wife, Beverly. He keeps active at gardening, swimming travel and many gatherings with friends.

JACK C. LEDFORD, born Sept. 1, 1920, at Blairsville, GA. Commissioned 2nd Lieutenant U.S. Army Air Corps, Oct. 31, 1941, Flying Class 41-H Kelly Field, TX.

Jack C. Ledford

Served as Flight Instructor at Goodfellow and Carswell Fields until joining the 45th Bomb Sdn., 40th Bomb Gp. at Pratt, KS in January, 1944. Served as Aircraft Commander and Assistant Group Operations Officer.

After WWII accepted Regular Commission, USAF. Served in Command and Staff positions in Nuclear Weapons Systems, Strategic Bomber (B-36), Tactical Fighters (F-100), and Reconnaissance Units. (RF-101, U-2, SR-71).

Earned BS Degree in Physics, Ohio State University; MBA, George Washington University; Distinguished Graduate, Industrial College of the Armed Forces.

Awarded Distinguished Service Cross, Distinguished Service Medal with Oak Leaf Cluster, Legion of Merit and 22 other U.S and Foreign decorations.

Voluntarily retired from USAF in September 1970 as Commander 12th Air Division, SAC, in rank of Brigadier General.

Served as Vice-President, Southern Arizona Bank, Tucson; and then Vice-President, Southeast Asia, Hughes International.

With wife Polly, now retired and living in Tucson, when not traveling and chasing tennis and golf balls.

"I am very proud of the first B-29 Unit, the 40th Bombardment Gp. (VH), and to have served with such wonderful guys!"

LOUIS LEMOS, born in Modesto, CA Oct. 5, 1917. Graduated High School in 1937 and entered the Army Air Corp October, 1941.

Attended aircraft maintenance and power plant technical school at Chanute Field, IL from December, 1941 to June, 1942. Remained as instructor in Power Plant Branch until July, 1943.

Completed B-29 Armorers Remote Fire Control Course at Lowry Field, CO, August 1943 and went to the 58th Bomb Wing at Smoky Hill Field Salina, KS where I was assigned to the 40th Bomb Gp. at Pratt Field,

Louis Lemos

KS.Assigned to the 44th Bomb Sdn. and right gunner on Maj. McWilliams combat crew. We flew B29 #6297 to Chakulia where we flew ferry missions over the Himalaya Mountains (The Hump) and combat missions out of Chakulia and Hsingehing, China.

We left CBI February, 1945 for Muroc Army Air Field, CA and was assigned to sub-depot in the B-29 engine section.

Returned to civilian life September 1945.

TED LINDSTROM, "Lindy", born in St. Paul, MN, Mar. 5, 1918. Went through schools in St. Paul and finished up at Central High in June 1936. Joined Minnesota National Guard, 216th Coast Artillery (Anti aircraft) August 1940. Inducted to Federal Service January 1941. Sent to Camp Haan, January 1941 (Riverside, CA) discharged Aug. 13, 1941 and returned to St. Paul, MN. Pearl Harbor Dec. 7, 1941 returned to San Francisco January 1942.

Ted Lindstrom

Worked for the U.S. Engineers Department and returned to the military August. Spent a short time at the Presidio of Monterey and then to March Field for a few months and landed up in Pratt, KS, left Pratt for Camp Anza, CA (P.O.E.). Left for India on the U.S.S. Mount Vernon with a brief stop in Melbourne, Australia. Spent one year in India (Chakulia), left India and went to Melbourne, Australia and had a short shore leave. From there on to New Guinea, Manus Island, landing on Tinian Easter Sunday 1945. Returned to U.S. November 1945. Discharged Dec. 1, 1945, Camp Beale, CA.

Hope this will be of some help for the book. Came back to the U.S.A. on A.P.A 214 - USS Natrona. Spent 26 1/2 years with the Fire Department - retiring Apr. 1, 1978. Done nothing since.

GLEN E. LISTON, was born May 5, 1908 at Wayne Co., IL. He was a successful farmer, born and raised on the farm.

Inducted into the service Mar. 16, 1942, at Scott Field, IL. Discharged Dec. 10, 1945 at Jefferson Barracks, MO.

Basic training was at Ft. Warren, WY. Then eight weeks of truck driver school, at Ft. Warren. He spent some time at Ft. Dix, Wrightstown, NJ.

Glen E. Liston

He was a private two months, then a corporal 42 months. He was a member of the 28th service gp., attached to the 40th Bomb Gp. He served in Chakulia, India and on the island of Tinian, with the 20th A.A.F. for 22 months.

Drove general duty vehicles at B 29 bases, hauling equipment, supplies and personnel to various areas.

Decorations and citations he held were; Good Conduct Medal, Meritorious S.V. Insignia G. O. 79 Hq. 20th A.F.-Asiatic Pacific Theatre Campaign Ribbon, three Overseas Bars, Victory Ribbon and American Theatre Campaign Ribbon.

Glen is deceased. His widow Bess, lives on the farm, Route 3, Fairfield IL, 62837.

C.P. LOWMAN, (Pete), born in Richmond, VA, Oct. 5, 1919. Enlisted in A.U.S. September 1940. Assigned to 246th C.A., Ft. Story, Virginia Beach, VA. Accepted for AAF Officer Candidate School September 1942. Received commission December 1942 and was assigned to 45th Bomb Sdn., 40th Bomb Gp., 6th AF in David, Panama January, 1943 as Squadron Intelligence Officer.

C.P. Lowman

Returned U.S.A from Galapagos Islands July 1943 when the Squadron began B-29 training in Pratt, KS. Completed Combat Intelligence School at Harrisburg, PA and Air Officers Anti Aircraft Observers Course at Camp Davis, NC.

Moved to Chakulia, India when Group began combat operations in March 1944, and later to Tinian in March 1945. Awarded Air Medal and Bronze Star. Returned to U.S.A. October 1945 and was separated from the Service as Captain.

Married Betty Lee Fry of Richmond, VA in January 1946 and has three sons. Resumed employment with Exxon Corp. in 1946 and held a number of executive marketing positions in U.S.A. and Europe prior to retirement from the Company in 1978.

Now maintains residency and divides time between Virginia Beach and Isla Del Sol, St. Petersburg, FL.

GEORGE M. LUNDQUIST, born Apr. 10, 1921 at Aurora, NB. Attended rural grade school and Aurora High School. Entered Army Air Corps October 1940. After basic training and tech school at Chanute Field, was assigned to 20th Pursuit Gp. Attended Aircraft Maintenance Officers School and commissioned September 1942, was assigned to 45th Bomb Sdn., 40th Bomb Gp. in Panama then on to Pratt, KS, Chakulia, India and Tinian. Served as Flight Engineer and Maintenance Officer.

George M. Lundquist

Released from active duty January 1946 as Captain.

Employed by U.S. Bureau of Reclamation for three years. Recalled during the Korean Conflict and again released from AD July 1953. Retired from USAF as Lieutenant Colonel.

Employed July 1953 by USAF as Quality, Systems and procurement engineer with SPACE AND MISSILE SYSTEMS ORGANIZATION. Retired June 30, 1973.

Married Mary Nichols of Wichita, KS and reared a daughter and son. Our son has followed his Dad's footsteps and is serving with the USAF.

ARTHUR J. MACER JR., born in Westfield, NY on Mar. 10, 1921. Left college to enter service in July 1942.

After an aborted attempt to become a pilot—from September 1942 to January 1943—assigned to Bombardier School at Big Spring, TX in April 1943. Completed course and commissioned in July 1943. Immediately assigned to Navigation Training at Hondo, TX and graduated with a rating of Navigator-Bombardier in November 1943.

Arrived at Pratt, KS in November 1943. Left for overseas with Capt. Landrett's crew in March 1944. Went by ship to Casablanca

Arthur J. Macer Jr.

and by ATC to India. Arrived at Chakulia in April 1944. In November 1944—after serving with the Tanker Gp.—was assigned to Lt. Robert Winter's crew. In March 1945, joined Maj. Chester Woolsey Lead Crew as Navigator. Credited with 18 missions while in the CBI and completed my 35 missions from Tinian. Awarded the DFC with OLC, Air Medal with three OLC, Asiatic-Pacific Theatre Campaign Medal with six Battle Stars, and the Distinguished Unit Citation. Separated from the service in November 1945.

Married Phyllis Todd in August 1946. Have two daughters and a son. Retired in October 1984 from Renold Inc. as President of the Engineered Products Division. We have attended all the Reunions except for the one held at Ft. Worth.

FERRELL J. MAJORS, born May 13, 1918 in Argonia, KS. He completed the tenth grade in high school. Joined the Air Corps Jan. 7, 1943 and was stationed at St. Petersburg, FL, Sioux Falls, SD, Pratt, KS, Chakulia, India, China A-1.

Ferrell J. Majors

Was strafed by Jap Zero and forced to land at Chittagong. POW in Rangoon, Burma from Dec. 14, 1944 to Apr. 29, 1945. Flew on the C-109 deferred service. Was a Radio Operator on Bob Shenk's crew.

Received the usual awards and was discharged as M/Sergeant. in October 1945.

My wife, Marion, passed away Jan. 1, 1987. We have two children and one grandchild. President of Ferrell and Co. Inc., a wholesale supply business.

E.R. MANFRIN, Maj., USAF Ret. Born Sept. 6, 1916. Graduate Boys High Brooklyn, 1934. Two years Coast Artillery NYNG; Enlisted US Army 1936. Honolulu 1936-39; 40th Ord. NJ and MD to 1942; 99th Inf. Div.,

1943; AAFTC Yale University to the 40th Bomb Gp. Pratt, KS as S-2, 1943; CBI-Tinian 1944-45; Air Defense Command, NY 1945-50; Armed Forces Occupation-Germany 1950-53; Ent AF Base, Colorado 1953-57. Retired Major USAF May 1957.

E.R. Manfrin

Recipient Air Medal, 345 Combat Hours; Air Force Commendation Medal; Presidential Unit Citation w/two Oak Leaf Clusters; New York State Conspicuous Service Cross and seven others.

Graduated: Ordnance Field Service School; Army NCO Course; Intelligence School, Harrisburg; Army Language School (Spanish)-Monterey; Command and Staff School, Montgomery; Survival School, Stead AFB; Strategic Intelligence School, DC.

Retired May 1957 USAF.

Civilian: US Forest Service, US Postal Service. Associate Degree Broadcasting (1978). Presently freelance writer/photographer.

ROBERT S. MARTIN, (Bob), 40th Bomb Gp., 25th Sdn. I was home on a delay enroute in August 1945 when the war ended and was discharged out of Santa Ana, CA. I returned to my trade as a pipefitter after the war. Went into business with a partner as Martin-Willardson Company in 1963.

Robert S. Martin

In 1972 I formed my own company, Martin Mechanical, doing piping for air conditioning systems in large commercial and industrial buildings throughout the Southern California area. I'm currently attempting to semi-retire, turning the business over to my two sons. I enjoy golf and bi-annual trips to Hawaii. My wife, Eileen, and I celebrated our 46th Anniversary this year.

IRA V. MATTHEWS, born Aug. 30, 1919, Townley, AL. Raised on farm near Fayette, AL. Educated in Fayette public schools, AAC Flying School and Air University. Graduated Pilot and 2nd Lieutenant, Maxwell Field, AL September 1941. Joined 40th Bomb Gp., October 1941, Borinquen Field, Puerto Rico. Flew B-18, LB-30, B-24 and B-29 aircraft from Curacao, Aruba, France Field, David, Panama, Galapagos Island, Pratt, KS, Chakulia, India and Hsing-Ching, China. Completed combat tour and returned to ZI March 1945.

Ira V. Matthews

Remained in USAF, served in SAC 1946 to 1961, with two tours in Korean War, last SAC assignment, B-52 Wing Cmdr. Served in MAAG, Laos, Indo-China 1961-1962. Last USAF assignment, Dir. of Maint.-Engineering, MOAMA, Brookley AFB, AL. Awards: Legion of Merit, DFC, Air Medal and Bronze Star. Retired March 1967. Married former Wynelle Mitchell of Fayette, AL March 1945. Has two daughters, Margaret and Elizabeth and five grandchildren.

2nd Career from 1968 to 1982, Assistant to the President, Mobile College, Mobile, AL. Retired December 1982

WALTER L. MAURER, born in Oakland, CA, Nov. 17, 1917. Drafted into Army Air Corp Feb. 11, 1942, and discharged in October 1945.

Walter L. Maurer

After Boot Camp in Biloxi, MS sent to Central Fire Control School in Denver, CO. After training in Pratt, KS sent to Chakulia, India and then to Tinian Island. Was Armament Crew Chief for the "Himalaya Hussy", Capt. Lyons and "Last Resort", Maj. Roberts.

After separation from service I went to work for the Pacific Telephone and retired in 1980. Father of two children. The boy was four months old when I left for the service and the girl was born when I returned.

44th Bomb Sdn.

KENNETH A. MAUSOLF, born in Alpena, MI, May 1, 1924 and I graduated from Alpena High School in January 1943. I entered the military in January of 1943. After basic training in Clearwater, FL I attended radio school at Sioux Fall, SD, then to Madison, WI. After training there I went to Boca Raton, FL, as a radar operator and mechanic.

Kenneth A. Mausolf

Went overseas as a replacement to Chakulia, India, 40th Bomb Gp., 44th Bomb Sdn.

After separation from the service, December 1945, I went to work as City Firefighter for the City of Alpena and upon retirement in July, 1986, I am working my own Heating and Air Conditioning business.

I am married and have one son and two stepsons.

TELEMACHUS MAVROFRIDES, "MARK" "MURPH", "MURPH" spent most of his life in Haverhill, MA, as a farmer and machinist before entering the Army Air Corps Mar. 11, 1941. Trained at Camp Edwards, Cape Cod, before joining the 45th Bomb Sdn. at Jefferson Barracks, MO, and at Ft. Myers, FL, and Tucson, AZ. In California, trained in small arms with Corporal—later General—James Stewart.

At Victorville, CA, had a young man of 18 assigned to train under him and helped him to get into pilot training. He is now General "Chuck" Yeager.

Telemachus Mavrofrides

Went from Pratt, KS, through Newfoundland and Egypt to India, in the China-Burma-India Theater, and flew the Hump about three times a week with supplies for China bases. Went to Tinian with the group for the rest of the war. His plane was "Black Magic."

Discharged as a Master Sergeant, 45th

Bomb Sdn., 58th Wing, after 18 months overseas as crew chief and flight engineer. Principal awards were the Air Medal and Asiatic-Pacific Ribbon with six Battle Stars.

Married to the former Elvira "Vi" Simmons, living at 480 Broadway, Somerville, MA, 02145, with summers at Westport, MA, PO Box 441, North Westport, MA, 02790.

Started a construction business in 1930 and still in it, with a business mail address at PO Box 144, Bradford, MA, 01830.

Greatest adventure in life was service with the B29s, traveling around the world with "a great group of guys," and meeting Barney Gallagher, Bobby Elms, Red Simonds and Ralph Daggett, all from home, all in B29 outfits, for a great party (with a Jeep and a jug) riding around Tinian on VJ Day.

JAMES McAULEY JR., born Apr. 7, 1926 in Philadelphia, PA. Graduated from high school January 1944 and entered the Army Air Corps in April 1944. Basic training Keesler Field, MS.

James McAuley Jr.

Graduated Aerial Gunner's School Buckingham Air Field, FL as a Tail Gunner. Graduated first B-29 combat crews to train at Davis Montham Field, Tucson, AZ. On May 1, 1945 assigned to 40th Bomb Gp., 44th Sdn. in Tinian. Flew fourteen combat, one weather, two photo, two supper dumbo missions. We called in help for a fighter pilot who had bailed out over the ocean, picked up by sub. We had one forced landing at Iwo Jima, flew with Capt. W. Shockley's crew.

Biggest thrill was dropping supplies to POW's in Japan after end of War. Discharged Jan. 1, 1946.

Married Rita Brown June 14, 1947. We have two children and six grandchildren. Worked 36 years for U.S. Postal Service, retiring January 1983.

JOHN D. McCRORY, born Jan. 24, 1922, at Florence, AL. Attended college two years before joining Army Air Force in 1942. Was discharged in 1945.

Basic training at Miami Beach and A.C. Mechanic School in Amarillo, TX, A.C. Electrical school at Chanute Field, IL. Attached to B-24's at Boise, ID and joined 40th Gp. in Pratt, KS.

Rank of S/Sergeant and followed 40th Gp. in Chakulia, India. A-1 in China and Tinian.

After service, used G.I. Bill to finish college with AB Degree, with cognate major in math and science at University of North Alabama. Employed as purchasing agent for an aluminum company for 15 years, then as project manager and estimator for a construction company, from which I retired in 1986.

John D. McCrory

Married and have five children, all of whom graduated from college. In addition, I now have a son-in-law and two grandchildren.

ANDREW F. McGLAUN JR., born Sept. 7, 1921 in Dawson, TX. Graduated Tahoka High School 1939. Enlisted Air Corp. January 1941. Gunnery and Bombsight Specialist at Lowry Field. Joined 25th Sdn.-40th Bomb Gp. at Pratt, KS. Overseas to Chakulia, India, China and Tinian, Marianas. Squadron Gunnery Officer-25th Bomb Sdn. and Group Gunner Officer for the 40th Bomb Gp. Discharged January 1946.

Andrew F. McGlaun Jr.

Became State and County Tax Assessor-Collector, Tahoka, Lynn Co., TX. Entered Office Supply Business in 1950, and now owns and operates: Frank McGlaun Office Supply, Business Copy Products, and Warehouse Furniture Company in Lubbock, TX.

Married Melvena Baker in December 1942. Father of two daughters and have two grandchildren.

FRANK W. McKINNEY, born in El Paso, TX Dec. 14, 1920. Joined Army Air Corps as Aviation Cadet in May, 1942 at Ft. Bliss, TX. After Bombardier and Navigation schools was assigned to 40th Bomb Gp. at Pratt, KS October 1943. Was with first group to Chakulia, India and flew missions as Bombardier and Navigator. In March, 1945 was assigned to Muroc AAF, CA as Instructor until separated from active duty at Ft. Bliss, TX in December 1945.

Continued my education, was licensed as Public Accountant in Texas, January 1950. Operated accounting practice in El Paso since 1947. Now semi-retired, but maintain an office to keep busy.

Frank W. McKinney

Awards include DFC with OLC. Air Medal with OLC, AP Ribbon with six Battle Stars, AF Commendation Medal.

Retired Jan. 1, 1974 as Colonel USAFR, commanding Security Police Department. Married former Mary Jane Marion of Pennsylvania July 1, 1945. We have six daughters and one son.

DANIEL J. McNEW, born Aug. 9, 1914 in Glade Spring, VA, South Western part of Virginia. Father was an Engineer for the N&W Railroad.

Daniel J. McNew

Joined the U.S. Army March 1934 and was assigned to the 2nd Coast Artillery at Ft. Monroe, VA. After serving five and half years in the Army I transferred to the U.S. Air Corp, 2nd Bomb Gp.; Langley Field, VA.

Attended A&E school at Chanute Field in 1940-41. Joined my organization in Borinquen Field, Puerto Rico in May 1941. Served as crew chief and flight chief, part-time as flight engineer.

When the 40th Bomb Gp. was formed I was assigned to that Group. My first unit of assignment was to HQ. & HQ. Sdn. This Sdn. was after we transferred to Panama, deactivated and I was transferred to the 45th Bomb Sdn. I remained in this Unit until the war was over. I was assigned as Crew Chief and Flight Engineer on the first B-29 but was taken off flying status due to color blindness. Was also turned down for pilots training in 1942 for color blindness. Remained the position of crew chief until the end of WWII.

Transferred to Germany after the war to the 5th AACS as line chief and acting Engineering Officer. Attended OCS in 1947 at Seikenheim, Germany and declined a commission after graduation.

Retired from the Service November 1954 and accepted a position with Army Aviation Research and Development, Ft. Eustis, VA. Held the following positions with the Army during my Civil Service employment: Chief, Engineering Div. Research and Development. Chief of Test, TATSA, Ft. Ruckker, AL-Depot Technical Advisor for the first Army Aviation Depot, Mannheim, Germany - Data Analyst and Aviation Advisor, Logistics Data center, Lexington, KY - Aircraft Technical Representative and Logistics coordinator for Army Aviation Command, St. Louis, MO.

Retired November 1969 from Civil Service. Moved to Florida in early 1970. Started my own business as realty investment. Sold my business in 1978 and now have just begin to work. This work consists of 90% looking for something to do and 10% doing it.

My hobby is traveling and meeting old friends.

JOSEPH W. McWILLIAMS, Col., born Dec. 20, 1919 - Hall Summit, LA. Attended Northwestern State University, LA, where he met his future wife, Helen McKinney McWilliams. They were married Sept. 2, 1942. "Mac" as he was fondly called, was commissioned Second Lieutenant Pilot, Maxwell Field, A/A. Class 41C. "Mac" loved to fly, he was a pilots-pilots, always concerned about the safety of his crew and fellow airmen.

Joseph W. McWilliams

"Mac" served his country bravely in three conflicts. WWII (Caribbean-CBI), Korea and Vietnam. His heroics over Japan saved many lives and a mission from disaster.

Besides the usual campaign medals "Mac" was the recipient of the Distinguished Flying Cross and the Air Medal with four Oak Leaf Clusters. "Mac" received regular commission in the Air Force after WWII and served with the Strategic Air Command until his retirement in 1963.

Besides his love for his country and flying, "Mac" loved his family more. Helen his lovely wife, gave him four beautiful children. They are: M. Ann McWilliams, Teacher-Bio-BS, Masters, E. Claire McWilliams-Teacher-Special Ed.-BS, Robert L. McWilliams-BS-Science, Dr. Joseph G. McWilliams, Math Professor-MD, BS, Masters, PhD. Two grandchildren: Vivian C. McWilliams, Elizabeth A. McWilliams.

After his retirement in 1963, "Mac" was employed with NASA-Lockheed Aircraft until 1971. Then he tried his hand in retail business until 1977 when illness forced him to retire for good.

Although "Mac" suffered much pain the last five years of his life, he never lost his quick wit, his broad smile, nor his love and concern for his family and fellow man. He gave it all....He'll be missed!

WENDELL MEADOR, enlisted Nov. 21, 1940. Basic at Barksdale and Jefferson Barracks, Radio School Scott Field. Arrived Puerto Rico, 44th Sdn., August 1941. Thence to Guatemala, Pratt and Chakulia. Completed missions with Swancutt and Andy's crew. Returned A/P to Albuquerque.

Wendell Meador

Fought in the famous Battle of Borinquen (slept soundly). Member of the "Was On The Rock Bunch" and won the war with the 25th Sdn. in China.

Continued with Air Force, served in Germany, Norway, Japan, Korea, Spain, Alaska and Stateside. Retired CM/Sergeant June 1967.

Employed by Boeing in the Seattle area as an Electrical Production Planner. Worked on 707, 737, 747, and AWACs E3A A/P June 1967 to August 1983.

WALTER H. MESSERSMITH, born in Lafollette, WI on Dec. 11, 1919. Moved to Port Angeles, WA in 1925.

Walter H. Messersmith

Entered Army Air Corps at Tacoma, WA on May 1, 1942. Following basic training at Sheppard Field and radio school at Scott Field, I joined the 44th Sdn. at Guatemala in November 1942.

Returned to Pratt in June 1943 and was assigned to the 25th Sdn. as radio operator on Maj. Daniel T. Rogers crew.

Left Pratt in B-29 number 288 and arrived in Chakulia Apr. 12, 1944. No. 288 was replaced with No. 351 there. We flew first mission over Bangkok and several flights over the Hump to Hsinching. Crew was returned to the States Aug. 9, 1944 and I was stationed at Grand Island, NB as instructor in Last Ditch Training School.

Was discharged Oct. 6, 1945 at Portland, OR. Worked with an irrigation company here in Wenatchee for 33 years and retired on Oct. 1, 1985.

RICHARD A. MONTGOMERY, born Sept. 19, 1917 in Pittsburgh, PA. Enlisted in the Army Air Corps, Feb. 16, 1940. Sent to Langley Field, VA for recruit training. Trained as Radio Operator at Chanute Field and Scott Field, IL. Stationed at Borinquen Field, Puerto Rico with 25th Bomb Gp. until formation of the 40th Gp. in 1941. Remained with 40th through various moves; (Borinquen to Guatemala City; to Pratt, KS; to Chakulia, India.) Assigned to Capt. Cornelius C. Meyer's crew as Radio Operator at Pratt. Shot down with rest of crew over Rangoon, Burma Dec. 14, 1944. Captured by Japanese and held as POWs until May, 1945.

Richard A. Montgomery

Married Margaret Bruder in July, 1945, had one son, Richard Jr., and three daughters, Janice, Luanne, and Jeanne. Discharged in January 1946. Re-enlisted in November 1946 and remained in the Air Force until retirement in June 1972. Currently operating a one-man clock repair shop in Riverside, CA.

RICHARD H. MOORE JR., born Ft. Worth, TX. Graduated public school there in 1940. Attended N.T.A.C. (now University of Texas, at Arlington). Inducted U.S. Army, Camp Wolters 1943. Basic training Shepherd Field. Gunnery school Buckley Field and Lowry at Denver. Served Herrington, KS, Clovis, NM, Salina, KS. Assigned Lt. Herbert Wright's B-29 crew and flew to Chakulia, India and 25th Sdn. Flew combat missions from there and China. Transferred to Tinian flying with Capt. Massey's crew and Wright, completing 30 missions.

Richard H. Moore Jr.

Received usual medals and Air Medal with three clusters and D.F.C. After discharge in 1946 as Staff Sergeant received LLB from University of Texas and direct commission as 1st Lieutenant USAF JAG Dept. and later retired as Captain (USAF res.) Served as Asst. District Attorney, Texas, Civilian Attorney Corp of Engineers, U.S. Army, Galveston. Since 1954 in private practice of law with interests in ranching, oil and other investments.

BERTRAM H. MORROW, "BERT" born Mar. 16, 1921 in Easton, PA. Graduated from High School in 1938. Entered LeHigh University 1939. Enlisted in Air Force June 1942. Graduated from Flying School 43-H. Was flying instructor, Courtland Army Air Force Base 1943-1944.

Bertram H. Morrow

Entered B-29 program 1944. Transition Maxwell Field; OTU Tucson, AZ. Came with 40th as a replacement crew in spring of 1945. Only claim to fame—flew on mission to Osaka July 1945 (Presidential Unit Citation to 40th). Had best crew in the 20th Air Force. Didn't we all? Reverted to Reserve status January 1946.

Married, had four children with first wife who passed away three years ago. Worked 37 years with Equifax Services as General Manager of North Jersey area. Now retired and living in retirement colony.

WILLIAM ROBERT NEIL, born June 7, 1923 in California, PA. Graduated from High School in 1942, drafted into the Army Corp Feb. 27, 1943. Went to Miami Beach for Basic Training. Sheppard Field for A.M., Chanute for Hydraulic Spec. School. Joined the 44th at Pratt, KS. Went to Chakulia, India and Tinian. Worked on the line and changed engines. Was discharged from Ft. Knox, Nov. 22, 1945.

William Robert Neil

Worked at Colonial Rubber Company in Ravenna, OH for 27 years. Moved to Texas in 1980, worked at Cypress Welding Equipment Company in Houston until early retirement in 1986. Now live in Spring, TX with my wife Betty.

BILLY MACK NELSON, born in Paris, TX Jan. 6, 1920. Enlisted in Army Air Corp Oct. 5, 1939 and discharged Aug. 21, 1945. With 40th Bomb Gp. from inception in Puerto Rico until discharge. Attended Air Force Tech School at Chanute Field, Rantoul, IL. Served two and half years as Flight Engineer and three years as Crew Chief.

Billy Mack Nelson

Stationed at Borinquen Field in Puerto Rico, Panama; and after helping to modify first B-29's at Pratt, KS was sent to Chakulia, India and Tinian Island.

Married Neta Nelson in November 1946, had one daughter and two granddaughters. Retired from Shell Chemical Company, Deer Park, TX in March 1982 after 33 years. Joined 40th Bomb Gp. Association at Arlington reunion 1981. Deceased June 16, 1987.

ELLIS ALBERT NEWMAN, born Mar. 5, 1917 at Ransom, PA. Graduated from Wyalusing High School, Pennsylvania June 1935. Enlisted in the U.S. Army; 18th Inf. Ft. Hamilton, NY. January 1936. Reenlisted-5th Bomb Sdn. Mitchell Field, NY January 1939. Transferred to 19th Bomb Wing, Albrook Field, CZ, March 1940. Joined 29th Bomb Sdn. Maint. Det. Albrook Field, CZ, August 1942. Transferred to 25th Bomb Sdn., Salinas, Equador, November 1942. Assigned to 770th Bomb Sdn., 462nd Bomb Gp., Walker Field, KA, June 1943. Moved with 462nd Bomb Gp. to Paradobi, India, April 1944. Moved with 462nd Bomb Gp. to Tinian, April 1945.

September 1943 returned to USA and continued service in the Air Force at Spokane, WA; Great Falls, MT; Fasberg, Ger.; Portland, OR; Minneapolis, MN.; Chanute Field, IL; and Ankara, Turkey. Retired as C.W.O. W-2 in September 1957.

Graduated from California State University at Long Beach and taught school in Chino, CA until retirement in 1973. Presently living in Sauk Rapids, MN.

WILLIAM C. NIEHAUS, "Bill", born Feb. 6, 1921 in Trenton, NJ. Bill entered the Army Air Corps in July 1942 and was discharged in October 1945. As a Radio Operator-Mechanic-Gunner. He flew 15 combat missions in B-24s based in the Aleutians. As a radar observer-mechanic-bombardier, Staff Sgt. Niehaus flew 23 combat missions in the B-29 while based in India and Tinian Island. During this time he was a member of the 20th Air Force Bomber Command, 40th Bomb Gp., 44th Bombardment Sdn.

He participated in the air offensive over Japan, Aleutian Islands, China, Central Burma, India, Burma, Western Pacific, and the Palembang Sumatra Campaigns. He was a charter member of the "I Bombed Japan Club," and is credited with downing three zeroes. He received the following decorations: Distinguished Flying Cross, American Theater Medal, Good Conduct Medal, Asiatic Pacific Service Medal with two Bronze Stars and one Silver Star, Air Medal with three Bronze Oak Leaf Clusters, and the Distinguished Unit Badge.

Following his discharge, Bill married the late Ruth A. Williams of Pennington, NJ. He was employed by New Jersey Bell Telephone Company as a Right Of Way Agent, retiring after 37 years of service. Bill passed away suddenly on Apr. 17, 1987. He is survived by two daughters, three grandchildren, and one sister.

HOWARD E. NORAIN, born Nov. 22, 1923 at Chicago, IL. Received draft greetings from Uncle Sam in the Autumn of 1942 and inducted into Service February 1943, sent to Keesler Field, MS for basic training. Attended Air Force Mechanics School at Amarillo, AFB, TX, Electrical School at Chanute Field, IL and B-29 School at Seattle, WA.

Howard E. Norain

Arrived at Clovis, NM AFB early 1944 and assigned "Line" duty on B-29 aircraft and later entered combat crew training. Upon completion of training period his crew, under the command of John Meinha, was assigned a B-29 out of Kearney, NB. Arrived in Chakulia February 1945. Two missions were flown from Chakulia. Crew arrived at Tinian Island June 1945 aboard the U.S.S. General Robert Calnan after a 35 day trip from Calcutta. Fourteen combat missions were flown from Tinian including the "VJ" flight on Sept. 2, 1945.

Awards include Victory Medal, American Theatre Ribbon, Asiatic-Pacific Ribbon with three Bronze Stars and Air Medal with Oak Leaf Cluster. He was separated from service Dec. 15, 1945.

Married, he is now retired, and makes his home in Chicago.

JOHN O. NORDHAGEN, 45th Bomb Sdn., 40th Bomb Gp., born Feb. 8, 1918, Choteau, MT. Enl. Air Corp. January 1941 and Assg'd 17th Bomb Gp. McChord Field, WA (1st B-25's and source of many "Doolittle's Raider's") Graduated Acft. Mech, Chanute Field, August 1941. Graduated Pilot flight training, Stockton, CA, July 1943. Comp. B-17 trans. Hobbs, NM and assigned 40th Bomb Gp. at Pratt, KS, October 1943.

John O. Nordhagen

Assigned to crew with Capt. Robert P. Haley, and we flew the first Bell built B-29 (#26222-Dueces Wild to India) in 12 days with an unscheduled stop at Presque Isle, ME. Crew was later taken over by Capt. Carter McGregor, and we flew a number of missions together, with a stint in C-109's for some of us. Assigned/w C.A. Woolsey and lead crew early 1945. Returned to ZI late July 1945.

Recalled AD June 1951 and flew C-54 on Alcan Run from Gt. Falls, MT. Flew SB-29, 1952, at Nagoya, Japan w/3rd (later 37th) Air Rescue Sdn. Accum. 850 combat flying hrs., DFC w/2OLC, AM w/6OLC, DUC (2) Asia/Pacific and Korean Theater, Sr. Pilot.

Virginia and I have a son with a daughter and son; and a daughter with two sons.

Spent 30 years in Aerial Application and Gen'l Aviation Operations, and continue to do some maint., sales, etc. Virginia is about ready to retire after 30 years in Federal employment, currently FmHA.

JAMES E. NUNNALLY, born Apr. 20, 1924 in Jacksonville, TX where he attended public schools and junior college, entered the service in February 1943 and was discharged with rank of Sergeant in November 1945.

James E. Nunnally

After basic training at Sheppard Field, radio-operator-mechanics training at Scott Field and Truax Field, he was assigned to the 58th Bomb Wing at Pratt, KS in January 1944 and served with the 40th Bomb Gp. at Chakulia, the 40th forward detachment at Hsinching and at Tinian.

After WWII he received an MA degree in physics at the University of Texas at Austin where he was also employed by the Military Physics Research Laboratory. Subsequent employments included Convair (B-58 project), Texas A&I College and the University of Denver before finally becoming a medical physicist at M.D. Anderson Hospital, marrying Helen Terrell of Tyler, TX and being employed by South western Medical School and the VA Medical Center at Dallas.

JAMES J. O'KEEFE, entered the Army Air Corps in November, 1942. Went through Bombardier School in the spring of 1943 and through Navigation School in the summer of 1943. Joined the 40th at Pratt in October, 1943.

James J. O'Keefe

Flew missions on the crews of Murr Skousen, George Weschler, Rod Wriston, and Leland Jones.

Discharged in September 1945. Attended the University of California and the University of British Columbia. In business for several years, then went into junior college teaching.

Married Charlotte in 1949. Two children: a daughter, Laura, and a son, James Aldrich O'Keefe.

Herb Aldrich located me for the Reunion Committee. The reunions I have attended have been among the most moving experiences of my life.

Have contributed stories about the men of the 40th to several collections of Air Force stories. In my stories I have tried to show the great respect and affection which I felt for those men.

CHARLES L. ORLUSKY, born in Denver, CO on May 19, 1925. Drafted into Combat Engineers in September 1943. Transferred to Air Corps December 1943. Discharged December 1945.

Sent to Chakulia, India, Chen-tu, China, and then Tinian Island.

Cartoon's - Crate's N' Crappers accounted for most of my time then and now.

The Hump Happy series, "Duce's Wild," "The Outlaw," and "Bonnie Lee," along with

Charles L. Orlusky

the 45th Squadron's Patch. Remember Kagi-Suti the Fire God?

After separation from active service, worked at home construction, commercial art, designed and built parade floats. Design and build wood mosaic furniture, work as portrait artist in winter. Summer is for fishing.

As for the third "C" we're' building them indoors now.

FLOYD F. PARK, born Dec. 17, 1916 at Coeur d'Alene, ID. He attended high school in Illinois and Indiana and two years college in Michigan. He enlisted in the 23rd Inf. Ft. Sam Houston, TX in 1939 and transferred to the Army Air Corps the same year. He received technical training at Chanute Field and assigned to the 25th Bombardment Gp., which found its way to "tent city" Puerto Rico and from which the 40th Bomb Gp. was activated. He remained in the 40th Bomb Gp. throughout its history with assignment as Crew Chief.

He retired in the grade of CWO, W-4 with 27 years service. After retirement he worked at General Dynamics, Ft. Worth, TX as Technical Writer. He accepted early retirement from G.D. after five years and for the past 15 years has worked at St. Joseph hospital in the Purchasing Dept. At age 70 he has received the honor at the hospital as "Employee of the Quarter" and has one chance in four of receiving the "Employee of the Year" award.

Floyd F. Park

His military awards include the Air Force Commendation Medal, Bronze Star Medal with cluster, Air Medal and all campaign medals and Presidential Unit Citation awarded to the 40th Bomb Gp.

RICHARD P. PATCHES, "DICK", born Oct. 26, 1924 at Lebanon, PA. Graduated

Richard P. Patches

High School June 1942. Enlisted in Army Air Corps Oct. 26, 1942.

Attended Radio and Radar Tech Schools; assigned to 25th B.S., 40th B.G. Pratt, KS November 1943. Assigned as Radar Operator on "Woody" Swancutt's crew; also flew on "Bob" Gaughan's Crew. Completed 15 Combat Missions and 24 Hump Trips. Awarded DFC, Air Medal with OLC, along with usual Campaign Medals and Battle Stars. Was on first crews returned to States from India.

Married childhood sweetheart, Kitty Lou Stohler, June 9, 1945. Have two daughters and a son.

Remained in Air Force with tours of duty in Canada, Okinawa, Japan, Germany and various Stateside assignments. Retired at Hill Field, UT, January 1965 as Senior Master Sergeant after 22 years service.

After retirement worked in Real Estate and Mutual Fund and Insurance sales - was Division Sales Manager for ITT Hamilton in Kansas City. Transferred to Tempe, AZ and spent last eight years as Pneumatics System Technician at local hospital. Retired completely January 1987.

JOSEPH EDWARD PHALON, born Aug. 15, 1918 in La Crosse, WI, attended St. Mary's Grade School, Acquinas High School and graduated from Marquette University. Enlisted in the Army Air Corps on Aug. 26, 1942 and discharged with a 50% medical disability on June 16, 1947.

Joseph Edward Phalon

He attended Cadet Training School at Yale University in 1942, while Ronald Reagan was there as an Announcer and Glen Miller was the Band Leader.

He attended the Weather Observer Course at Chanute Field, IL, AATTC at Yale University, Flight Engineers School at Salina, KS, Boeing B-29 School, Seattle, WA.

He flew over the "Hump" on many occasions while stationed in India. Also flew many missions from Tinian and other South Pacific air strips.

He was also featured in an article in Readers Digest and Life Magazine on "Ten Men on a Raft" in which he wore a life saving vest made by the wife of another officer.

Was a part of the "Fire Bombing Raids" in Japan. He was awarded three Purple Hearts and many other military awards.

During the war, because of his Engineering Degree from Marquette University (Milwaukee, WI) he served in the capacity of Flight Engineer for B-29s.

He attained the rank of Major prior to his forced retirement due to injuries sustained during the war. He was discharged June 1947 at the Rank of Captain.

Battles and Campaign: India-Burma-China Offensive, China Defensive, Air Offensive Japan, Central Burma, Bombing of Palembang, Simetra. Decorations and Citations: Asiatic-Pacific Campaign Ribbon with Silver Service Star and Bronze Service Star, WWII Victory Medal, Purple Heart, American Theatre Ribbon, Air Medal with two Oak Leaf Clusters and DFC.

After the war he married Ann M. Erickson, his childhood sweetheart. They had two children, John Patrick and Ann Marie. He also had one grandchild, Ann Catherine McLaughlin.

Since leaving the Army Air Corps he was involved in a number of business ventures, including starting several firms. He passed away as a result of an accident Apr. 3, 1985 and is buried in his family plot in La Crosse, WI.

OTTO PIPEK, enlisted at Mitchell Field, Long Island, NY in October 1939 and discharged on July 4, 1945 from Chanute Field. Was made a Flight Officer at Pratt, KS in December 1943. Was with the group at Puerto Rico, Panama, Galapagos, Pratt where some of us were transferred out to Ardmore, OK. Then to Boca Raton, FL. Finally to Langley Field, VA where I was sent to Chanute Hospital to be discharged for a medical.

Otto Pipek

I was the bombardier on the B-18 that ditched from France Field, Panama.

I received the Air Medal at Panama, and Service Ribbons. After discharged went to work for Postal Department in Flushing, NY, from which I retired and moved to Florida.

PAUL M. PISARCIK, born Dec. 23, 1919 at Bitumen, PA. At age 7 moved to Cleveland,

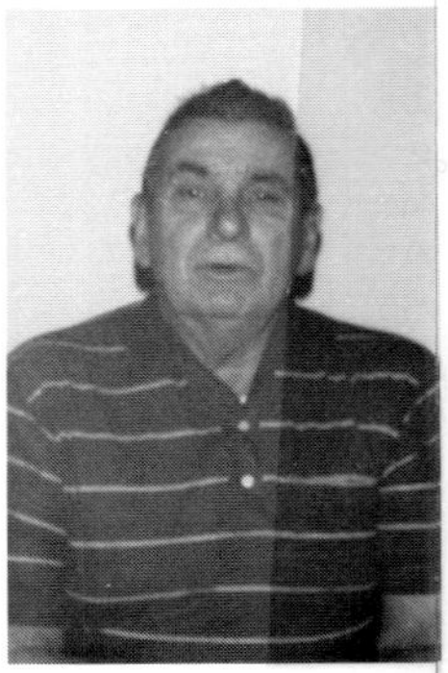

Paul M. Pisarcik

OH, which I consider my hometown. Attended grade and high school in Cleveland.

Drafted into the Army February 1942. Basic training at Shepherd Field, TX and a transit camp in Puerto Rico. Assigned to the 44th Bomb Sdn., 40th Bomb Gp., at Borinquen Field, Puerto Rico. Assigned to the Squadron Supply Section. Felt pride in joining this elite group, as all its members were said to be all volunteers, and I became one of its first draftees.

Remained with the Group throughout its travels from Puerto Rico, Panama, Guatemala, Pratt, KS, Chakulia, India and Tinian Island.

At Pratt I was transferred to the 25th Bomb Sdn. as Squadron Supply Sergeant, a post which I held for the duration.

Discharged October 1945. Went home to Cleveland, where I still reside, married and ran Three Supply Warehouses successfully until retirement in April, 1985.

ANGELO PISCIOTTA, born in St. Louis, MO, Mar. 22, 1921. Worked for Curtis Wright for three years before being drafted into the Army Air Corp, May 7, 1943, and discharged October, 1945.

Took basic training in Lincoln, NB. After later training in Pratt, KS, I was sent to Chakulia, India and then to Tinian Island. I was a welder on B-29's.

Angelo Pisciotta

After separation from the service, I went t work for St. Louis Car Co. Then worked fo Dee's Auto Repair for 25 years. Later worke for Allen Foods before retiring in 1984.

Married Millie Serra and father of two chil dren and three grandchildren. Millie wa pregnant when I went overseas, so I did no see my son until he was 16 months old. W had a daughter after I got home.

40th Bomb Gp. and 45th Bomb Sdn.

ENRICO E. PISTERZI, "Hank", born July 13, 1915 in Sunnyside, UT. Attended lower grades in Arvada area. Graduated Regis High School 1934, Denver, CO. Enlisted U.S. Army Air Corps Jan. 10, 1942. Discharged Aug. 25, 1945, Ft. McArthur, CA.

Enrico E. Pisterzi

Attended Airplane Engine and Mechanics School, Love Field, Dallas, TX. Joined 40th Bomb Gp. at France Field. Remained with 40th through Panama, David, Galapagos Islands, Pratt, KS, Chakulia, India. Unable to continue tour of duty with 40th due to POW status after Rangoon Fiasco. Served as Line Mechanic until Galapagos Islands. Then served as Flight Engineer until B-29 program. Duty on B-29s from Kansas to Rangoon was as Tail Gunner.

"Yard Bird" lowest Rank, T/Sergeant highest rank. Awards other than Good Conduct, Battle Ribbons, etc., were Air Medal with one Oak Leaf Cluster, Distinguished Unit Citation, Aerial Gunners Badge, Asiatic-Pacific Campaign Medal with four Battle Stars and American Campaign Medal.

Completed eight Hump trips, one of which ended in crash landing in Sichang, China in June 1945. Was on third combat mission at time of Rangoon Fiasco.

After separation from Air Force was employed by Mountain Bell Telephone Company. September 1945 date of hire; remained for 29 1/2 years. Retired Feb. 20, 1975.

Proud to have been a "small" part of the 40th Bomb Gp. Super People.

STANLEY POPLASKI, "Pop" USAF M/Sgt. (Retired) joined the 40th Bomb Gp., 45th Bomb Sdn., in January 1944, Pratt, KS. He was assigned to Capt. Bob Shanks crew as tail gunner. Other members were Etherington, Fletcher, Benedict, Majors, Cochran, Oglesby, Basche, Lentz and Sommers.

Stanley Poplaski

A native of New Britain, CT, now residing in Green Bay, WI, Poplaski enlisted in the Air Force in 1940 when he was 22 years old. He was sent to Hickman Field, HA where he graduated from A and E School in October 1941.

Poplaski dodged the enemy at Pearl Harbor and encountered the enemy in the Battle of Midway and Guadacanal, Solomon Islands. Back in the States in 1943 he went to Biggs Field, TX and requested B-29 School at Boeing Aircraft, Seattle.

Upon graduation he was sent to Pratt, KS, and he and the Shanks crew went by boat from Newport News, VA to Casablanca. Flown by military aircraft to Chakulia, India, the crew flew B-29 missions over the Hump hauling fuel to China and took part in the first bombing mission over the Japanese mainland.

Poplaski was wounded during a fighter attack over Bangkok, Thailand, Hank Pisterzi replaced Poplaski on a mission to Rangoon, Burma when the Shanks crew had to bail out of a crippled aircraft and all were taken prisoner by the Japanese.

Without a crew Poplaski joined a pool of standby personnel for other crews. In 1945 he left India by boat for Tinian Island via Australia and New Guinea. Poplaski flew his last mission over Kobe, Japan and having accumulated enough points for discharge he shipped back to the States and attended Tri-State College, Angola, IN for two years.

Poplaski re-enlisted in the Air Force to become a career man in September 1948, and went by boat to Germany where he participated in the Berlin Airlift. Instructor Training School at Chanute Air Force Base, IL was his next challenge in 1949. He was stationed at Lowry Air Force Base, CO and at Tachikawa, Japan in 1953 where he maintained C-124 aircraft.

In 1963 he went to Tripoli, Libya, N. Africa with Air Sea Rescue where they covered the Mediterranean and Middle East areas. Poplaski retired after 24 years service in 1966 after serving at McChord AF Base, Washington, as a dock chief on C-124 aircraft. He married WAF S/Sgt. Lenore "Kelly" Selissen and they parented four children. Presently he is maintaining golf course equipment at Royal Scott Country Club.

Major Awards include: Silver Star with Oak Leaf Cluster, Air Medal with two Oak Leaf Clusters, Asiatic Pacific Theatre, seven Battle Stars, Purple Heart with two Oak Leaf Clusters.

J. IVAN POTTS, JR., Received commission at University of Kentucky in 1942. First assignment was Sdn. Adjutant, 152nd Observations Sdn., 26th Observation Gp. Ft. Devens Army Field, Massachusetts.

Activated 11th Airdrome Sdn. at Hunter AAF, Savannah, GA. Applied for pilot training and received wings in Class 43K. Attended Advanced Twin Engine Instructors School, Randolph Field, TX. Became twin engine instructor at Moody AAF, Georgia in 1944. Completed B-17 Instructors School, Lockbourne AAF, OH. Volunteered for B-29 program and assigned to 25th Bomb Sdn., 40th Bomb Gp. (VH), Chakulia, India in 1944.

Completed eight Hump trips and 34 com-

J. Ivan Potts, Jr

bat missions, CBI and Tinian. Awarded DFC with OLC, Air Medal with three OLC's, Army Commendation Medal, PUC with OLC, Asiatic Pacific Campaign Medal with four Battle Stars, American Campaign Medal with one Battle Star.

Personal Citation From Gen. H.H. Arnold. On Sept. 18-19, 1945 was crew member on Gen. LeMays crew which set four Air Force records. Flight was from Hokkaido, Japan to Washington, DC in 27 hours, 30 minutes.

Separated from active duty as Captain. Colonel TN-ANG, retired. Married Katherine Dale of Nashville, TN in 1949. Have one son. Was Ford-Mercury dealer, Shelbyville, TN 1955-1980. Presently Assistant Director, Business Development Center, Middle Tennessee State University.

It was a great honor to be a member of the 40th Bombardment Gp. "The Finest Group of Men I Ever Knew."

ARTHUR F. REIBE JR., born Adams,WI 1921 - attended elementary school there High School and one semester Jr. college at El Dorado, AR and Arkansas National Guard.

Arthur F. Reibe Jr.

Late 1939 joined Army Air Corps at Barksdale Field, Louisiana-Air mechanics school at Delgado Jr. College, New Orleans, LA. 1940 assigned NO Army Air Base 122nd Observations Sdn. Air National Guard as mechanic/observer/gunner in B-47 aircraft flying anti-sub patrols in the Gulf.

Attended Lowery Field, CO bombsight school-returned to the 30th Bomb Gp. at New Orleans early 1942 as Sergeant bombardier-B-17s.

Appointed Warrant Officer in bombsights and aircraft engineering October 1942 at Baer Field, IN. Reassigned to 11th Anti Sub Sdn. Ft. Dix, NJ with B-34 aircraft.

At Olmstead Field, PA early 1943 was assistant armament officer. Married my

New Orleans sweetheart and made Chief Warrant.

Joined 28th Air Service Gp. in New Jersey as assistant engineering officer. Assigned B-29 school at Wichita, KS late 1943. Joined 40th Bomb Gp. after initially being in the 444th Bomb Gp. at Great Bend, KS, early 1944.

Discharged at Randolph Field, TX late 1945 from Mariannas Islands. Joined the 40th Bomb Gp. while in Chakulia, India.

Retired from a large Chemical Refinery in 1983 after 33 years.

Had two sons-one in 1947 and again in 1955. Rejoined 40th Bomb Group Association 1981.

DANIEL T. ROGERS, "Dan", born May 18, 1915 at Latta, Dillon Co., SC and entered military service as a Flying Cadet in The Army Air Corps in February 1941. First assignment as pilot was with the 25th Bomb Gp. at Borinquen Field, Puerto Rico. He joined the 44th Sdn. of the 40th Bomb Gp. in February 1942. He moved with the Group to Panama, Guatemala and Pratt, KS. At Pratt he was reassigned to the 25th Bomb Sdn. and flew B-29 Aircraft No. 42-6288 to Chakulia, India. He was on the mission to Bangkok and flew six trips over the Hump to China. His crew from the 40th Gp. and a crew from each of the other three Groups of the 58th Bomb Wing were selected to return to the States with Gen. Wolfe and his team in August of 1944. Decorations received include campaign and theatre ribbons; Presidential Unit Citation and the Air Medal. He retired from the USAF as a Command Pilot and Lieutenant Colonel after 20 years active duty in September 1961.

Daniel T. Rogers

After retirement he received a BS in Economics and a Masters Degree in Education from Francis Marion College of Florence, SC. He married Ethel McLaurin, his childhood sweetheart, from Dillon, SC on Aug. 26, 1944. They presently have two sons, one daughter and seven grandchildren.

WILLIAM A. ROONEY, born LaCrosse, WI, Aug. 29, 1917. Moved to St. Louis, MO, 1939. Drafted, Clayton (St. Louis), MO June 4, 1941. OCS, May, 1942. Assigned to 2nd Air Force, then to Panama. Joined 45th Sdn., David, Panama, January 1943. Air Force Intelligence Officers School (Harrisburg, PA) August to October, 1943. To India via Norfolk, Oran, Naples, Bombay, Calcutta, February to April, 1944. Forward Area (China) S-2 for 40th, May to November 1944. Transferred to XX Bomber Command, Kharagpur, India, November 1944. Returned to States from India. Discharged Captain, October, 1945. Married (Roberta), son (Timothy).

William A. Rooney

Spent business career in advertising. Retired, 1974. Became communications consultant. Published book, 1985, "Architectural Ornamentation in Chicago." Received Distinguished Service Award, Chicago Chapter, American Institute of Architectis, 1986. First Secretary of 40th Bomb Group Association, 1981. Served as Editor of 40th Bomb Group Association MEMORIES from start up in 1984 to present. Contribute to editing and publishing 40th Group Newsletter.

MORTON C. ROTH, born Dec. 9, 1922 in Bridgeport, CT. Attended college 2 1/2 years. Joined the Army Air Corps on Feb. 15, 1943 and served with the 25th Sdn. 40th Bomb Gp.

Morton C. Roth

Stationed at Kearns, UT (Basic), Denver, CO, Pratt, KS, Salina, KS, Norfolk, NB, Chakulia, India, Tinian, Mariannas. Was in charge of "Spiritus Frumenti" (booze) on Tinian.

Remember the eruption of Mt. Vesuvius while in Bay of Naples and being bombed by Germans while in Bay of Naples aboard ship "Champollion."

Awards included the Soldiers Medal, five Battle Stars and The Presidential Citation. Discharged as a Sergeant on Nov. 26, 1945

Married Bernice Corwick in 1950 and have two sons and two daughters and eight grandchildren. Have been self-employed for 35 years in window treatments and retired in December 1981.

FREDERICK W. SAMPSEL, born Aug. 3, 1917 at Mansfield, OH. Graduated from Mansfield High School June 1935. Took two years of Art training. After two years changed to Architecture. Excelled in sports. Pitched Semi-Pro and Triple A until 1939. Went to Los Angeles last of 1939 for additional construction and architectural training. Met my wife to be, Mary Rands of Ogden, UT. After start of War, arraigned to become a Cadet in the Air Corps on Jan. 13, 1942. Due to misinformation was sworn in as a Private.

Frederick W. Sampsel

Was sent to Sheppard Field. In February was sent to Borinquin Field, Puerto Rico, Assigned to Hq. and Hq. Sdn. Later assigned to 45th. After Bomb Gp. was split at Pratt, assigned to 396th Sdn. Passed Flying Cadet Exam but at David, Panama received an unfortunate injury which stopped future cadet training. After Galapagos and Pratt was sent to Topeka General Hospital where I was discharged Nov. 22, 1943.

Built many outstanding structures during career. Due to several back surgeries went to work for California State Architect until 1970 when I resigned to go to the Philippines for eight years for LDS Church for large bldg. program. Was Artist, Architect, B-1 Contractor. R.E. Broker and LDS Bishop.

LOUIS L. SANDRICK, (Sandy), born Jan. 12, 1916 in Pleasant Valley, PA. Enlisted in U.S. Air Force on Oct. 31, 1939. Attended Aircraft Mechanic School at Casey Jones in Newark, NJ for 24 weeks. After graduation was sent to Puerto Rico, then to Guatemala, back to United States to Pratt, KS for training on B-29's.

Louis L. Sandrick

Was assigned to Capt. J. White's flight crew as Left Gunner and Ass't. Engineer. We were sent to Chakulia, India by way of Gandor Bay, N. Africa and Egypt and assigned to the 44th Bomb Sdn. Also was in

Panama. Ending service in Tinian Island and returned to civilian life in August 1945. Awards received during service Good Conduct, Air Medal with two Oak Leaf Clusters, Distinguished Unit Badge, American Defense Service Medal, American Theater Service Medal, Asiatic Pacific Service Medal with four Bronze Stars.

Married Catherine Maslak in Detroit, MI in May 1946. Had five children two girls and three boys. The youngest son a Priest in the Ukrainian Catholic Church.

Worked in the Post Office for awhile; for Michigan National Guard for three years and the the railroad for 30 years, then retiring in 1979. Now traveling to visit our children from the East Coast to the West Coast.

ROGER F. SANDSTEL, born at Holdrege, NB, Aug. 5, 1918. As a farm boy in Nebraska remember well the great depression, droughts, dust storms and crop failure of the 1930's. Received a B. Sci. degree from the University of Nebraska, 1948, and a Ph.D. degree from the University of Minnesota 1954. Married Gwen Swanson 1949. Have three sons. Employed at the New York State College of Agriculture and Life Sciences, Cornell University for 26 years. Retired as Professor Emeritus 1983.

Roger F. Sandstel

Drafted into the infantry, October 1941. Transferred to the DEML and served as clerk for a short time at Ft. McDowell and Camp Stoneman, CA. Enthralled by fighter planes chasing around overhead and applied for and was accepted into the Army Air Corps 1942. Commissioned a 2nd Lieutenant and a pilot at Douglas Army Air Base July 1943.

Trained as a B17 pilot at Hobbs, NM and a B29 pilot at Clovis, NM. Flew a B29 with a crew of nine from Harrington, KS via South America and Africa to the 45th Bomb Sdn. at Chakulia, India. Finished the war a First Lieutenant with this great outfit after completing 21 missions as pilot and nine as airplane commander. Flew our war-weary B-29 from Tinian across the Pacific to Mather Field, thus completing a trip around the world. Awarded the DFC, Air Medal with three Oak Leaf Clusters and Battle Stars.

NORMAN SCADOVA, born Aug. 14, 1924 in Altona, NY near Plattsburg. Attended schools there. Joined the C.C.C.'s (Civilian Conservation Corp) in February 1941. Moved to Keene, NH in 1942, where I still reside. I was drafted February 1943 took basic training in Atlantic City, NJ.

Norman Scadova

Went to Camp Kohler near Fresno, CA to Signal Corp School, then to Salt Lake City, UT to Radio Operator's School. Joined the 40th at Pratt, KS and remained with 44th Sdn., 40th Bomb Gp. through Chakulia, India, and Tinian Island. Flew nine missions over Japan between June 28 and Aug. 8, 1945. Ribbons received were Good Conduct, Battle Ribbon-five Stars, Air Medal, and Presidential Unit Citation. Was separated October, 1945. Married Frances Hyland in 1947. Have two sons and three daughters. Worked 24 years at American Optical, retired January 1987.

I'm proud to have served with the 40th.

LOUIS E. SCHERCK, born Lynn, MA, Oct. 13, 1905. Graduated Brown University 1928, PhB Degree. Graduated Special Class Harvard Business School. Investment Banking in Boston and New York until 1935 when moved to Houston, TX to engage in oil and gas exploration in Gulf Coast and West Texas areas. Volunteered and received commission as 1st Lieutenant Air Force May 12, 1942. Completed Officers Training School in Miami, FL and Combat Intelligence School, Harrisburg, PA. In August 1942 to 6th A.F. Allbrook Field, Panama Canal Zone as Asst. Intelligence Officer. Promoted to Captain May 1, 1943. In August 1943 assigned to 40th Bomb Gp., Pratt, KS for B-29 Program. In April 1944 assigned to 40th Bomb Gp. S-2 Chakulia, India with forward base Chen-tu, China. Promoted to Major June 1, 1944. Served in CBI Theater until April 1945 when transferred to West Field Tinian, Marianas. Completed 12 Hump trips and six combat missions as aerial observer.

Louis E. Scherck

In August 1945 assigned to 20th A.F. Headquarters Intelligence Section Guam, Mariannas. Discharged from service Ft. Sam Houston, San Antonio, TX, Dec. 19, 1945. Awarded Air Medal with Oak Leaf Cluster, Bronze Star, Asiatic Pacific Medal, American Campaign Medal, Army Commendation Medal, Victory Medal, and Distinguished Unit Citation Award.

Home, Houston, TX. Married, three daughters, ten grandchildren and 13 great-grandchildren. Presently engaged in oil and gas exploration and investments.

SAMUEL C. SILL, born Hemet Nov. 18, 1920, raised in San Bernadino, CA. Entered Army Air Corps September 1942. Basic Training, Biloxi, MS; Radio training, Sioux Falls, SD; Radar training, Boca Raton, FL. Assigned 44th Sdn. Commanding Officer Col. Cornett's crew at Pratt, November 1943.

Samuel C. Sill

Arriving Chakulia, assigned to Maj. Eigenmann's crew and teamed with Capt. Ohr., visual bombardier, to form Pathfinder bombing team. Many hours of practice flown to perfect lead crew and pathfinder accuracy. Missions from Chakulia and A-1 China completed tour of duty with Eigenmann's crew. Again teamed with Capt. Ohr, assigned to Maj. Tisserat's crew continuing raids from Chakulia and A-1 prior to transfer to Tinian. Raids intensified against Japanese mainland plus many hours flown training replacement crews.

Returned Stateside July 1945; married Roma Earlywine whom I met in Pratt in 1943; was honorably discharged September 1945. We have four children. Having both retired we are enthusiastically enjoying the rewards of a full life.

WAYNE H. SIMS, born Sept. 6, 1912 at Fresno, CA. Attended local grade school, high school, and Fresno State College. Volunteered for the Army Air Corps on Jan. 14, 1942. Was sent to Shepherd Field, TX for basic training. After five weeks was sent to Borinquen Field, Puerto Rico to complete basic training. Joined 40th Bomb Gp. there. Went to France Field, Canal Zone; David, Republic of Panama; Galapagos and then to Pratt, KS, then to Chakulia, India, a short stay at Chegtu, China, back to Chakulia and then to Tinian. Discharged Oct. 15, 1945.

After discharge returned to Fresno and went back to my former job with the Local Utility. After a few years there I quit and went to work for a large Construction Company. I worked on jobs in the local area, Southern California, Washington State, Upstate New York, Alaska, Saudi Arabia, and South Vietnam. I retired in September

Wayne H. Sims

1977 and returned to Fresno where my wife and I are now living.

BERNARD SLONINA, "Benny", born Mar. 25, 1916 at Yonkers, NY. Family moved to Middleport, PA, where he grew up and attended school.

Bernard Slonina

Enlisted in the U.S. Army Feb. 20, 1936 and was stationed at Ft. Belvoir, VA. Transferred to the Air Corp Dec. 10, 1936 where he was attached to G.H.Q. Langley Field, VA. Attended Aeronautical School in New Jersey, before leaving Langley Mar. 22, 1941 for Borinquen Field, Puerto Rico, where he was a charter member of the 40th Bomb Gp. Remained with the outfit the entire time of activation; Borinquen Field, France Field, David Field, Galapagos Island, Howard Field, Pratt, Chakulia, India, Tinian, March Field, and Tucson, where the 40th was deactivated.

Along with some of the "old gang" went to Ft. Worth AAF (now Carswell AFB) and pioneered the B-36 program. Spent 1953-54 at K-13 Korea, going from the big ones B-36 to the small ones, F-86. After returning to the states came back to Langley Field. As a part of the 429th Sdn. was on the ground floor of the Air re-fueling, using KB-50's (modified B-29's).

Attended many engine and tech schools. Awarded many Unit Citations, as well as personal medals with OLC's and commendations. Retired from the military as a M/Sergeant. November 1958.

After retirement, worked as NASA Langley, entering the space program as an Aero Space Mechanic and later an Engineering Technician. Did experimental full scale testing starting with the original seven astronauts, also VTOL-STOL, F-15, Flex Wing, Flying Chair, Lunar Module, etc.

Two daughters, Barbara and Mary, five grandchildren. Now retired with wife, Virginia, in Poquoson, VA.

EARL F. SLUSSER, born Aug. 26, 1922 at Wisconsin Rapids, WI. Graduated from high school 1941 and volunteered for service shortly after Pearl Harbor.

Earl F. Slusser

Had basic training at Miami Beach and attended Technical School at Embry-Riddle School of Aviation in Miami.

After more technical schools at the Glen L. Martin Plants in Baltimore and Omaha he was assigned to the 40th Bomb Gp., 44th Sdn. at Pratt, KS.

Stayed with 40th Gp. to Chakulia, India and Tinian Island as engine mechanic and crew chief on B-29.

Attained rank of T/Sergeant and was discharged Nov. 14, 1945. Married Alvina Weir 1946. In heating and cooling business for 26 years and Maint. Mech. at 3-M Nekoosa, WI, for 15 years until retirement in September 1986.

JOSEPH P. SOKOL, born Dec. 26, 1923 in Duncan, NB. Entered service Feb. 12, 1943. Graduated from cadets as pilot, Class 44 G, George Field, IL, Aug. 4, 1944. Took B-17 transition at Lockbourne, OH, and B-29 training at Almogordo, NM. Joined 45th Sdn., 40th Bomb Gp., May 1945 at Tinian. Flew 13 missions.

Joseph P. Sokol

Was separated in February 1946. Recalled to active duty July 1953. Served as Air Traffic Control Officer in various stateside assignments, and in Germany, Morocco, and the Philippines. Retired as Lieutenant Colonel in January 1971. After retirement from USAF, worked for various Hwy. Construction Companies until retirement in 1986. Married Irene Mueller in 1949 and we have four daughters. Enjoying retirement by playing a lot of golf.

ARTIE T.L. SPENCER, born Sept. 20, 1918 in Frankfort, WV. Did farm and road

Artie T. L. Spencer

work until I went to work for Westvaco Paper Mill at Covington, VA in 1939.

Enlisted in the Army Air Corps on Oct. 10, 1942. Went to Miami Beach for boot training then to Mt. Union College, Alliance, OH for a refresher course for five months. I was then sent to Scott Field, IL for radio training and then to Clovis, NM for combat training. Was then assigned to Lt. Hug's crew. We were sent overseas as a replacement crew in January 1945 by way of Brazil, Africa and Karachi to the 45th Sdn., 40th Bomb Gp. in Chakulia, India. From there we went to Tinian Island. I flew 21 combat missions over Japan and Rangoon, Burma.

I was discharged on Oct. 29, 1945 as Staff Sergeant. I married Virginia Earehart in December 1945. We have three daughters and one son. Went back to work at Westvaco. Retired in 1983.

DONALD G. STARKEY, Lt. Col. USAF-Ret., born May 1, 1918 near Pine Grove, WV. After high school, completed two years of college and taught two years of school. Entered USAAF as cadet in November 1941. Graduated from Lackland AFB as Aerial Navigator on July 25, 1942. Joined 40th Bomb Gp. in Guatemala City in September same year. Flew patrol missions to the "Rock". Returned with the group to Pratt, KS. Was Sdn. Navigator on James I. Cornett's crew, 44th Sdn., for approximately two years. Flew to Chakulia, India, in April 1944 and returned to U.S. in December same year after completing tour. Reverted to inactive status in December 1945. Recalled during Korean Conflict by the 443rd Troop Carrier Wing. Between wars, received MA degree in Psychology from SMU. Spent 20 years in Aerospace Industry as ergonomics engineer supporting NASA.

Donald G. Starkey

Married Barbara Rae Moore from Dallas, TX, in 1954. Have two sons. Retired from Air Force in 1978.

FLOYD D. STEINER, (Dick), I was born Sept. 24, 1922 on a farm near Mondovi, WI; graduated from Eau Claire, WI, High School in 1940 and enlisted in the Army Air Corps in July 1942. I went to Navigation school at San Marcos, TX, graduating and was commissioned in August 1943. After completing bombardier school I was assigned to the 468th Bomb Gp. at Salina, KS and after we crewed up we were sent to Clovis for RTU and went on to India as a replacement crew to the 45th Bomb Sdn. We lost our airplane enroute from Natal to Accra and arrived at Chakulia without an airplane or first pilot. Jim Cowden was our first crew commander until we bailed out on the Omura Mission on Nov. 21, 1944 after being hit by fighters over the target. Our bombardier, Ira Redmon, was killed on this mission and Leland Jones, Co-pilot, was injured. The crew broke up after this and I completed my tour of combat from Chakulia and West Field, Tinian, with Glenn Landreth, John Mewha and Chuck Thornsberry. After the war, I stayed in the Air Force for 31 years, retiring at Travis AFB on May 1, 1973.

Floyd D. Steiner

I received the DFC and the Air Medal with three Oak Leaf Clusters for service with the 40th Bomb Gp. during WWII. I served in Korea and Vietnam, remaining on flying status for my entire service career, in addition to various stateside and overseas assignments in Japan and Thailand. I was a Plans and Programs Officer for about 20 years.

Majil, my wife of 44 years, and I, both went to the University after my retirement and earned degrees, she in fine arts and I in government/journalism. We are fully retired now and live in the Sierra foothills three miles from Nevada City, CA. Our two sons live in Santa Rosa, CA; one has a vineyard and raises wine grapes and the other in the furniture business.

CHARLES WAYNE SULLIVAN, born in Marion, IL, Oct. 15, 1922. Enlisted into the Army Air Corp, Oct. 9, 1942.

Attended school at AAFTS in Madison, WI and Boca Raton, FL. Spent 17 months in the India-Burma China campaigns as a radar bombardier on the B-29. Served with Maj. Roberts on the "Last Resort" when it crash landed in China. Was forced to parachute from a plane over Iwo Jima after a bombing mission.

Received the DFC, Air Medal with two Oak Leaf Clusters and four Battle Stars. Discharged Sept. 30, 1945.

Charles Wayne Sullivan

Married Florence Kuzminski in 1947 and settled in Chicago. Father of five boys and three girls. Worked as a conductor on the Pennsylvania Railroad (Conrail) for 33 years. Died of a heart attack on July 10, 1983.

FRANCIS SUNDERLAND, "Frank", born Jan. 7, 1923 in Philadelphia, PA. Graduated from high school in Philadelphia. Went into Army Air Corps on Jan. 4, 1943 and was discharged on Nov. 15, 1945.

After two months of Basic Training in Miami Beach, FL, attended Power Operated Gun Turret School and Central Fire Control School at Lowry Air Field, Denver, CO. Was one of the first C.F.C. Mechanics assigned to the 44th Bomb Sdn., 40th Bomb Gp. (VH) at Pratt, KS. Then went to Chakulia, India and Tinian Island.

Lowest rank held was Buck Private and highest rank was T/Sergeant.

After separation from the service finished my apprenticeship at the Philadelphia Naval Shipyard as a Shipfitter. In May 1947 I entered the U.S. Post Office in Philadelphia as a Letter Carrier. After 40 years and ten months of government service, I retired as the Manager of a Medium Large Station of the Philadelphia, PA Post Office with 75 employees.

EVERET E. SWANSON, born in Kane, PA on Jan. 18, 1923. Graduated from high school in 1941 and went right to work for Curtiss Aircraft. Was drafted in February of 1943 and sent to St. Petersburg, FL for basic training. I requested gunnery school and was shipped out 11days later. Went to Buckley Field, Lowry Air Base and Pratt, KS. Left for overseas in February or March of 1944 and was stationed in Chakulia, India and on the island of Tinian.

Everet E. Swanson

Was top gunner on Maj. Weschler's crew flying in the Princess Patsy and Superstitious Aloyisious. Received the D.F.C., Air Medal with three Oak Leaf Clusters and a couple of Unit Citations. Had one half credit for a Jap fighter over Mukden during 35 missions and many Hump trips.

Retired from Tennessee Gas Pipeline Company in 1985. I am married and have three children. 25th Sdn.

CHARLES M. TAYLOR, born Sept. 29, 1915 in Chatsworth, CA. Entered Army Air Corps in December 1940 as an Air Cadet. Graduated from Brooks Field, TX Sept. 26, 1941 as a Lieutenant, Air Corps Army, Flying Class 41-G.

Charles M. Taylor

In 1944 left Pratt, KS for the CBI Theater as a B-29 Pilot with the 40th Bomb Gp. Completed 35 combat missions with a total of 646 flying hours. With the Award of the DFC, this statement (of record) was made: "For extraordinary achievement while flying the longest assigned non-stop bombing missions in the history of aviation."

Other assignments during 28 years of Service are: 1951 - Korean Conflict. Awarded Bronze Star Medal. 1957-58 - T-3 Fletchers Ice Island (Floating Ice Cap Near Thule AF Base - Greenland). Commander of the AF Gp. stationed on T-3 for Scientific Survey.

Upon return to "Stateside" from T-3 I was honored on the TV "This Is Your Life" along with the "Ham Operator" who brightened some of our days on Ice Island.

1960-66 -With "Inspector General" (IG) based in Ballistic Sy. Div. (BSD), Norton AF Base and Washington, DC. Toured and inspected bases (USAF) worldwide.

1966-67 - Deputy Base Commander at AF Da Nang base, Vietnam.

In December 1967 was awarded Vietnam's "Armed Forces Honor Medal" (comparable to our "Medal of Honor") by Brig. Gen. Tran Van Minh (Republic of Vietnam). Translated as follows by Awards Branch USAF "Foreign Decorations."

"As Deputy Commander, Col. Taylor cooperated and provided assistance for the people of Da Nang after Vietnamese aircraft crash landed in a populous area December 1966 and again in February 1967 the Viet Cong rocketed the Da Nang airfield and one rocket fell into Da Nang City. On being informed of the accidents, Col. Taylor organized rescue teams in cooperation with the 41st Wing and provided emergency care for the victims. In addition, Col. Taylor also devoted himself to providing facilities and construction materials for an orphanage at

Da Nang in line with the restoration program for the City."

1968 -Retired as Lieutenant Colonel from SAC, AF Base, Vandenberg, CA.

1971 - Moved from our home in Sherman Oaks, CA to South Padre Island, TX.

1976 - Moved to "Hill Country" in Texas.

1985 - Col. Taylor deceased June 14, 1985 after surgery in V.A. Hospital.

A.C. THOMAS, JR., born June 2, 1920 in Darlington, SC. Graduated High School 1938; entered service Mar. 4, 1940; left for Panama Mar. 29, 1940. Stationed France Field, Hqs., Sdn., 6th Bomb Gp. (M). Attended Aircraft Mechanics School, Rio Hato; returned to France Field; then transferred to Rio Hato; Salinas, Ecuador; Aqua Dulce; David; Howard Field; Pratt, KS.

A.C. Thomas, Jr.

Attended Electronics School at Chanute Field, then to Oran, Africa; Italy; Suez Canal; Bombay; Chakulia, India. Was in Hsinching twice with Capt. Dorsey B. Thomas - once we crashed on landing - Katie #298. From Calcutta to Australia to Tinian; left Tinian July 1945 (point system) to Siapan - from Siapan to U.S. - discharged Aug. 30, 1945.

Attended University of South Carolina. Graduated from the National Institute of Drycleaning and was in the drycleaning business for 35 years.

Married Elizabeth Morrell in 1949 - have two wonderful daughters and four grandchildren. Now retired - buying and selling real estate as a hobby.

WILLIAM J. TOPPIN, born in Harbor Beach, MI, Jan. 24, 1922. Joined Army Air Force in March 1943 from College reserve. After basic training in Atlantic City, I completed Armament school at Lowry. Following a few short assignments at different

William J. Toppin

bases, I was assigned to the 40th Gp. and 44th Sdn. in December 1943 at Pratt, KS. I continued in the Armament in both India and Tinian. Final separation from service occurred in November 1945.

I eventually returned to college and graduated in 1949 from Michigan State in 1949. Began employment at General Motors Diesel Division soon after in 1950 and spent 32 years in various service and sales administration activities until retirement in 1983.

Currently enjoying retirement in Michigan with wife, Janet, with primary interest in antiques, golf, in addition to some challenging activity in developing programs and operating my personal computer.

HARRY E. TUCKER, born in Hanover Co., VA, July 21, 1916. Married Marjorie L. McGhee Sept. 26, 1940. One son, now a cardiologist and one daughter, Jo Anne Bosher. Each have two sons and a daughter. Stanley was four months old when I entered the service in April of 1943.

Harry E. Tucker

My Air Force experiences include Atlantic City, basic training; Ft. Logan, CO; Pratt, KS; Chakulia, India; Tinian and the thrill of flying in the victory armada over Tokyo.

In October, 1945, the day after a tornado swept over the Island, I took off in a B29 for discharge and home.

I was employed before and after the service with a life insurance company for 45 years, receiving my CLU degree in September 1950. Retired in March, 1982 as Department Manager and an Assistant Secretary of the Company.

Over the years I have been active in the Church, Boy Scouts and Masonry.

ALEX A. URBANIC, born Middletown, OH Feb. 10, 1919. Graduated high school 1937. One year in C.C.C.'s 1938-1939, Oregon. Enlisted Army November 1940, Denver, CO. Basic training Barksdale, LA and Jefferson Barracks, MO. Mechanics School Rantoul, IL (Chanute Field).

Assigned 44th Bomb Sdn. Puerto Rico, September 1941. Moved to Guatemala City, Guatemala to Galapagos five months. Back to Guatemala. Then back to the States. Pratt, KS, Gunnery School, Denver, CO. Smokey Hills, KS, then back to Pratt. Sent to Ft. Meade, MD put on a boat and shipped to Casablanca, Africa. Flew to Karachi, India. Sent on detached service to maintain C109 for three months. Back to Chakulia, then to Tinian, Saipan, to Hawaii for R&R. War is

Alex A. Urbanic

over so we go to Seattle, WA to Ft. Harrison, IN. Discharged September 1945.

Got a job at Bendix-Westinghouse. Worked for 25 1/2 years. Married in 1951. Had two children. One of each. Have two grandsons.

JOE D. VALLEY SR., born Mar. 19, 1916 at Wisconsins, second oldest settlement Prairie du Chien.

Graduated from Prairie du Chien High School in 1936. Mechanical Background and experiences.

Joe D. Valley Sr.

Enlisted in U.S. Army Air Corps Aug. 16, 1941.

Spent time at Milwaukee *Camp Grant* (Boot Camp) at Jefferson Barracks, MO. Mechanics Aircraft Tech School at Chanute Field in 1941. Attained PFC. Cpl. - and Sergeant at Midland A Air Field at Midland, TX, in 1942 where he worked as Airplane Mechanic, then Crew Chief. Then Aircraft Inspection Department, and had some flying experience on Twin engine Beechcraft AT 11 practice Bombers.

Sept. 15, 1942 transferred to 861st Bomb training Sdn. at San Angelo, TX where he helped develop the air field and serve as Aircraft Inspector and then Line Chief and considerable flying on twin engine aircraft. Promoted to Staff Sergeant at San Angelo Oct. 1, 1942. Transferred to Glenn L. Martin Factory B-26 training school at Baltimore, MD in 1943 and then Apr. 1, 1943 helped activate Dodge City Army A.C. Pilot training school. Air Field 61st Sdn. There was crew chief of "Boot Hill Dust Storm" a B26. Then Line Chief and then Aircraft Inspector, in 61st Sdn., and there promoted to Tech. Sergeant. There was able to Do A lot of Co-Pilot time on the B-26 and made several landings at Pratt B29 Base - observed B29s and the 40th Bomb Gp. there and applied for Flight Training at Lowry Field and began Flight Engineer B29 training Apr. 1, 1944. Took some B24 and B17 FE training before going on B29s, at Clovis, NM and there forming our future Combat Crew consisting of:

1st Pilot, Mills L. Bale, Navigator Pat W. Daly, F. Engineer Joe D. Valley, Co-Pilot John F. Laxton, Bombardier Eric Buzza, CFC Gunner, Glen O. Sally, Then Bill Rifel, Left Gunner Clyde Beckley, Right Gunner Conrad Becker, Tail Gunner Harry Pudlofsky.

Served some time at Lincoln, NB and received issue B29 #224739 at Harington KS. Ferried it to West Palm Beach - Puerto Rico - British Giana - Natal Brazil - Accra, Gold Coast - Nigeria - Kartume - Anglo Egyptian Sudan, -Saudi, Arabia - Karatchi and then home base 40th Bomb Gp. 45th Bomb Sdn. at Chakulia in November 1944. Was welcomed by Col. Butch Blanchard. Was part-time FE for Col. Oscar Shaff and William E. Skaer. 224739 was taken away and we received for our crew #224738. Honeywell Honey. Mills Bale flew as Co-Pilot on a Singapore Mission and had to bale out and was unable to continue with our crew. Nedric Baugh took over as our 1st Pilot. We made seven round trips to A1 in China and seven missions to Singapore from Chakulia. #224738 was 1st B29 to lose 4000 ft. altitude in the clouds over the Hump and recover and continue on to A1. We were at 38800 ft. and all four engines quit. Need for quick thinking said I should reduce turbo pressure at that altitude and they all came back in. Completed 29 missions in CBI and West field Tinian with the 40th Bomb Gp. Returned 224738 to Mather Field at Sacramento Oct. 20, 1945. Was in 40th Bomb Gp. Riverside until Jan. 18, 1946. Flight officer on Guam Aug. 28, 1945; Second Lieutenant Sept. 25, 1946; 1st Lieutenant Mar. 25, 1949; Captain Apr. 4, 1954; Major in AF Res. 1960. Retired from AF Res. as Major Mar. 19, 1976. Awarded DFC, Air Medal, #30LC, Asiatic Pacific Com. American Campaign, Good Conduct, Armed Forces Reserve and others.

Continued to operate business Valley Air Cooled Engines at Prairie du Chien. Established 1932 and still operating 55 years in same location. Still active with 40th Bomb Gp. The very finest group of individuals.

RICHARD A. VEACH, (Dick), I was drafted from the University of Nebraska Apr. 2, 1943 and soon applied for pilot training. I graduated in Class 44G in B-25s at Mather Field.

Richard A. Veach

I completed B-17 first pilot training at Hobbs, and was then assigned to B-29 Copilot training at Pyote with Maj. Schindler as AC. After our assignment to the 40th, we picked up a new 29 in Topeka and flew it to Tinian, arriving May 15, 1945.

On May 19, I flew my first mission, followed by 15 others in the next 52 days, which may have set some kind of a record. We never had an abort, and always hit the primary, with photos to prove it!

Once, after bombing on three engines, we received an advisory from base to land at Iwo because of anticipated high gas usage. Instead, we returned slowly but confidently to West Field, landing long after all others were in. We found inquires from base "Are you still up?" to be rather amusing after the ground crew dipped our tanks and found more gas left than anyone else in the squadron!

That experience, plus our other good performances, led to our selection as 1 of 20 crew assigned to Lead Crew school at Muroc.

Since the war had ended just before we completed our school, we were sent home for discharge. I immediately re-entered the University and graduated in1947. A 39 year career with AT&T then followed, from which I retired in June, 1986.

I have a wife Harriett, and a married son and daughter. I live in Omaha, NB.

WARREN W. WALTERS, JR., "Bud", born Feb. 8, 1915 at Trappe, PA. Attended grade school and is a graduate of Collegeville High School. Received B.S. Degree in Chemistry from Ursinus College in 1938. Employed by the Pennsylvania Department of Highways as a Construction Inspector in 1939.

Warren W. Walters Jr.

Drafted in June 1941 for one year. While in training as a Radio Operator in the Army Inf. at Camp Wheeler, GA enlisted in the Army Air Corps for Navigation training. Graduated from Kelly Field Navigation School Class of 42-4.

After graduation was assigned to the Ferrying Command, which became the Ferrying Div. of the Air Transport Command, at Morrison Field, West Palm Beach, FL and later assigned to New Castle Air Base, New Castle, DE.

Was transferred to the 44th Sdn. of the 40th Bomb Gp. at Pratt, KS in October 1943. Assigned to E.O. Berry's crew as Navigator. Several months after arrival in Chakulia, India was promoted to Sdn. Navigator. Credited with 26 combat missions from India, over the "Hump", out of China and from Tinian.

Awarded DFC, Air Medal with Oak Leaf Cluster, Asiatic Pacific Campaign Medal with five Battle Stars, Distinguished Unit Citation, European Theater Campaign Medal, American Theater Campaign Medal, American Defense Service Medal, WWII Victory Medal and Armed Forces Reserve Medal.

Separated from active duty as a Captain and remained in the Air Force Reserve until retirement as Lieutenant Colonel in 1968.

Was manufacturing engineer in the production of electron tubes for Tung-Aol in Weatherly, PA 1946-47. Was employed by Western Electric, Co. in Winston-Salem, NC as project engineer in 1947. Retired from Western Electric as Senior Engineer in 1947.

It was a privilege to have served with the 44th Sdn. and to have known so many dedicated Americans.

ROBERT E. WATSON, CMSGT. USAF (Ret.), born May 20, 1922, Colorado Springs, CO. Completed grade and junior high in Boulder, CO. Moved to Austin, MN, where I completed high school. Joined the Army Air Corps at Ft. Snelling, MN Aug. 10, 1940. Received basic training at Chanute Field, Rantoul, IL.

Robert E. Watson

Attended Aircraft Armament school at Lowry Air Base, graduated in January 1941. Assigned to the 40th Bomb Gp. at Borinquen Field, Puerto Rico. Stayed with this group from Puerto Rico to Panama to Guatemala, where I met my wife, Trans. To Pratt, KS in June of 1943 to train on the B29's, from there to Chakulia, India, from there to the Island of Tinian. I returned to the U.S. August 1945. Was discharged at Camp McMcoy W I after six months of civilian life I reenlisted in the Air Force at the time of reenlistment I was assigned to the 29th Maint. Sdn. at Grand Island, NB, from there a nine months (90 day?) TDY trip to Alaska. Returned to the states and was assigned to Rapid City AFB. In September 1949 was sent to Lowry ABC for schooling on the B29 and B36 CFC System. I was selected to stay at Lowry as an instructor. I taught the CFC System for approximately nine months then was assigned to classes on the B47 and B52 Navigational Systems after this training I was assigned to teach the Nav. Systems for the B52 and B47. In 1959 was sent to Ft. Worth, TX for training on the B58 Nav. System. In April of 1960 was transferred to the 512A field training detachment at Hunter AFB, GA. In November of 1960 the B47's were phased out of Hunter so the 512A was moved to DMAFB, Tucson, AZ. In July of 1964 I was transferred to Edward Air Force Base where I worked on various ProtoType Aircraft. In November 1967 I received Systems Commands Meritorious Achievement Award for a modification of the Electronics Systems on aircraft used for the training of potential Astro-naughts.

I was promoted to Chief Master in April 1968.

I was transferred to Barksdale Air Force Base at Shreveport, LA. In May 1968. Assigned to the 2nd Avionics Maint. Sdn. (SAC) as the Bomb Nav. Sys. Supt. In November of 1968 a 90 day TDY Trip to Guam, B52 support to The Vietnam War effort.

I retired from the Air Force in August of 1972 and returned to Tucson where I have a home. After some minor maint. on the house I decided to go back to school and get a degree. I received a B.S. Degree in Business Administration with a computer Major. I began teaching for a private business college where I taught Computer Programming, Math, and Accounting for nine years. Now I am completely retired! I spend time in my work shop and some time in writing programs on my computer for personal use in the home. Rejoined the 40th in 1984.

M.O. WEBB, S/Sgt., of the 395th Bomb Sdn. born Nov. 20, 1919 in Burkburnett, TX. Entered U.S. Calvary, training at Ft. Bliss, TX. Took examinations and re-enlisted in Air Force. Trained at Shepherd Field, Wichita Falls, TX. Sent to Boqueron Field, Puerto Rico. Joined 40th Bomb Gp. as P.E. instructor. Flew in B18 and LB30. Served in France Field, Panama as radio operator, flying B24 patrolling Panama Canal. We flew from "The Rock".

M.O. Webb

Sent to Pratt, KS by boat via San Francisco. Flew B-17 and B-26 waiting for B-29. Left for Chakulia, India by way of Newfoundland and North Africa. Hit on bombing raid over Japan, losing one engine. Flew for seven hours to Siberia where we bailed out Aug. 21, 1944. Walked out in 20 to 30 days. Interned in Russia until Jan. 30, 1945. Returned to States and discharged in 1945 as S/Sergeant with Major McGlinn's crew. Went to work for Amoco 1951 - retiring 33 years later.

RALPH H. WEINBERG, born Oct. 11, 1918 in Philadelphia, PA. Received two years of credits at Temple University. Joined the Army Air Corps Nov. 1, 1941. Attended Kelly Field Navigation School, graduating June 1942. Retained as instructor. At Hondo, TX taught celestial navigation; Roswell, NM Bomb School. Stationed at Pratt, KS, Chakulia, India, Chengtu, China, and Tinian.

Ralph H. Weinberg

Remember the pictures taken flying "The Hump," on missions to Formosa being hit by air to air bomb. Losing a gunner and wounding me and our radio operator on photo mission over Singapore. Jap fighter hit oil line causing one prop to windmill and just barely making it to British Base. On mission to Tokyo seeing a Kamakazi ram the plane ahead of us and being hit by the debris resulting in a steep dive and windmilling prop. Pulling out at 100' and limping into Iwo Jima.

Received the DFC w/Cluster, Air Medal w/ three Clusters, Purple Heart, Presidential Unit Citation, American Defense Service Ribbon, Asiatic-Pacific Campaign Medal w/ Cluster, Victory Ribbon, Longevity Service Award Ribbon, Armed Forces Reserve Ribbon w/Hr Glass, Chinese Republic Medal.

Discharged Nov. 1, 1945; became A.F. Reservist in 1947 and retired as Lieutenant Colonel in 1964.

Married Eleanor L. Weinberg and have one child and three stepchildren, and 12 grandchildren. Worked in manufacturing of ladies hosiery 1946-50, Sales 1951-57, Real Estate Broker 1957-64. 1964 to present managing health care facility.

NEIL W. WEMPLE, born Feb. 26, 1918, Milford, CA. Graduated from high school in 1936. Have BA in Commerce from San Jose State College. Entered U.S. Army Air Corps as Flying Cadet November 1940. Graduating from Brooks Field, TX as a pilot 2nd Lieutenant July 1941. First active duty; 44th Bomb Sdn., Borinquen Field, Puerto Rico, July 29, 1941. Served continuously in 44th until Sept. 1, 1946, longer than any other officer, becoming its Comdr. in January 1945 and promoted to Lieutenant Colonel in June 1945. Flew 27 missions with the 44th in WWII.

Served over 18 years in SAC, promoted to Colonel January 1951. Had duty at SAC HQS, 92nd, 6th and 509th Bomb Wings, and 15th, 16th AF, Air Univ. and AF Systems Comd. Served 29 years in USAF and retired August 1969. Flew 36 different aircraft over 5700 hours, one thru ten engines, including 1100 jet hours. Held Wing/Base Comdr. and numbered AF Personnel Dir. positions.

Married Helen Hidden of Portland, OR in

Neil W. Wemple

Tapachula, Mexico, January 1943. Have three children and two grandchildren. Have real estate brokers license, and sold real estate for 12 years after AF retirement.

WILMER R. WILKINSON, born in Nampa, ID on Nov. 13, 1923. Graduated from Nampa High School 1942. Entered Army Air Corps as aviation cadet and was sent to Coe College, Cedar Rapids, IA, under the College Training Detachment Program. Then to West Coast Training Command where I received my commission and Pilot's Wings at Williams Field, AZ, Class of 44-F.

Wilmer R. Wilkinson

Spent six months as Flight Instructor in P-38s, then sent to Roswell, NM B-17 training. Was sent overseas in February 1945 to the 58th Bomb Wing where I saw a B-29 for the first time at Kharagapur. Was assigned to 40th Bomb Gp., 45th Sdn. as replacement pilot. Transition training received at Chakulia before being sent to Tinian, where I was assigned to John Hug's crew as Co-Pilot in June 1945.

Graduated from University of Idaho in 1952. Currently employed by Kaiser Aerotech as Contracts Administrator in Rocketry.

Married; two children, four grandchildren.

J. MERRICK WINSHIP, "Jack" born May 15, 1905 at Sunrise, WY. Went to lower grades and high school in that area. Came to California in 1923 and made my home here ever since then.

After boot camp and tech school training at Greeley, CO, was assigned to 40th Bomb Gp. at Pratt Air Force Base in Kansas. Stayed in the group from Pratt, KS to Chakulia, India and Tinian Island in South Pacific.

My lowest rank was Private and highest rank was Tech Sergeant. Awards received included the Good Conduct Medal, Battle Ribbons with Stars, etc.!

J. Merrick Winship

William Zimmerman

Sheldon S. Zweig

After leaving the service because of age, July 1945, went into Retail Merchandising until retirement in 1969.

I also raised many species of exotic birds, including many rare parrot types.

EVERETT WOLFSON, born July 16, 1924, Providence, RI, grew up in New York where I attended grade school and high school and then enlisted in the USAAF on Oct. 24, 1942.

Everett Wolfson

Completed basic training in Miami Beach, FL and was assigned to Airplane Mechanics School in Amarillo, TX. From Amarillo I was assigned to Airplane Electrical/Electronic School at Chanute Field, IL where I volunteered for the B-29 program and was assigned to the B-29 plant for engineer training. The engineering program was discontinued and I was transferred to B-29 Gunnery School at Denver, CO. From Denver I was assigned to Pratt, KS, where I was assigned to Maj. Garth Doyles crew as left gunner/electrical specialist, 25th Bomb Sdn., 40th Bomb Gp.

I completed 47 missions including "Hump" trips where the entire crew was transferred home to the United States with War Weary Planes while the rest of the unit was sent to Tinian.

I was awarded the DFC, the Air Medal with Oak Leaf Cluster, a Battle Star for each of the following: "Central Burma Campaign", "India-Burma Campaign," "China Campaign", "Air Offensive against Japan", and the bombing of PalemBang, Sumatra.

I was discharged Sept. 28, 1945 and returned home where I married Barbara Friedman of New York. We have three sons, who give us great joy.

Currently I am semi-retired after 30 years as an insurance financial planner.

WILLIAM ZIMMERMAN, born Aug. 18, 1921 in Lock Sheldrake, NY. Graduated from high school in 1936 and entered service in August 1942. Attended aircraft mechanic school at Lincoln, Electrical specialist at Chanute, B-29 school at Seattle, and gunnery school at Lowry.

Transferred from Lowry to Clovis for flight training and was assigned to the crew of Lt. Herbert Wright. We were sent overseas as a replacement crew in August 1944 by way of Brazil, Gold Coast, Egypt and Karachi to the 25th Sdn., 40th Bomb Gp. in Chakulia.

After completion of 26 missions with Lt. Wright and others, having earned the DFC, Air Medal with two Clusters and three Battle Stars, was returned to civilian life in September 1945.

Married Loretta Tremper in 1955 and had two sons and two daughters. Accepted a job with the New York State Correction Department as a correction officer and retired in 1982 with the rank of Deputy Warden. Rejoined the 40th Bomb Gp. at the Dayton Reunion.

SHELDON S. ZWEIG, born Dec. 11, 1921 in Newark, NJ. Drafted Summer, 1942 in Air Force. Trained at Radio School, Scott Field, IL and Radar School, Boca Raton, FL.

Assigned 40th Bomb Gp. Pratt, KS, 1943. Radar Mechanic 25th Bomb Sdn. Stationed at Chakulia, India A-1, China, Tinian Island. Rank Staff Sergeant.

Awards: American Service Medal, Asiatic-Pacific Service Medal, Distinguished Unit Badge, Good Conduct Medal, WWII Victory Medal.

B.A. 1950 History, University of Colorado, M.A. 1953 History/Education University of Colorado, Boulder, CO. M.A. 1976 Guidance-C.W. Post College, LI University, Long Island, NY.

History teacher 18 years. Guidance Counselor 16 years, retired July 1986.

Married Adele Buris, Elizabeth, NJ, 1947. Children: Jeffrey, musician and Garry, teacher.

It was a privilege to be a part of the 40th Bomb Gp. and a wonderful team of dedicated, courageous G.I.'s

B-29 after emergency landing and camouflage

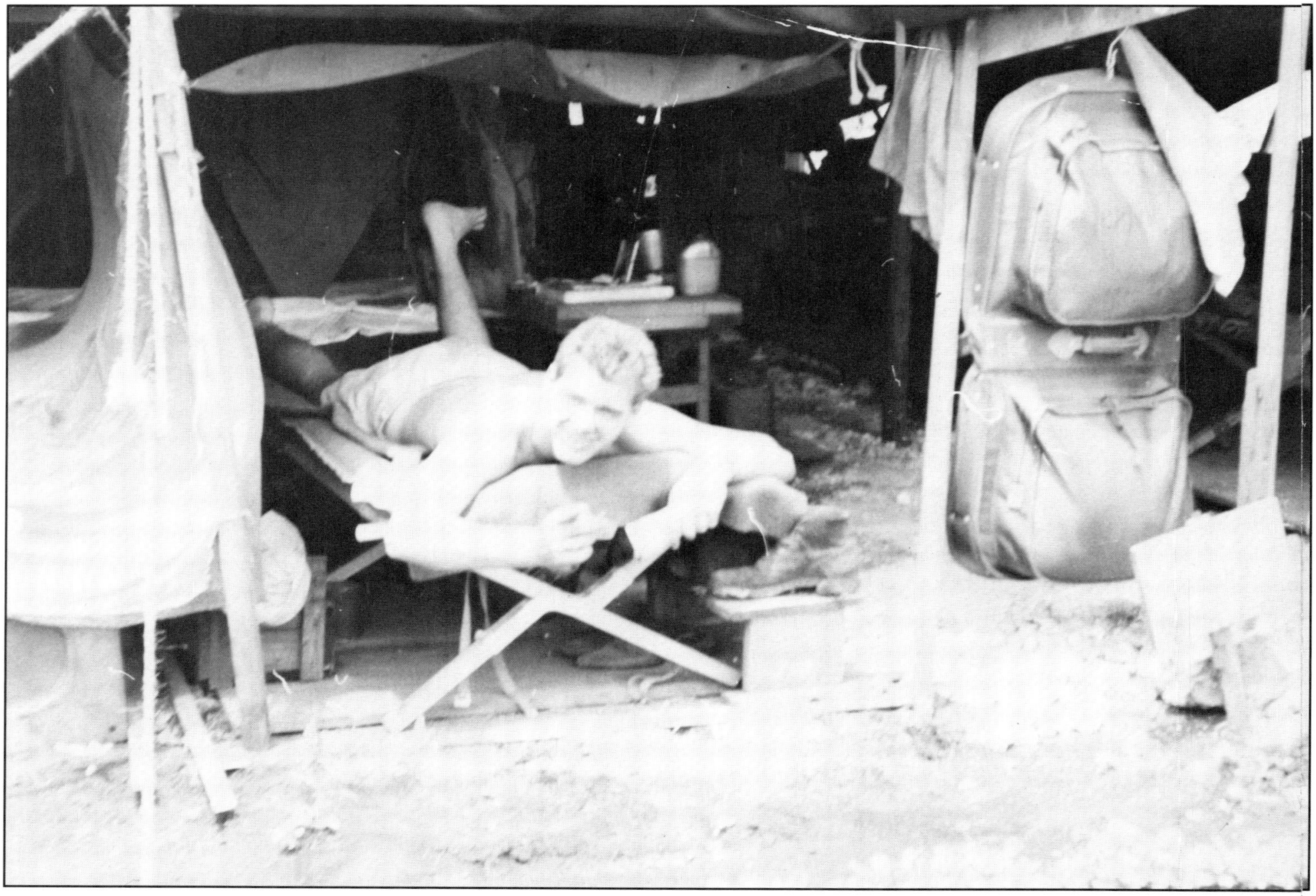

40th Bomb GroupVeteran taking a break

Instrument Crew 44th Bomb Sqdn. India L. to R. Robert I. Cook, Howard Eppler and Joseph Koziol

Front row third from left Glen E. Liston, other unknown.

Barracks, Chakulia India

Sqnd. Quarters area Lt. John Constandy, Lt. Nate Hicks. "Genie" crew member

Lt. Robert Pollard in rickshaw, Calcutta India. bombardier of the B-29 "Ding How"

Far left Lt. David Miles Lustig, Navigator. Far right 1st Lt. Robert "Con" Conley Co-Pilot. Hsinching area China

40th Bomb Group Basketball Team

272

—NOTES—

RIAL NO. 42-24643
There'll Alway
As we stir a Toddy this Heavenly Body
Is winging her way through the sky.
Her pose is a sign that the going is fin
And America's still flying high!
The pace has been hot and we've been through a lot
And none of us look any younger.
But "Mussy" is sunk and Tojo feels punk
And Hitler is strictly from hunger!